Ernest Thompson Seton and his wife Julia M. Seton

BY A THOUSAND FIRES

BY A
THOUSAND
FIRES

NATURE NOTES AND EXTRACTS FROM THE LIFE AND
UNPUBLISHED JOURNALS OF ERNEST THOMPSON SETON

JULIA M. SETON

Illustrations by Ernest Thompson Seton

DOUBLEDAY & COMPANY, INC.
GARDEN CITY, NEW YORK

1967

Dedicated to

DANIEL SETON BARBER

whose joy we hope it will be
to carry on the traditions of
his Grandfather

LIBRARY OF CONGRESS CATALOG CARD NUMBER 67–19073
COPYRIGHT © 1967 BY JULIA M. SETON
ALL RIGHTS RESERVED
PRINTED IN THE UNITED STATES OF AMERICA
FIRST EDITION

CONTENTS

C.1

PROLOGUE

I have listened by a thousand fires as the Buffalo Wind blew through our lives.

At first my own ears heard it not for what it was—they were not attuned. But always I knew it was there, though for long I was disturbed and puzzled by what I did not understand. I did not *hear* but I felt it, albeit unrealizing.

Always it came when we were alone together. Sometimes by day, sometimes by dark. A moment of unworldly peace, a silence like a soundless sound; then an exaltation of perfect harmony between us and—what?

It is almost fifty years ago tonight when first we met, and my way had not been his. The channels of our being had run wide afield, our aims and ambitions were in diverse paths for the most part.

But when first we touched hands in a casual introduction, we knew.

That time it was by a mere symbol fire—a painted cruciform on a hardwood floor, the arms each lighted by a candle, a shaded electric bulb at the crossing of the ways.

The Woodcraft Ritual spoke in words that were to shape the rest of my days.

Since then, our fires have been in many parts of the world and of many various kinds: in the maple woods of New Hampshire, in the pine timberlands of the North, in the pinyons of New Mexico, in the swamplands of the South, in the Canadian Rockies, in the Wind River Cave of South Dakota, in a sheep camp in Colorado, in the tepee of a Cheyenne Indian, in a country house outside of London, by a fireplace at Bonn University, a short moment on a New Year's Eve in Czechoslovakia, in his onetime studio revisited in the Quartier Latin, in the Pavilion of South Shields, the town where he was born, by the dying embers of the council fire which gave me my ceremonial Indian name, in the dirty square of Juarez, Mexico, in the skunk yard where we loved those pets we were raising, at the grave of Buffalo Bill, by the last of the campfires after a Navaho *Yei be chi*, by a fluttering little bonfire outside St. Francis' Cathedral at Santa

Fe, by the light of my cigarette one night on the French liner
Lafayette, in the winter woods of what the next day we bought as our
permanent homeland, by the vigil fire on our Memory Hill, in the
kiva we built on our place, by the first fire of our new home, by a
single candle as we kept vigil over a departed friend—but oftenest
and most easily induced by our own fireplace in Seton Castle, our
chosen home, into which we had joyously put so much of our physical
energy, our worldly goods, our plans and dreams—yes, more, our love
for the home, the estate, the land we had selected of all the world,
for our baby and for our work.

It was by campfires, inglenooks, hearth fires, and even one ill-fated
fire when the main building of our Institute burned to the ground,
taking with it our records of the previous twenty-five years, manuscript notes for books to come, besides the material possessions which
were housed therein.

But ever the spirit that was his came through the joys or the
sorrows, the hopes or the griefs, with a brilliance that was crystal
clear, a shining light that carried all in his world to a triumphant
finish.

Always a hand touch—a grip—a moment—then in a voice vibrant
from another world: "The Buffalo Wind is blowing!"

And so would come a flood of revelation, an unceasing flow of
inspiration such as could not be courted. Many a time have I sat
by the embers, in motionless silence for hours, while the words came
in unhesitating rhythm of passionate life—for we did not measure our
life together with a shallow cup. Each time we dipped, we brought
up the chalice brimming full and running over.

I have hoarded the treasure of those years beyond belief. But I
know now that the memories are not for me alone. I must heed his
own injunction given for another cause:

"When you discover the folksiness of some tree, the compact of
bee and bloom, the all-aboutness of some secret . . . you must in
some sort write it down and pass it on to another . . . that the liquid
gold turn not to vitriol in your hand; for those who have won power
must with it bear responsibility."

Twenty years ago tonight the Buffalo Wind blew a long last breath
that for the first time left no spoken word behind it. I heard it then,
and knew it for what it was. As it passed beyond our ken, so did his

spirit go out as he had wished—in triumph, in peace, in honor and in love.

May that Buffalo Wind blow for me while I give to you with open hands the heritage that is mine.

JULIA SETON

Seton Castle
Santa Fe
New Mexico

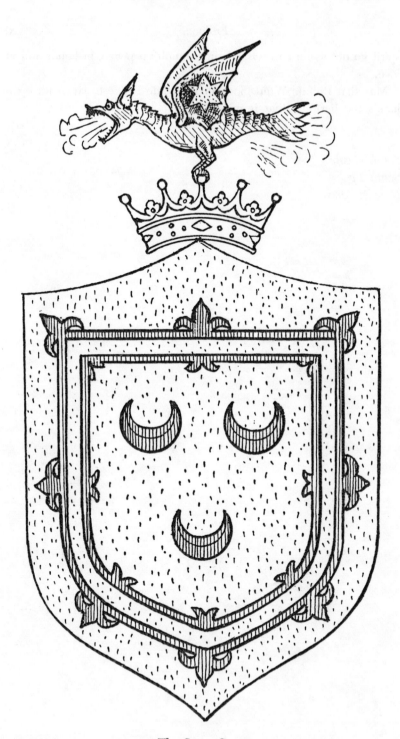

The Seton Crest

BIOGRAPHICAL NOTES:
ERNEST THOMPSON SETON

1860: Born August 14, South Shields, Durham, England.

1866: Moved with family to Canada, first to Lindsay, Ontario, then when ten years old to Toronto. Educated in the public schools. In 1879 was Gold Medalist in the Ontario Art School.

1879: Went to England to study art. Won seven-year scholarship to study at the Royal Academy.

1881: Forced to return to Canada because of illness.

1882: Went to Manitoba where his eldest brother was homesteading near Carberry. Was later appointed Official Naturalist for the Province of Manitoba.

1883: Went to New York City. Century Publications commissioned him to do 1000 animal illustrations for their 12-volume dictionary.

1890: Went to Paris where he studied painting under the French masters Gérôme, Fouguereau, Fremier, and Mosler. He studied in Paris intermittently for the next six years.

1898: His first book of stories, *Wild Animals I Have Known,* appeared. It was a best seller. The book is now regarded as a classic.

1902: Founded the Woodcraft Indians, the first outdoor organization for boys. Later incorporated as the Woodcraft League.

1910: Was chairman of committee that established the Boy Scouts of America. Wrote first Scout Handbook. Was installed as first Chief Scout, a post he held for five years.

1925: *Lives of Game Animals,* an 8-volume work giving the life histories of all the game animals from Mexico to the Arctic, appeared. This won for him the John Burroughs Medal and the Elliott Gold Medal of the National Academy of Sciences, the highest award a naturalist can receive. Seton's *Lives* still regarded as the definitive work on the subject.

1930: Moved to New Mexico. Settled on a 2500-acre site south of Santa Fe. The site was part of the old Sebastian De Vargas

Grant. Here he and Mrs. Seton established a school for youth leaders and a camp for young people.

1946:   Seton died. Active and in full command of his talents to the very end, he had influenced three generations during his lifetime. Through his books, now translated into nearly every language, he will continue to delight and instruct generations yet to come.

BIOGRAPHICAL NOTES:
MRS. ERNEST THOMPSON SETON
(JULIA MOSS SETON)

1889:   Born in New York City.

Mrs. Seton was educated in New York City. She received a Master's Degree from Hunter College there. She is an authority on Indian culture, particularly Indian philosophy, music, and dance. She lectures throughout the world on this subject and has written ten books. Mrs. Seton lives in Seton Village in a home she completed last fall. She continues to write and lecture as well as manage the Village and Museum.

PART ONE

HEARTH FIRES

CHILDHOOD

South Shields

One of my cherished ambitions was achieved when I was able, together with my husband, to visit South Shields, the place of his birth. It is a small, quiet little town in Durham, England, on the south bank of the river Tyne where it empties into the North Sea, some sixty miles south of the Scottish border. It is but nine miles from Newcastle, the great commercial city of the north; is, indeed, the seaport of that town.

We two took a long walk through the town, not much larger than it had been seventy years before when he had known it so well. It had still a remarkable featuresqueness all its own. I had a feeling that it had changed little since he had lived there. Indeed he knew every turn of a street, almost the very shops that had been there all these years. It was like turning back the pages of time with scarce even a flutter of the paper.

He was anxious to see the strand, and we went first to that. The famous harbor in which was first invented and launched the lifeboat that has saved so many thousands of lives is a mile across, improved by two massive breakwaters. It is the great central nucleus and hub of this little world.

Lining the shore of the river Tyne just above the mouth are still to be seen hundreds of merchant ships from all parts of the world, as well as fishing boats from the North Sea, the Dogger Bank, and the Cornish pilchard fisheries, with herring trawlers from the open sea, and even cod boats from the far-off banks and fogs of Newfoundland. And over, and forever over all, were screaming hosts of white-winged winnowing gulls.

Back of these, north and west, were rising slopes covered with the houses of coal miners, for deep under these low hills are still to be found the most famous coal deposits of England. Wedged in between were innumerable factories taking advantage of cheap coal and abundant low-priced help.

As we strolled, he told me of the old octagonal wooden pavilion in what was essentially the plaza of the town, and of how the old sea dogs used to sit about smoking their pipes and weaving their yarns.

And suddenly we were upon it—just as he had described it. It was noon, and only a few old men were there. A lump was in my throat as we made our way slowly in and took a seat along the inner edge of the open building. How wonderfully soft and musical their voices seemed to me as we listened in silence to their talk!

We sat in reverie, calm and content in this little oasis of quiet until the other occupants, one by one, arose and left.

Soon, as if he had never stopped his reminiscing, he took up his story:

"Nearer to the ocean was a settlement of a different class, the men known as shipowners of the Merchant Marine.

"Needing to be near their business, shunning the smoke of the low town as well as the factories of Upper or High Shields, these men showed their appreciation of the ocean breezes by building a little settlement of their own near the junction of the river and the sea.

"Here grew up the Terraces—Wellington, Ogle, Winterbottom, Chaloner, Albion. Also the Master Mariners' cottages, Westoe and Cledon Villages.

"Here it was that my father built his own plain solid three-story house of brick, now No. 6 Wellington Terrace, and in this his numerous progeny were born—fourteen of us in all.

"The names of our neighbors come clearly back to me now. All were in some measure shipowners, and most of them relatives— Stephensons, Rennoldsons, Lees, Snowdons, Hewisons, Biddlestones, Maxwells, Fenwicks, Stoddards, etc., nearly all of them names of fame in Border history.

"Here and hereabout it was that my people had dwelt since the great crash of their fortunes in the Stuart rebellion had sent them scurrying out of Scotland."

A period of silence, and again he took up his memories.

"From our windows on the south, we had a wonderful view of wheatfields and meadows, with their pleasant variants of animal life in the grass, and skylarks singing in the sky, far away to Cledon and on towards Sunderland and down the coast to Souter Point, where moans the unearthly siren on fearful nights of fog.

"Our easterly view of the sea was shut off by bosky hills and terraced houses; but toward the north we could see across the mile-wide gray-green harbor, flecked with boats, to the other shore called Tynemouth, where stark and somber stood ever and unchanging the dark and towering ruin called Tynemouth Abbey, a grim reminder of the Church's power a thousand years ago, a grim reminder of the terror of the sea kings, the Vikings in the days gone by. For here it was that Red Eric landed with his husky berserks clanging their shields and flashing their spears; here, after he had gathered at his will all that appealed, he had set the torch, and all he left is what we see today."

The Old Sea Dogs

Joseph Logan Thompson, Ernest's father, was considered a well-off man in the little seaport of South Shields. All the town was interested in shipping, and all their wealth came from gambling on the weather and sailing the Seven Seas.

In this life, varied in its far-reaching interests, there was one outstanding figure all-important. That was the Captain, and everything depended on him.

He was the commander, navigator, pilot, and financial agent of the ship. All of which sounds perfectly logical. But one office is perhaps not so obvious. He was also the doctor.

Each ship had on board a medicine chest with 24 bottles in 24 separate bins, and a book of "Symptoms." If a man seemed ill, the Captain would examine him and locate his trouble by number, according to the symptoms. Thus, suppose a man had chills and pains. The Captain would consult the book. The point where the *chill column* crossed the *pain line* said No. 6. The man had probably a cold combined with inflammation; but the instructions gave no name to malady or remedy; merely said: "Rub the parts with No. 6, and make him swallow one teaspoonful of the same in hot water every hour." This No. 6, I have been told since, was essence of capsicum.

But everything was done by number. There happened to be a run on No. 18 (I think it was calomel). The bottle was empty. But the Captain's mind was mathematical in training. He took equal parts of No. 10 and No. 8, both somewhat neglected heretofore; and when these were used up, he mixed 13 and 5 to take their place. He always maintained that such combinations gave equally good results.

The vital importance of the Captain is becoming evident. The captains could make or break their owners in the Merchant Service. The Captain dictated all the details of the voyage, and even the voyage itself when it began at a foreign port. Often it was his duty to decide where and when to sell the cargo he had brought, and what to load with for the return; whether indeed there was to be a return cargo or else go back under ballast.

There was nothing to prevent the Captain from sailing to New York with a cargo of coal and manufactured articles, intending to come back to Newcastle loaded with wheat and hides. But, changing his mind after study of the New York markets, he could go instead with cheap finery to the coast of Africa, where he might exchange his trinkets and cotton for palm oil, rice, and sago. He could then take that to Newcastle, or again change his mind and land it at Málaga, coming back with a load of light wine and raisins.

There were no cables and practically no mails, so all decisions were up to the judgment of the Captain. It is evident why these men could make or break the owner—and usually did one or the other.

And then the anxious moment for the owner, when his ship was sighted off the bar, and some aspiring youngster or would-be pilot came flying hotfoot to the door to announce that the *Spring* or the *Annie Lee* or the *Marathon* was off the bar; and to receive the customary shilling for the good news—a sum of money that meant joy for a week and glory for a month.

How real it all was! What actuality in the now half-forgotten, wholly enfeebled phrase "Wait till my ship comes in!" In those days it meant probably fortune, at least temporary affluence.

But it all turned on the Captain. And the Captain said it all turned on the ship. How those men did love their ships! They always personalized their boat, and of course called it *she*. "The ocean's my home and my bark is my bride" was real then. The Captain was literally the "boat's swain"; and the head steward, called the "ship's husband," took second place, a quaintly triangular situation that was established on the high seas and accepted as normal.

Then came the landing, and the speedy appearance of the bluff old sea dog at the house of the owner. Yes, the owner first, long before wife or family. And then the quaint rugged honesty of their primitive methods and procedure—the logbook of course, to show when and how they lost that mizzenmast in the cyclone. But no bills of lading; a few scrappy papers perhaps, a lot of details purely from memory, surprise in the owner when the ports of call were named, a rough casting up on a blotter—and last, a fat bag of real gold pushed across the table. Oh, so simple!

But it all turned on the Captain. Most of these skippers were honest as they were rough; and when a "bad 'un" got somehow into command, it took only one or at the most two voyages to have him properly labeled.

The Ballast Hills

The sea played a vivid part in Seton's childhood—indeed there was no early childhood without the sea. We strolled down to the ocean strand, and here he took up the retrospect. He told me how a very clever captain always arranged to come back with a cargo; this added greatly to the profit.

If no cargo was carried back, he had to come under ballast; that is, the vessel was filled with the nearest available earth and stone, till she was down to her watermark, and so came safely home. In such case, of course, the return voyage was a dead loss.

Having arrived at the home port, South Shields, the ballast had to be dug out by hand, and shipped on little cable-drawn trolleys. These trolleys brought the ballast across the town to a stretch of wild sand hills along the shore of the ocean, here to be dumped.

These sand hills, being covered with bent grass, were originally called the "Bents," but the continual dumping of ballast at last covered the sand with various kinds of clay and loam, and then piled up so that the whole stretch was known as the Ballast Hills.

Of course, the assemblage of this material from all over the earth resulted in a remarkable variety of foreign plants and flowers, with occasional strange reptiles and insects.

But this man-made geological epoch was ended about 1875 by the general adoption of water ballast in tanks. This could, for one tenth the cost of solid ballast, be pumped in as the vessel sailed, and pumped out as soon as she sighted home.

The Ballast Hills are wholly changed today. When last we visited them in the 1930s, these wild heaps had been graded, planted, and beautifully laid out. They now constitute the Town Gardens, of which the residents are justly and intensely proud.

Gold Coast Disaster

Ernest's father, indeed all their near kin, were shipowners in the Merchant Marine. Joseph owned a dozen of these sailing ships, and in years of good luck was very prosperous. He was highly thought of by his men, so that when he got a good captain, that man stayed. Thus they had good captains in charge of their dozen sailing vessels, and on most years fortune smiled. A successful voyage, indeed, meant a hundred per cent on the outlay.

Then came a turn. One of their vessels "missed stays" three times, that is, failed to respond to her rudder, so ran aground, in crawling up the Bristol Channel; which meant three unloadings, and a dead loss at the end. One vessel went down in the Indian Seas. Next a captain turned bad. Then a businessman whose notes Joseph had endorsed "went broke."

A single disaster on the Gold Coast of Africa was the final blow. It was one of the last mishaps which resulted in the final financial failure that sent the family to Canada.

The Gold Coast had unusual perils and offered unusual rewards. The sailing vessels had to face the dangers of tropical tornadoes and of the "doldrums" or months of dead calm. There were few good harbors on the coast; and the Negroes of the Cameroons, with whom the crew must trade, were notorious for treachery and ferocity—frankly pirates.

But the rivers abounded in gold dust. This the Negroes washed out and, when a ship was in, brought it in little quills, eager to swap it for rum, weapons, calico goods, etc.

It was customary to wait for calm weather; then the British vessel would anchor off the coast. The Negroes came in a fleet of canoes, anxious to trade.

The White Captain, of course, despised all men whose skin was of different color from his own. But he kept his pistols ready and had the men armed for any contingency.

The first day of this particular trip, the Blacks, both men and women, swarmed on the decks, and a lively business was done in fabrics and rum for gold dust. But one of the sailors knew a few words of the Negro speech and warned the Captain that they were planning some sort of coup.

The third day, the men pointed out to the Captain that there were no women in the canoes. That surely should have been a signal for caution, but the Captain declined even to put up the boarding nets.

He was so contemptuous that he sent a boat ashore that morning with water barrels to be filled at the clear stream.

It was the mate in charge of this boat who told the final chapter. They were near shore when the battle cries of the Negroes began and the shots from the sailors' guns and pistols were heard.

The ship was taken, looted, and burned; while the second mate, with four men in a small boat, escaped southward, to land after two weeks in Portuguese territory, and thence relay the sad news back.

And so, blow after blow fell quickly; and a goodly fortune for those days was wiped out. All of this the children, at least the younger ones, heard long afterwards. At the time, they knew only that they were going to Canada. Pictures of log houses with pointed spruce trees all around, and bears and wolves in the background, gave Ernest thrills of mixed interest and fear.

The Dishonest Woman and the Cherries

Seton had a remarkable memory for the little events of his early childhood. On that first visit of mine to South Shields, as we passed beyond the house that had been his babyhood home, he suddenly burst out:

"How well I remember an injustice that that neighbor wrought on me. One day I was playing with some cousins in the back yard of this house. On a window sill in our view was a large bowl of cherries. We could see the mother of the family preparing to bake a pie.

"She was a kindly soul, and knowing little boys, she came to the door with her hands full of fruit.

"'How old are you?' she said to the first boy who approached.

"'Six,' he answered.

"'Here then are six cherries for you. And how old are you?' she asked of the next beseeching eyes.

"'Seven,' was the reply.

"'Then here are seven cherries for you.'

"The next boy was five and he received five cherries. It seemed fair to me, though I regretted my own extreme youth.

"As she turned to me, she apparently noted that her supply was running low.

"'And how old are you?'

"'Four,' I said, putting out my hand in anticipation.

"'Then here are yours,' and she put into my little waiting paw *three* cherries.

"All my gratitude for the gift was swallowed up in indignation at the injustice of it. I have never forgotten or forgiven her for the highhanded dishonesty—she robbed me of one of my cherries."

The Name of Seton

Never has there been such obvious confusion over the name of a famous artist or writer as there has been in the case of Seton; and many are the fantastic tales that have come to me as an explanation of the fact—and it is a fact—that he has been known as Thompson, as Seton-Thompson, and as Seton.

Let us once and for all settle the matter with a statement of the early history and the later events that have led up to this apparent discrepancy. In his autobiography, now out of print, he tells the story himself. In effect, it is as follows:

The Setons were of the Scottish nobility. During the turbulent days of the Jacobite uprisings in 1715 and 1745 they were on the wrong side of politics, siding with the Stuarts, sustaining Bonnie Prince Charlie. After the fatal battle of Culloden in 1746, in which the Highlanders were scattered in flight by the troops supporting King George, many of the clansmen sought hiding in England, among them Alan Cameron, a brother—or a cousin—of Cameron of Lochiel. He was a man of importance, so a price of £1000 was put on his head.

He took refuge among the shipyards of South Shields. There, in order to hide his identity, he assumed the name most common in the little town. That name was Thompson; and being a man of education, he spoke English well enough to complete his disguise.

His grandson was Ernest's father, Joseph Logan Thompson.

To continue in Seton's words: "In the earlier rising, our great-grandfather, Lord Seton, the Earl of Winton, had taken part, and lost everything, fleeing for his life to Italy, where he died. His only grandson, and his lawful heir, was George Seton, of Bellingham, Northumberland, my father's first cousin.

"In 1823, after the general amnesty, this George Seton appeared before the Bailies of Cannongate, the highest tribunal in Scotland; and proved himself the only grandson and lawful heir of George Seton, Earl of Winton. The Bailies acknowledged the validity of the claim, and George Seton was served with the title of Earl of Winton.

"He died without issue; but named my father as his heir and the lawful successor to the title, as he was the only male survivor of the line.

"My father's grandmother was Ann Seton. She never ceased to urge our people to make a stand for their rights. My father always meant to do so; but his natural indolence effectually stopped all action.

"On her deathbed, his grandmother, in these her last words, enjoined him: 'Never forget, Joseph, you are the heir. You are Seton, the Earl of Winton. You must stand up for your rights.'

"According to the law of Scotland, and under the original grant of the title, the earldom should be transmitted through a female when a male heir was lacking; said female was to carry the surname

Seton as though a male. Therefore, though lineally Cameron, my father's surname was Seton.

"These facts were common knowledge in our family, and frequently Father said that he felt it his duty to take his real name and assert his rights.

"In 1877, my father's sister, Mrs. Harry Lee, came to stay with us in Toronto. She was a very handsome lady of aristocratic habit and appearance. She took an intense interest in family matters and did all she could to stir my father to action in the matter of his true name and his titular rights.

"There was no lack of documentary proof; but the scarcity of funds, combined with my father's constitutional dislike of effort, resulted in nothing but a great interest on the part of the family and an emphatic announcement on the part of about half of us that we would take our real name at the earliest convenient date.

"One or two of my brothers did indeed begin to use the hyphenated name 'Seton-Thompson.' I was unable to take legal steps, being but seventeen years of age; but announced that at the age of twenty-one I would resume our name of 'Seton.' Father cordially approved; Mother was silent.

"I never wavered; and when I came of age I carried out my original plan. The necessary formalities were complied with; and on the first day of February 1883 my full and proper legal style became Ernest Evan Thompson Seton.

"Under this name I wrote all my first articles; under this name I illustrated the Century Dictionary. By this name, and this alone, I was known for years.

"Then one or two of my pious brothers got the idea that there was something irreligious in the family being divided between two, or virtually three, surnames; for one group was 'Thompson,' one 'Seton-Thompson,' and one 'Seton.' I could smile at their sophisticated platitudes—and did. I went my own way.

"After three years the subject again became acute. Against my father and a few cranky brothers I could stand. But when they got hold of my mother it was another matter. She was the only being on earth to whom I owed an avowed and absolute loyalty. They convinced her that the split was impious, and a reflection on both parents.

"So one day she put her arms around my neck and kissed me;

then invited me to kneel with her and pray for heavenly guidance. She prayed as few but my mother could pray; then rose and said: 'Oh, my boy, I want you to give up the name of "Seton," and be known as "Thompson" as long as I am alive.'

"Thus I was attacked in the weak spot of my wall.

"'Mother darling, I'll do anything you wish me to do—although I am wrong in doing this.'

"Then Father came, and it was agreed that I was to wear the name 'Seton-Thompson' as a *nom de plume* as long as Mother was alive; but when she should be called away, I would be free to resume what was my legal name.

"So it was arranged; and I continued 'Seton-Thompson' until the death of my mother in 1897.

"I was now released from my promise.

"There was no doubt about the form of my legal name; but so many copyrights had been taken out in the other form that it was deemed wise to have the matter cleared up in the courts.

"On November 28, 1901, the Supreme Court of New York decided the question.

"In a word, 'Seton-Thompson' was a *nom de plume;* 'Seton' is my family name."

His Father

Although of a most genial disposition, with the utmost kindliness and tolerance toward life in general, Seton held within him two deep-rooted hatreds which seemed to contradict his generous philosophy of living. One of these antipathies—that against General Custer—he retained all his life. More of that later.

The other—and this was the more personal and therefore the more bitter—he did finally efface; not by a willing effort indeed, but realizing the psychosomatic content of the thought during the last months of his life. That was his intense and uncompromising hatred of his father.

The subject is a difficult one to treat. Those of Ernest's brothers who were consulted were of the opinion that the whole topic should be avoided. Therefore, though against his own judgment, he wrote very briefly about it in his autobiography.

Nevertheless, Seton felt that the matter should be taken up, since the character of his father, his approach to life, his daily contact with his wife and with his children through all their formative years, were so positive that the effect on their development was fundamental.

Personally, I feel that this was so in the case of Ernest more than in that of the others because apparently he was more sensitive than his brothers, and felt things more intensely. Another fact, be it blessing or curse, was that Seton not only had a lasting memory of details of behavior of both himself and others; but in every case his memory of the occasion always brought back to him all the emotions he had felt at the time. Every impression bit in just as deeply as when it had first come to him. His later feelings were not a *remembrance* of the hatred he felt in his childhood, but the *same hatred itself* fanned to even greater heat by his own long sympathetic experience with children of his own and of others.

It was difficult for him to make any compromise with the fact that his father had lived in an era of vastly different psychological approach to child rearing. All arguments eventually brought him back to the same statement that his father was "the most selfish man I ever knew, or heard of, in history or in fiction."

Ernest seems to have been more closely akin in temperament to his mother Alice; and for that reason, often her confidant. It was on one such occasion that she told him of her legacy.

When her mother, Mary Snowdon, died, she left to her daughter £4000. "That goes into the bank," declared Alice, "to be the start in life for my sons." There were then ten.

At once Joseph flew into one of his customary rages and said: "Nothing of the sort, I'll take care of that. You turn that over to me."

"Poor Mother," murmured Seton as he told me the tale, "was terrorized as usual. The details I did not hear, but I do know that she said pleadingly, 'If it has to be spent, may I have a pony chaise and a boy to drive? I find it so hard to get about.' She was nearly always in a state of pregnancy.

"'Nothing but nonsense,' said Father. 'You can call a hack when you can't walk.' But he gave her no money to pay for the hack. So Mother as always was sacrificed.

"Then Father launched into an orgy of extravagance in the line of his own tastes. Nothing bad or even reprehensible. He bought an acre garden in town opposite his house, built expensive greenhouses, and hired a corps of gardeners. He bought a dozen different fancy rifles, and spent most of his time at the rifle ranges proving them. He bought microscopes and other scientific instruments. He had the best telescope in South Shields.

"As a result, he utterly neglected his business. Thus he squandered my mother's fortune and the inheritance of his ten sons; and never once seemed to think he had done wrong. 'Was he not our father —next, as it were, to God?'"

Joseph, Seton recalled, never referred to his own father except in terms of severe disapproval, calling him a tyrant, a hard task-master, a despot, etc. Yet he was of the very same type himself —an absolute ruler in the house, justifying his every act by his claim to "proper respect." The mania for enforcement of this attitude grew with the years to fantastic proportions until the phrase became a byword in the household.

"We were taught to treat him like the Pope, or a Roman emperor —to stand aside and at attention whenever he approached or passed. If he entered the room where we were sitting, we were trained all to rise and stand meekly behind our chairs with downcast eyes until he was seated. If one of us looked at him with more than a brief glance, he would say: 'At whom are you staring, sir? A more modest demeanor would comport more suitably with your station.'

"If he rose to leave the room, one of us was expected to promptly stand and go to open the door for him. Mother was always at watch, morning and evening, at the front door so that he would not have to open it for himself. I have heard her quote a hundred times: ''Tis sweet to know there is an eye to watch your coming, and to brighten when you come.'

"All very well when performed voluntarily, but he considered it his due, and was deeply hurt if ever he had to open the door for himself. 'Am I no one,' he would say indignantly, 'that you treat me as if I were merely one of yourselves?'

"If any of us said 'he' in his hearing, referring to himself, we were sternly rebuked. 'He! He! What do you mean by HE? Am I but one of yourselves? I'll trouble you to say "*Father* did this or *Father* did that." Never again let me hear you say "*He* did that," or any equivalent phrase.'

"If any of us played with him a game of chess, Mother used to warn us privately that we must not win. He would not like it; it savored of disrespect. I learned to avoid the game altogether. But our youngest brother good-naturedly consented to be the goat as a regular thing, and was most careful never to win, although he could have done so on a majority of occasions.

"Times without number he beat me black and blue with the hard leather and sharp-cornered ironbound heel of his slipper for some trivial transgression often beyond my understanding, which was construed into disrespect, or disobedience, or loss of temper. It was generally the last, for he had commanded me to keep my temper, and therefore anger was disobedience. Yet when he flogged me, he himself was always in a rage.

"As I review the history of the countless home floggings I got as a child, I can remember two, or perhaps three, in which I was guilty as charged and deserved the beating. Consequently I did not resent them, though the same effect would have been achieved in a bigger, better, and more permanent way by a serious rebuke or a different punishment without indignities or humiliation.

"All of the other floggings by my father left in me nothing but a sense of burning injustice, of bitter hatred. I was *not* the demon he described me as being; I did *not* have the 'brand of Cain on my brow'; I was *not* wholly given over to 'criminal thoughts'; I was *not* a reprobate, any more than he was.

"In the many family groups that we met at school, the elder boy in each protected the younger, but also bossed him; the eldest was the acknowledged chief of their clan. My father had laid down the law that no one in our family was to give orders but himself. We older brothers were to protect the younger, but not give them orders, or in any way boss them.

"This absurd and unnatural ruling had the usual effect of half authority; it bred ever growing discord and quarrels. My attitude to my younger brother finally became: 'If you are going to sass me and defy me, you may fight your own battles.' So, never very congenial, we grew ever wider apart.

"Quarreling was, in itself, a boyish peccadillo. But when my father, in his czarist role, forbade any further quarreling, quarreling became disobedience; that is, disrespect, an absolute capital and heinous crime.

"This mania reached its climax about the time I was fifteen. He had forbidden us to quarrel; it was like Peter the Great forbidding his peasants to grow whiskers. Of course we quarreled, under urge of natural laws.

"Then my brother Walter found that he could shift all blame to me quite easily, by saying: 'Ernest went into one of his rages; that awful look came into his face; you know what a temper he has, Father.'

"That settled it. 'Yes, I know it. He has disobeyed me again; he has treated me with disrespect; with defiance, virtually contempt.'

"Then came the usual beating. White with rage, he would hiss at me: 'I'll beat it out of you! I'll flog you within an inch of your life!' until Mother would beg and implore him on her knees to cease.

"'Have mercy, Father! Remember he is only a child! Temper justice with mercy!' Then, with angry words, Father would order Mother out of the room.

"One day, after one of these painful scenes, Mother took me to her room and said through her tears: 'Oh, my boy, don't you see the mischief you are making with your temper? It will certainly be your ruin. Won't you try to curb it; won't you pray for help, won't you let your mother pray for you?'

"'I'll do anything for you, Mother,' and we kneeled down together, and she poured out her soul and her prayers before God. I kissed her and promised I would do my best.

"And I did try. Again and again my plaguing brother riled me till I knew not what to do.

"Then on one occasion the trial came when Father happened to be present. He turned on me in fury.

"'Your devilish temper again!'

"I answered back: 'I didn't say anything or do anything.'

"'No, but I saw it in your face,' was his fierce retort.

"'I'm not responsible' I burst out, 'for what's inside of me. I got that from you. I'm responsible only for what comes out.'

"'What! You insolent, ribald monster! I'll flog you within an inch of your life!'

"Then he seized me by the neck and went at me in a white fury. He was a big, strong man, weighing nearly two hundred pounds; I was a sickly, small boy. He doubled me over his left knee, held my legs under his right knee; and with a hand clutching my neck, he pounded me till I shrieked in agony, and Mother threatened to go for the police if he did not cease.

"It was days before I recovered. During that time three ideas grew in me.

"First, I was not his son at all; I was a foundling picked up somewhere.

"Second, I would run away as soon as I could form a feasible plan.

"Third, I would never again try to curb my temper, or take impudence from my little brother.

"The last idea alone called for immediate action.

"The opportunity came all too soon. On the vacant lot where the neighborhood played ball, we differed as usual. I said: 'See here, I'll take no more sass from you. I'll smash you just as I would any other fellow, you dirty little brute; and if you tell Father, I'll kill you!'

"'Er—er—will you? You dasn't.'

"So I went at him without restraint, and gave him a severe pummeling. He ran for the house. I followed, giving him my boot behind at each opportunity. He yelled: 'I'll tell Father. I can get you licked any time. You'll see! You'll be sorry for this!'

"'You tell Father and I'll kill you before night.'

"He knew by my face that there was danger ahead. Anyhow, he decided not to tell. Moreover, he found that I was able and now ready at any time to give him a licking without regard to consequences; and the good results were evident soon.

"I think that was our last quarrel; it certainly was our last fight.

"Though of refined manner and speech, Father had a cruel side that often shocked me.

"When we were on the farm, he claimed for himself the right of killing all cows, calves, and pigs that had to be butchered. He was a good rifle shot and always dispatched the creature with one shot through the brain—then left the real work to the rest of us.

"According to his own statement, he on three occasions, for trifling reasons, ordered one or other of his sons out of the house forever. I know that he told one of my full-grown brothers to begone because he went into the toilet room at a time when Father himself usually went.

"Another brother, at the age of twelve, was told to get out for good and all 'and live the life of a beggar as you deserve' because he had eaten some grapes that Father had been cultivating. And, as Father himself later said to me, 'He should have gone had not your mother risen up and said: "Then I go too!"'

"My relatives in England told me of a typical case. My eldest brother, only one year old at the time, was commanded by my father to take a certain position at the table. Because of his babyhood, he did not understand.

"'I'll be obeyed,' shouted my pious father, and repeated the command. Getting no response, he began to slap the baby with his flat hand, but more and more heavily, shrieking: 'Do as I tell you! Do as I tell you!'

"In spite of Mother's tears and the baby's screams, he kept on till the child fell unconscious; and the fond parent was only stopped by my aunt Mary [Tate] going for the police.

"Aunt Mary herself told me the story, with bitterness and contempt, though it was thirty years agone. Mother refused to confirm or deny it, but I do know that Father bragged that he had a similar battle with my second brother Willie, and it took an hour's flogging and exhorting before the child collapsed in the corner. These things he himself told me proudly, as a warning to mend my ways.

"As he grew older, he more and more often reviled us boys for coming into the world to be his crushing burden. We all thought, but did not dare to say: 'Why did you bring us into the world if you did not want us?' Certainly Mother did not desire such a brood.

"Poor Mother! She bore the brunt of it all. Once in later years, in a moment of breakdown, she sobbed out to me: 'I could not have lived with him a year, had I not fed him on the most outrageous flatteries; and it all came back on me, because he believed them and thought himself perfect.'"

One later incident, although recounted in his autobiography, I should like to repeat here because it is so entirely characteristic of Joseph's attitude toward his family.

Ernest, after two and a half years of study—and starvation—in London, returned to his father's house in Toronto. He was sick and weak, but looking forward to natural history adventures, a renewal of all the joys in wild life that had been absent during the period he had been abroad.

Soon after his arrival his father called him into his study one day. He took down from a high shelf his cash book, a ponderous volume, opened it at "E" and then in characteristic fashion solemnly spoke:

"Now, my son, you are twenty-one years of age. You have attained to years of manhood, if not of discretion. All the duties and responsibilities which have hitherto been borne for you by your father you must now assume for yourself. I have been prayerfully remembrant of your every interest, and I need hardly remind you that for all that is good in you, you are, under God, indebted to your father—and, of course, to some extent, your mother also.

"You owe everything on earth, even life itself, to your father.

"While it is hopeless that you should ever discharge *this* debt, there is another to which I must call your attention at once."

He now pointed to page after page in the cash book—the disbursements that had been made for the boy since his birth. There they were, every item with day and date perfect—undoubtedly correct—even the original doctor's fee for bringing him into the world. The whole amount was $537.50.

"Hitherto," he said, with traces of emotion in his voice, "I have charged no interest. But from now on I must add the reasonable amount of 6 per cent per annum. I shall be glad to have you reduce the amount at the earliest possible opportunity."

Ernest was utterly stunned. He staggered to his feet and started off, refusing his father's offer "to furnish without expense a full copy of the indebtedness."

The fond parent's parting words were: "God bless you, my son. In the natural course of events, you cannot much longer be an inmate of my house; but I must prayerfully trust that, wherever your lot is cast in the near future, you will never forget the debt you owe your father, who is to you on earth the next to God."

Suffice it to say that within the next couple of years Ernest paid every cent of the bill to his father, who accepted it as his absolute legal and ethical due.

The Other Side of Father

"However true in detail the foregoing description of my father, it would, if left standing by itself, give a very unfair picture. He showed another nature altogether when the right conditions brought them into view.

"He was indeed indolent, resentful of having to work for a living, selfish and of a dangerous temper. Yet he was a man of exemplary morals, and temperate in all his habits of life.

"As a young man, he loved a glass of wine and the fragrance of a good cigar. Nevertheless, he thoughtfully and wholly gave these up when his numerous sons appeared. As I heard him put it once: 'I do not wish my sons to smoke or drink; therefore I will set them the good example of total abstinence.'

"He was usually grave and always dignified. His tastes were eminently literary, and his speech correct, refined, and scholarly at all times, with a tendency toward grandiloquence. I never heard him utter a coarse, profane, or vulgar word. I never knew him to listen to an improper tale.

"His natural bent toward science made him a careful and critical reader of the latest works dealing especially with astronomy, chemistry, and mechanics.

"He loved to discuss recent discoveries in art and science, and kept himself well posted. Like most of his generation, he was strongly opposed to Darwinism and the rest of the modern school; he was pre-eminently a classicist and a fundamentalist.

"His manners in public were those of the courteous, old-fashioned gentleman type that dominated English society a hundred years ago; and as long as he was treated with 'proper respect,' and not called on to 'work for a living,' he could be a most agreeable companion.

"Many a pleasant walk I had with him down the ravines and over the fields north of Toronto. There were times when we seemed in absolute accord, two really harmonious companions with common interests abounding. Then, suddenly, some trifle would happen, something that savored of 'disrespect,' a flippant answer, an overlong delayed response, a little nothing that was wrongly construed. And a storm was started that swept all good things out of life for days.

"Yet it is to my father that I owe my interest in art and science; it is to him that I am indebted for a certain dogged persistence that enables me to say that I never took anything in hand without completing it. It might be well done; it might be ill done; but it was done, was the best I could do, and was always carried on to a definite prearranged finish."

Mother and Her Superstitions

Many an hour Seton and I spent at various times talking of his childhood. I came to realize how closely akin he must have been to his mother, and recognized many of her sterling qualities in this, the son who was by all accounts her favorite.

His devotion to his mother was absolute. Although she had faults, he condoned every failing, and expressed the deepest admiration for the angel he considered a martyr to his father's selfishness. From many different occasions, I quote the following:

"My mother was the most rigidly pious and conscientious person I ever knew. Not only was she careful to read the Bible, morning, noon, and night, but also certain holy books by prominent religionists. Besides which she prayed many times a day—she prayed without ceasing.

"Her whole life was saturated with religious thought and colored by the assumption that she was being closely watched by an ever present Deity who was, above all things 'a jealous God and quick to anger.'

"If one of us set anything on the Bible, he was rebuked. Her glasses might be set *in* the Bible as a place marker, but not on top; nothing must be set on top of the Holy Book.

"Not only did she believe that the Bible was written by the finger of God, but she was convinced that it had been written in English exactly as it appears in the King James version. Any attempt, therefore, to revise, retranslate, or rearrange was dreadful blasphemy.

"She could at any time get absolute guidance from God by closing her eyes in prayer, opening the Bible at a venture, then dropping her finger at random; the exact text touched was inevitably the word of God for the present emergency.

"She was of the type that has been credited with overdeveloped veneration; the type that filled the convents of Dark Age Europe, or the Flagellant ranks of the Middle Ages. Nothing appealed to her more than the possibility of, in some sort, wearing the martyr's crown. Yes, even though it soared no higher than drinking cold tea when she preferred hot; or eating the gristle end of a steak while others got the tenderloin.

"Mother had little time for intellectual pursuits, although she was much interested in history and had a marvelous memory for facts and dates. Her gifts and life might easily have led her into gossiping but that she safeguarded herself and those about her by the continual observance of certain principles. 'Never,' she ruled, 'say anything that reflects on another, unless first you try it by three rules: Is it true? Is it kind? Is it necessary?' She lived up to this, and I know of no more practical way of applying the Golden Rule.

"Although burdened and overworked with the care of her vast household, she found time not only to make many garments for us, darn our socks, and mend our underclothes; she also managed to turn out numberless quilts and garments for the church's Dorcas Fund, destined to be of help to others in the city, less fortunate than ourselves.

"In assembling the scraps and patches for these quilts, she soon used up all available stuff in the house or other sources; but invented a mode that at that time at least was not used elsewhere. Having made a cover of scraps and an underlining, she laid the latter out on the frame; then, overlaying that with newspapers, three- or four-ply thick, tacked these down at one or two places; then laid on the cover and quilted as usual. These quilts were extremely successful, warm and far more enduring than one might expect. The crackling of the papers wore out very early.

"Many a time have I seen Mother and cousin Polly working nights on these kindly gifts, long after the rest of the household were in bed.

"These devoted sacrifices seemed to fill the place of recreation in my mother's life. I do not remember her ever going to a public entertainment; I never knew her to go to a private social affair if it interfered at all with her prayer meeting or her self-imposed burden of contributions for the clothing of the poor.

"Her bent inclined her not only to the severest orthodox religion but also to a multitude of little superstitions.

"Each time we moved into a new house she was most careful about the first household object to enter; it must be a basket or tray on which was a Bible, a loaf of bread, and some salt.

"On New Year's morning, the first one to cross the threshold must be a man, of dark complexion, and of spotless record.

"We were always cautioned to break the bottom of the egg shell after it was emptied, 'lest we balk the good fairies.'

"If the rooster crowed before the door, she would say: 'Now we can count on visitors today.'

"If one of us swept the table crumbs into the fire, she rebuked us, saying: 'Those belong to the sparrows; God will surely punish you for this someday by making you go hungry.'

"These were among the countless little thoughts and traditions that made the atmosphere of the household; and it must be admitted that all were at least in the right direction, none of them was likely to contribute a harmful tinge. The sum total was for kindliness, which, after all, is the only thing worth while."

Mother's Real Self

"But the little foibles and superstitions were merely the specks of dust and the superficial scratches on the blazing, shining jewel. Through all of my mother's life, her religion was her daily, hourly comfort; and she lived in all sincerity the doctrines that she preached. She was early inured to sacrifice; and, when her many (fourteen) children arrived, each a new care, a new drain, and a new opportunity for self-effacement, she met the stress with a martyr's courage and a mother's joy.

"Every one of us had all the standard diseases of childhood—whooping cough, croup, measles, scarlatina, colic, cramps, mumps, etc.; and every one of us was nursed by our ever loving mother. In the case of the last four children, she was without medical aid except her own experience. She never murmured, she never complained, was always cheerful, she never gave up. And when it became obvious to us youngsters that our father was a failure, she did all she could to screen him and set him in the best light possible.

"In moments of depression which, from time to time, descended on the whole family, it was always Mother who reacted first and most completely. She always led us back to happier thoughts by her smile and her ready jest. Father might see only the cloud; Mother could always see the silver lining.

"Never very strong, she spared herself not at all; broken down by overwork and over-childbearing, she continued to the last the true and loving mother—a martyr, but a joyful one, to her calling.

"Her gentle, unselfish conscientious care of us was unremitting, as it was lifelong. I do not believe there was ever a night when she did not creep about after hours to see that each of the younger ones was well covered in bed and sleeping the sweet sleep of healthy youth."

PART TWO

A LANTERN LIGHTS THE PATH

BOYHOOD

The Hen Coop

Having been brought up to believe that in merit and in wisdom their father was just one degree less than God, and in availability about two degrees better, Ernest never forgot the occasion when first he entertained a doubt of Joseph's omniscience.

It was in the fall of 1867. Ernest was seven years of age. A hen had hidden her nest in the field and hatched out a brood of chicks in late October. Here was a predicament. How could they possibly survive the winter?

Only by bringing them into the house—which meant the kitchen. To accommodate them, a pen and a sleeping box were needed. One of the brothers, or one of the neighbors, could have made it in an hour. But no, Father was trained in sea thought. The chickens must be kept in a coop of the style used on ships.

So, with much labor, the brothers constructed a long stupid sea-coop, a foot wide and a foot high, but 15 feet long; with a bench on top of it, and fastenings to hold it to the bulwarks of a ship.

The fact that it was too long for the kitchen, and no use as a bench, was ignored. "I see that coop to this day under the kitchen table," reminisced Seton in later years, "projecting 4 feet at each side, with its ridiculous bench and elbow rests, that were never once used.

"I can smell those unhappy chickens, and hear yet the sigh of relief from the womenfolk when the last of them died and was cast onto the dung pile."

Too Much Rulership

"My father was not only one of those dominating personalities that were typical of his time, the Mid-Victorian age; he was an extremist. He felt it to be his duty to settle every detail of our lives and thoughts, never doubting that his own was the best possible wisdom. We were allowed to make no decision, large or small, for ourselves.

"This may have its advantages at times—then again, we lost the power of deciding.

"In the spring of 1869, Father and Mother were away overnight. My brothers and I were left in the charge of my cousin Polly, who acted as regent in the absence of our parents.

"I had always slept with my brother in the northeast room. But my cousin, knowing the love that children have for change, and wishing to please me, said: 'Now, Ernie, you may sleep in any room you wish.'

"I was terribly embarrassed by having it put up to me, for there were three rooms available; and never before had I had the chance to choose.

"With many doubts and much hesitation, I finally said: 'I think I'll sleep in the east room.'

"Accordingly I said my prayers and tumbled into the east room bed. But I could not sleep. I was worried. I did not know why; maybe I was making a mistake; perhaps it was wrong.

"So I arose at last, hunted up Cousin Polly, and sheepishly said: 'I think I want to sleep in the southeast room.'

"With a little readjustment, I was moved thither. But here my indecision was worse. I tossed and worried; felt a sense of sin, a load of responsibility.

"At last, at a late hour, after torments of doubt, I crawled back into my own bed in the northeast room, totally upset by the burden of decision and yet made unhappy by the thought that perhaps I was losing an opportunity. It was the first time I had ever been allowed to make a judgment for myself."

The Kingbird

From the few books on wild life that he could procure on the farm, Ernest had read of a bird that, though little larger than a sparrow, was of such courage that it would drive off any hawk—yes, even an eagle.

He had read of this; but through all his hours of observation and study he had never seen anything that corresponded to the description. He came to believe that it did not inhabit his part of the world, maybe it was only in books.

Then one day as he went for the cows with his brother George and a neighbor, Jim Parker, he saw two crows fly high overhead. At once, there sprang from a low tree a small bird that uttered a sharp note of attack. The daring little fellow darted at one of the crows, then at the other. The huge black birds, many times bigger and stronger than the assailant, dodged and swooped in obvious fear, then escaped as fast as possible into the woods.

Ernest was ablaze with admiration and interest.

"What is that little bird?" he asked eagerly.

"That is a kingbird," George told him.

"A kingbird!" gasped Ernest. "Here in our country! On our own farm!" And he gulped with joy.

That was his first encounter with the brave little winged arrow; but now he watched with better-trained eyes, and learned more about the hero-bird.

Finally in 1876 he wrote a poem embodying his observations and his worship.

We give it here though he did not put it out in its final form until 1879. It is not great poetry, but he considered it the beginning and foundation of all his work as a wild-animal story writer.

THE KINGBIRD
A Barnyard Legend

On a June bright sunny morning,
On the banks of Mississippi
At the old farmhouse of Wonga,
Rhoda just had fed her poultry;
Then she left them all unguarded,
Scattering here and there and scratching.
Altogether they were hundreds.

In the back part of the barnyard,
One old apple tree was waning.
Mid its gnarled and twisted branches
Her home nest a Kingbird builded.
Now she was away, refreshing,
But her mate the brittle charge kept.
Bound by love alone to keep them
Safe and warm till her returning.
Small he was, of modest colors;
Black his fantail was, but white-tipped,
Grey and white his colors elsewhere,
Flies his food, nor troubled others.
In the pines a quarter mile off,
Dwelt the Hawk, the fierce destroyer.
In the absence of protection,
Saw and seized the chance to ravage.
Mid the cheery din of poultry,
One keen-sighted turkey spied him,
Cried aloud "The Hawk is coming!"
Cried and fled away for shelter.

Have ye heard the cry of "Fire!"
'Board the ship when in midocean?
First an awful silent instant,
Then a din, a wild commotion.
Like to this the consternation,

Crazy useless strife for shelter.
Last in flight the gallant game-cock
Cov'ring the retreat of chickens.

Long ere half the yard was traversed,
Down! the Hawk was in upon them.
Fierce his yellow eyes were gleaming,
Keen for blood his crooked bill was,
More for hatred than for hunger.
Now! he just will seize the hindmost!
But with sudden burst of courage
Sprang the cock at the destroyer.

Up he leapt with such a veh'mence
He the Hawk entirely baffled,
And the latter, back returning,
Was again repulsed right bravely.

But the bravest cock can never
Long resist a Hawk's fierce charges.
Down! he came again from heav'nward.
And the head of all the barnyard
In the plume-strewn dust was hurlèd,
All his neck and body bleeding.

Long his duty to his young ones
Chained the Kingbird down, unwilling;
But his mate, returning, freed him.
Now no longer small fly-hunter,
Now no longer shunning notice,
Changed his mien and e'en his color.
On his once grey head, displaying
Flaming red crest of the warrior,*
Shrills his loud and stirring war-cry,
Launching through air like a meteor;
Filled with furious indignation,
Screaming darts upon the waster.

* The red crest is concealed except when he goes to war.

Ere he yet has stilled the throbbing
Of the heart of him he vanquished,
Smote him full between the eyeballs,
Dashed him fully three yards backwards;
Both in air arose together.
But the Kingbird, ever higher,
Dashing down with righteous fury,
With his trenchant bill assailing,
Tore the bloody feathers from him;
Both in air went whirling ever.

When the Hawk sought to have slain him,
It was empty air he struck at,
Till he wearied all his vigor,
Striking, ever hitting nothing.
Then the Hawk sought to escape him,
Stretched his pinions for the wildwood.

But the glorious Kingbird followed;
Ever hard and harder smote him,
Till with blood and terror blinded,
Dashed the Hawk against a pine branch,
Broken by the blast of winter.
Sharp! it paled his wretched body,
Held him shrieking in the pine tree,
Till the tiny Kingbird pierced him
Through the brain and so destroyed him.

Screamed the King in exultation,
Backward hied he to the farmyard;
Grey head once again, and harmless.
To his gentle mate flew straightly,
Just resumed his lowly duties,
As he had not wrought such glories.

Such the legend of the Kingbird,
Of the fearless crested Kingbird;
He of fowls is the protection.
Though a sparrow he in size is,
Yet an eagle he in spirit.

The First Boots

One memory of his mother's bedtime visits stood out in detail in Ernest's mind.

It occurred soon after the family had moved from England to the Canadian backwoods.

"My parents," he told me, "brought to the woods with them a host of little prejudices; English meant sterling, Canadian meant third-rate, in all departments.

"We children arrived in very pronounced English costume—cloth caps, Fauntleroy collars, knickerbockers, white stockings, and shining leather shoes, without tops, but held on by a button and strap over the instep. So togged, we went to school.

"Most of the local boys and girls went barefooted all summer, and in cold weather wore heavy cowhide boots. Those that the boys used had legs that reached above the calf.

"The contrast between us in footgear was even greater than that in our manner and speech, which furnished topics of merriment and mockery to the rest of the school. Very soon our sense of superiority was undermined by the sneers and jibes. We began to wish 'we were like the other fellows.'

"We made surreptitious attempts to go barefooted, carefully resuming our shoes before nearing home. But, oh, how pitifully unfitted were our white and tender feet for such usage! And we never really learned the mode.

"Convinced that no good shoes could be bought in Canada, Father had brought an extra pair of the low-cut 'pumps' for each. But he had not calculated on the rapid growth of our feet; so that next year, it was clear that the two youngest must inherit the shoes intended for all four.

"This was glorious news for us older two. Not only were we feeling the ignominy of low-cut girlish shoes; but the very practical fact that thistles were the most abundant growth in the land had been made painfully manifest. Now we knew why all the boys and men here wore long-legged boots when working in the fields.

"Just how I happened to come ahead of my elder brother Arthur in this case I do not now know. But the home authorities admitted that I, first of the four youngsters, now seven years old, must have a pair of new shoes.

"Shall I ever forget that day! Mother took me in the wagon to Lindsay, to the great shoe shop of the famous John F. Lyons; and speedily, to my joy and amazement, I was allowed to select a pair of real manly boots 'just like the other fellows had.' They were made of strong cowhide, had legs that reached up nearly to my knees, had two ostentatious straps or tugs to pull them on with. But—more than that—each had a shiny copper toe band like a golden moon in front. And last and most glorious, on the front upper part of the leg a square of blazing red leather on which, printed in gold, were two boys having a boxing match!

"I was overwhelmed with joy. There were few boots in school that could compare with these, and absolutely none to surpass them.

"In the matter of fit, I was easily pleased, so long as they were big enough and looked manly enough. As I remember it, that pair of splendors cost sixty cents. My attempt to leave my English pumps in part payment won no favor, my sole motive being to get rid of them forever.

"For the next hour or two I had to put in time while Mother shopped. But I walked up and down the chief sidewalk, wearing my new happiness, my pants carefully tucked in the top to give the admiring public a full opportunity, and I basked in the radiance of each passing glance. I tried to keep a straight face, but I was grinning and looking very conscious most of the time.

"We got home about three o'clock. My brothers could not arrive from school before four-thirty, and I was sore beset to put in the time until I could burst upon their gaze in my new magnificence.

"I went about various chores, selecting those that could not possibly tarnish my scarlet and gold. I watched the road and chafed until at last I saw my two brothers and some schoolmates loitering along.

"I was puzzled as to the exact etiquette of the occasion. Should I run, shouting in triumph, to meet them, or should I maintain my dignity and 'pretend,' letting them find out the miracle for themselves?

"I decided on a compromise.

"On the drive, halfway to our gate, was a log. To this I went with an ax, and began chopping as though I meant to cut it through. I didn't work hard at it, or do much chopping; but, standing on the log, I was up in the air and had high visibility. I was standing in a graceful position—rather a heroic position, I thought—as my brothers came in easy view.

"'Hello,' I said, 'what made you so late?' And, assuming the air of a tired businessman, I drove the ax into the log.

"'We're not l—,' one began; then the other exclaimed, 'Hello, what you got?'

"I tried to look inscrutable, unconcerned, but it was no use. I was on exhibition obviously. They were dazzled, and I broke into the broadest and weakest of grins. For the next five minutes I wallowed in their admiration and ill-concealed envy. It was the proudest moment of my life. Never before had I been accused of dress-pride; but on that occasion I was intoxicated, deliriated, with the vainglory of it.

"The rest of the waking hours of that day I tramped ostentatiously about, always with the pants tucked in the tops. I stopped many times during my evening meal to look under the table at my copper toes and shiny red leather. At bedtime, I wanted to keep my boots on while I said my prayers. But Mother said, 'No,' I must be properly undressed, and kneel at my bedside as usual.

"So we compromised by my putting my boots on the bed; then I bowed my head over them so I could smell the leather while I prayed.

"At last I was snugly away in bed as usual, except that the boots were tucked under my pillow.

"I was just going off to sleep as Mother made her last rounds to see if all was well with her brood.

"I called out:

"'Mamma! Mamma!'

"'Yes, darling.'

"'Come quite close, Mamma.'

"'Well, what is it?'

"'Mamma, when I go to heaven, will my boots go too?'

"'No, darling. People don't wear boots in heaven.'

"'Then, Mamma, I don't want to go!'"

The Cheese

The winter of 1935–36 Seton and I spent abroad, lecturing much of the time, and enjoying all of it. In December we were in France; and the holiday season having limited our professional engagements, we found no more interesting pastime than exploring the gastronomic possibilities of the country.

We have always agreed with the French in regarding good cooking and excellent wines as serious elements in life. They are there, as they should be, looked on as gifts from God, to be joyfully and thankfully partaken of, but not to be abused by overindulgence.

We had come to near the end of our meal one evening. A serving of delectable *fromage de brie* reminded him of a humorous incident which occurred in the early days of his family life in Canada, soon after they had come from England.

"Since we were going to live like Robinson Crusoe," he chuckled, "Father decided that we must make everything for ourselves.

"In the summer of 1868, therefore, having now an abundance of milk, we set seriously about the making of cheese. Father did all the bossing.

"The two eldest sons at home were able carpenters. Under Father's guidance, and taking advantage of the fine weather, they erected a strong cheese press, of massive oak timbers, each six inches square. In this was geared a mighty jackscrew, of the type used in hoisting a brick building or a locomotive; because 'high pressure is the secret of cheese.' As the boys worked to perfect their contribution, Father read up on the subject.

"A round vat with perforated bottom was procured; then some rennet which Mother had, under instruction, prepared from the stomach of a recent calf.

"The buckets of milk were now warmed, curdled with the rennet, and poured into a strong sack which was held in the vat, and fully lined it. The sack was sewed up, the sliding lid replaced, and the vat hoisted into position under the jackscrew.

"The boys took turns at the long arm of the screw, Father directing from a safe distance and uttering words of encouragement as the whey oozed out of the bottom and squirted out of the top.

"The mass was reduced to about half when the boys thought it time to stop. But Father thought otherwise. After a period of recuperation, he ordered them at it again, and the great screw went slowly down, till the mass was only about a foot thick.

"'Pressure is the secret of cheese,' Father repeated. 'You can't give it too much.' So, by another effort that only six-inch oak could resist, the mass was reduced to about ten inches.

"The whey ooozed out for an hour or so, then ceased. They left the cheese overnight in the press to set. Next day it was triumphantly taken out. It was a pleasant-smelling mass of yellowish-white stuff, somewhat like cheese, and just possible to be cut with a knife.

"'Hold on! The book says it needs ripening.' So the cheese was put away for a month to ripen. During that month it got somewhat yellower, and much harder—so hard that a hammer as well as a knife was needed to cut it.

"Father still insisted that it was not ready. So it was left till winter; then declared 'open for settlers.' We went at it with enthusiasm. It had indeed turned as hard as ivory; but a good hatchet and a sharp saw could break or cut a piece loose; and we children thought those pieces delicious—not for immediate consumption indeed, for they defied our teeth, but toasted on a fork. And for a while we had some pleasant evenings with that big round yellow bulk.

"The mass kept steadily ossifying. Even with a saw, it was not easy now to separate a chunk. But we were used to tools, and very ingenious; so we devised the plan of making a deep cut with a sharp saw, then driving an iron wedge into it. This would usually force off a piece; and, at the last moment when it flew, we learned to cover our eyes against the splinters.

"But the cheese continued to crystallize and petrify. The effort at separating a piece became prohibitory. The carpenter protested against the damage to the tools; and the cheese was rolled into a dark corner to be forgotten.

"Years after, when I went to visit the Blackwells, who had acquired our farm with its every appanage, I saw the barn door propped open with a large yellow boulder. Then I saw one of the boys with a hammer straighten some nails on it.

"'Where did you get that stone?' I asked.

"'Dunno. It was here when we come.'

"I examined it carefully, noted its shape, the marks where the tools had bitten into it, and the later marks where the rats had broken their teeth on it. The evidence was complete that that doorstop and anvil combined was nothing less than my father's cheese."*

Old Ellen

After we had established our home in Santa Fe we had the usual problems with help. Each time we thought we had the perfect maid or the permanent man, something would happen, and again we were on our own.

As we sat one evening in the kitchen where I had just finished pinch-hitting for the late-departed incumbent, Seton began:

"In England, 'the old country,' Mother had always at command an adequate staff of three or four maids. They came and went after the manner of their kind. But one there was that remained a fixture. That was Old Ellen, nominally the nurse, really the major-domo. She had nursed my mother as a baby, her mother had nursed my grandmother, and so they faded back into the mists of the forgotten, a long series of faithful retainers, bound to us by love, loyalty, and appreciation.

"When the crash in our fortunes made it clear that we could no longer keep the needed staff, it was not supposed to bear on Ellen's position. She was one of the family.

"But when we set out for Canada, Ellen was in a quandary, for her aged mother was still alive and needed Ellen's daily ministrations as well as her weekly salary.

"So Ellen, duty-bound in South Shields, saw us off with streaming

---

* The family committee, after consulting the records, decided that there is some overstatement in the foregoing. Practically none of the children, they say, was wounded by the splinters of the cheese; and only one rat—a very young one—had his teeth broken as indicated. Nevertheless, scientific light that came later implies that his father had stumbled on the making of casein, a form of artificial ivory much used in commerce today.

eyes and a final 'God bless you, Missus, I must bide wi' my mother. But she's eighty-two and feeble, and in God's time I'll follow you.'

"One year later her mother, old Mary Robertson, died; and Ellen, true to her instincts and her vow, took steerage passage on a sailing vessel, and found us in the woods.

"I have but a dim remembrance now of her arrival with two seaman's chests. It was in the spring of 1867. We had moved into the brick house. Ellen had been met at the station by a town friend who brought her out to the farm in a buckboard. She stepped into the back door to find my mother, soft-handed and reared in delicate nurture, down on her knees, scrubbing the floor—not wholly, I think now, without the pride of the martyr.

"This was too much for the faithful old creature. She broke down in a passionate outburst of weeping. 'Ye shanna dae it, ye shanna dae it! I've come to be wi' my ane folk, but I'll gae back if ye dinna promise ye'll never dae it again!'

"I do not think that any power on earth would have made her 'gae back.' But her sorrow was so real and Mother so unfitted for the work that, as far as I remember, Mother never again scrubbed the floor.

"Most of Ellen's kinfolk were sailors, but some were farmers; and Ellen took charge of poultry, geese, and small stock, as well as cooking, in the masterful way that is born of knowledge combined with common sense and physical fitness.

"A cat seemed a necessary adjunct to the farmhouse, and one was secured at Lindsay, our nearest town. But it was fully grown; and it is well known that a full-grown cat is apt to go home, yes, miles through unknown woods, to the place she knows the best. The big brothers were debating the question 'Will she stay or go back to the town?' when Ellen took the cat in her arms and thoroughly anointed its feet, all four of them, with fresh butter, then gently set the cat down with the remark: 'Once a cat licks her feet, she feels at home—and that butter will make her lick them all round.'

"Sure enough, as soon as set free, the cat began to lick off the butter; and by the time all four feet were licked clean, pussy was purring contentedly by the stove. Whether the notion be true or false, I know not; but this I do know: the cat stayed with us and supplied us yearly with more kittens than could be absorbed by any local demand.

"Those six per cent quarterly dividends that our cat declared were in such little favor at home that next summer she made her nest in a fence corner far afield. Here she was safe from human annoyance, but exposed to one danger hitherto unthought of.

"The kittens were yet small—barely had their eyes open—when in the absence of the mother the cowering brood was discovered by a prowling skunk that incontinently set about making a hearty meal of the kittens. The loud and distressed mews of the first victim attacked brought the mother cat racing and raging.

"Is there any creature on earth of greater courage than a mother cat? Had it been a flock of elephants or a troop of lions, she would have attacked them just the same. In a moment, the feasting skunk was in a death grapple with a passion of unbounded courage, terrific weapons, incredible strength, and absolutely matchless agility.

"The skunk fought with all his guns, muzzle-loader and breech-loader. But what can stand before the fury of a mother cat? The skunk fled in ignominious defeat. Perhaps for the first time in his life, his defense had been inadequate.

"How much he was injured we never knew. But the cat soon turned up at the house. How well I remember her plastered and disheveled fur as she came blinking her bloodshot eyes, half blinded with the musk, and stinking to heaven, filling the whole house with her unfragrance. We reverenced her heroism but could not endure her person. So she was forcibly invited to 'sojourn in the wilderness for many days,' the sun and rain to be her kindly purge. A chair that she had sat on before her condition was realized had also to stand in the sun and rain before it could be tolerated indoors.

"Old Ellen described the stench as a 'very parsey smell,' whatever that means. It seems to be a North Country word for any odor that is frightfully unclean. It was often used by the Tynesiders of the older generation. I have never heard it elsewhere.

"Ellen's particular pets were the geese. Each spring she set a goose in the kitchen closet and successfully brought off a brood of goslings. Every day during that long month, about ten o'clock in the morning, the gander would come to the kitchen door and trumpet loudly.

Then Ellen would open the door of the closet, the old goose would gravely cover the eggs with the down of the nest lining, and waddle out, answering the gander as she went. Outside, she was received with a rapturous quackering by the gander and the other geese as they bent their snaky necks down to the ground, bowing and congratulating the setting goose. After half an hour refreshment, the mother goose came waddling back, quackered her good-bys, left the gander at the door, uncovered her eggs, and resumed her job.

"One deep impression I have of dear Old Ellen. She always sympathized with us children when we were in trouble, even if it was punishment for wrongdoing. I remember once quarreling with my next brother over some maple sugar, with the result that Father decreed that both must go without sugar for one day.

"Harsh it seemed to us, though just; and bitter weeping was our natural reaction—till Ellen managed surreptitiously to convey to us all of her own share, which we ate in secret with the added joys of conscious sin and successful strategy. It was an early lesson in the value of advertising, for had we not proclaimed our sorrow by howling, no one would have been moved to compassion.

"It was Ellen who taught us the sovereign power of goose 'same' or gut-fat as a remedy for chapped skin and chilblains. It was Ellen who showed us how to dye our Easter eggs in two colors— one with the first dip, and the second dip in another color from which the egg was in part protected by a greasy rag; and still others by boiling in a cotton rag on which was a colored print. One which I particularly remember had a black and white check.

"It was Ellen who showed us how to make butterscotch—or more often made it for us herself. She was too conscientious to use the household sugar stock for this. But she found a way. She always ate her meals in the kitchen, and she was supposed to help herself to a fair amount of sugar. This she did, but carefully hoarded it, denying herself the luxury so that she might 'give the bairns a treat.'

"When the winter grew too cold for school, and when also the workshop was not possible for us youngsters, we were allowed to play in the big dining room where there was a wood fire. It became our daily way. After breakfast each morning we got out our knives and blocks of pine, to whittle, carve, or construct.

"Of course the floor was speedily littered over with chips, till, near noon, Mother would say to one or other: 'Now get the brush and shovel, and clean everything up.' We became quite expert.

"One day I had swept the whole floor and cast the chips into the fire; but found, next the kitchen door, there was a thin line of dust that I could not easily sweep onto the shovel. So I did as I had often seen done before—I gave it a swish, and scattered it—anywhere.

"Mother happened to be watching, and said: 'Oh, you must not do that; that is a slovenly finish.'

"'Why,' I said, 'Ellen does it that way.'

"But Ellen was there, and denied it savagely; and muttered something about my being 'an impident trash.'

"Mother sided with Ellen, and rebuked me, both for my act and for my statement. I was silenced, though not convinced.

"Years afterward, Mother told me that she knew I was right; all maids did it that way. Childhood observations are keen and correct. But she felt that at any price she must spare the feelings of the faithful old retainer.

"Ellen continued with us till her death in the October of 1869. So far as I know, she received no wages—nothing but board, lodging, and clothing—during those years of unremitting service.

"During her last illness my mother nursed her with the tireless devotion that she deserved. For two months she lingered, bedridden. Then one morning in October about ten, Mother came down into the big room where we four children were at play, and said simply and softly: 'Nellie's dead.'

"There was something of frightful restraint in her voice and manner. Her eyes—I see them yet—were a little red. Then she left the room. At the time I sensed only the tenseness and restraint. I know now that she went to her room to weep her heart out and to pray.

"That funeral I shall never forget. There was not enough snow for sleighs, so we went in rough jolting wagons; the plain coffin in the first one. It was bitterly cold for us youngsters. We were numb and dumb as we lined up by the grave.

"My younger brother Walter stood opposite to me. I can see him now, his copper-toed boots turned toes in, his elbows turned out, his face purple-red with cold, and his little red nose blowing unheeded bubbles that told of cold, suffering, and indifference to appearances.

"I heard the service, but only one part has stayed with me: 'Dust to dust, ashes to ashes,' and each of the four dominating words sadly emphasized by the sexton dropping a shovelful of earth on the hollow-sounding coffin.

"I do not remember that any of us wept then. We were possessed simply of a dumb, stony sadness, chilled to the marrow by physical cold, clouded in mind by a dull sense of loss.

"Old Ellen was gone!"

Religion and Ethics

During the years that we carried on our school for youth leaders at Seton Village, we conducted each week a Sunday service, nonsectarian, non-theological, with emphasis on high principle, not creed. Perhaps the theme of our worship is expressed in one of the Woodcraft Laws formulated by Seton many years ago: "Seek the joy of being alive." This was the doctrine that he lived by.

His childhood had been so permeated and distorted by the opposite approach that he carried throughout life a distaste for churches. His own explanation is convincing. He says:

"During our backwoods life, immediately after coming from England, the only available church was the Methodist meetinghouse, one mile away. Here services were held each Sunday morning at ten o'clock.

"The sermon was flat and dreary; the singing most doleful. One day, however, I invented a trick that lent some interest to the music. I covered my ears with my hands quite tight, then removed the hands, then replaced them, with varying intervals, making of the hymn a most intriguing succession of explosive howls. This diversion provided entertainment for one or two occasions, and helped to while away the time; but the 'government' discovered the practice and sternly suppressed it.

"At home on Sunday we had religious exercises that filled all the waking hours.

"It is hard to set forth in reasonable language the gloom and horror of that day. If a child laughed, he was sternly rebuked. 'Children, children, human beings with immortal souls to save should not give way to unseemly levity, above all on the Lord's Day.'

"If we walked with other than a funereal tread and mien, it would be: 'I hope that this haste is not in any worldly matter. On such a day, remember only the King's business demands haste.'

"All books were prohibited except the Bible, *Pilgrim's Progress*, and some Sunday school library books that told of a little prig who died and went to heaven.

"We youngsters, well versed as we were in at least the words of the Bible, discovered one amusing occupation which, after careful investigation, was, by authority, pronounced 'not contraband.' That was making Scripture alphabets. For example:

"A was a chieftain who founded a city,
B was an idol thrown down without pity.

"The first adventure was digging out the names from the Bible and rhyming the story; the second was inviting our friends to guess the name whose initial was given. A fragment of one by an elder brother comes to mind; I suspect his eyes twinkled as he wrote it.

"M was so punished he really was sore;
N made an ark; 'twas a very slow go-er.

"The minute and continual ransacking of the Bible in these pursuits gave us a rare knowledge of the Scriptures. I have seldom found even a clergyman who had as complete an acquaintance with the Bible as we had—albeit ours was purely superficial, our approach being wholly that of the word puzzle."

The Worship of Moloch

"It was characteristic of my parents," Seton said many times, "that whatever they did, they did wholeheartedly, sincerely, and with perfect consistency.

"Before we were a year in Toronto, complete affiliation with the hell-fire church had been effected with the extremists of the doctrine; and we children were driven through the fiery furnace.

"The theory of their religion was: 'Draw them by love the right way, and drive them by fear from the wrong.' But this was pure theory; they had lost sight of the first part some years before—a generation before at least, I should imagine. By the time of this story, the one continual preachment was the fear of hell.

"'Everything human is bad, and born of the Devil' was one summing up of our early religious training. 'The heart is deceitful above all things and desperately wicked' was the favorite text; and the total depravity of human nature was the logical and acceptable conclusion.

"God was pictured as an omniscient, omnipotent, offended, and forever angry being, implacable, terrible, and destructive. One day the preacher was expounding his grim doctrine to a listener of another faith, when the latter exclaimed at last: 'I see! Your God is my Devil.' Yes, that was the sum of our church training—to set up a hideous child-devouring monster for the worship of mankind.

"There was not a day of the week in which we children were not reminded that there was practically nothing in sight for us but hell—hot hell—and plenty of it. If one of us burned his finger, Mother would improve the occasion by saying gravely and emphatically: 'Now, that is what Hell is like; only it is all over your body, and lasts forever and ever.'

"This was weekday stuff, and occasional. But Sunday was wholly given up to detailed contemplation of our inevitable future; we certainly formed no partiality for the Sabbath. I remember many times escaping to my room and lying on my bed, slowly counting to one thousand, just to pass away the gloomy moments of that fearful day.

"The regular Sunday routine of those Toronto days was established and inescapable. We rose as late as we dared—about 7:45; read a chapter of the Bible and a Psalm; then private prayers, each of us in his bedroom before coming downstairs, when, at the table, we sat through a long grace and a short breakfast.

"Next came family worship, in which Father would read a chapter or two from the Bible; followed by a Psalm of David. Then all would kneel, while he read a long prayer, finishing with the Lord's Prayer in which we all joined.

"Now Mother would say: 'Children, to Sunday school.' We were hurried off to Cook's Church Sunday school on Elizabeth Street. We were due at 9:30; but we were always ahead of time—Mother saw to that. For one hour now, we had the horrors of the next world pumped into us. At 10:30, school was supposed to be over, but usually it lasted till 10:45.

"Home we went—to be hustled off to the Presbyterian church, to hear the Rev. J—— K—— dilate on the hot horrors of the world we most of us were bound to land in. He began at 11 o'clock, and it was near 1 o'clock when we escaped."

Seton remembered the Rev. Mr. K—— all his life, as a grim hard doctrinaire, of irreproachable personal life, in his eye a strange gleam which his followers called inspiration, as he expatiated on the immortal glory of the man who burned Servetus at the stake.

Continuing his reminiscences, Seton went on:

"Arrived at home, we had, after a suitable grace, our midday dinner. Then Mother would say: 'Now be sure you are ready for Sunday school.' Getting ready meant learning some complex doctrine out of what is called the Shorter Catechism. Shorter! Is that shorter? There was always the terrifying thought that someday we might be confronted with the Longer Catechism—or even the Longest!

"At 3 o'clock we had Sunday school in the basement of the church; and there, supposedly for one hour—really for an hour and a half—we had hurled at us texts, sermons, proofs, assurances, every kind of evidence of future inevitable overwhelming Hell.

"We were solemnly warned that it was our duty, our whole duty, to strive for escape from the fiery furnace ahead, but were at the same time assured that all our efforts would surely be in vain.

"By 6 o'clock we sat down to an adequate grace and a brief evening meal. By 7 we were all again at the Rev. Mr. K——'s footstool, listening to his lurid word pictures of our unspeakable depravity. It was near 9 o'clock when we surfeited youngsters were once more at home.

"Here, after a few minutes' respite, Mother would say: 'Now, get the books.' Each—there were thirteen of us at this time—was equipped with a Bible and a hymnbook. We sat about in a circle and dolefully sang half a dozen hymns and the Twenty-third Psalm.

"Then Father would say: 'Now we shall read from the word of God in Chapter . . .' After glancing over it to see if it was quite suitable to be read in public, he would intone two verses, the next in line would read two, and so on round a couple of times; after which we all kneeled down once more with our tired sleepy little noses rubbed hard into the varnish of those wooden chairs, while he read another long prayer, and finished up with the Lord's Prayer.

"Then Mother would say: 'Now, children, to bed; and don't forget your prayers.' Yes, another private set-to—with another chapter of the Bible, before we dared to trust ourselves to our pillows to dream of the horrors of the world beyond the grave, and wonder if it could possibly be less alluring than the Sunday we were enduring here."

The Sunday School Books

One Sunday afternoon our little daughter Beulah was devouring the latest "funny." She was gloating over the lurid details depicted, as do all of the modern youth.

As the three of us sat before the glowing hearth fire, Seton recalled the books that he had been allowed to read on Sundays— the ones that were in the Sunday school.

"It is hard to give an idea of these books," he murmured, "without using 'language.'

"Apparently the only equipment necessary for a Sunday school book writer was that he be a minister of the gospel who had failed as a preacher, or who at least had an array of Scripture expressions and a clinging belief in a faultless little milksop who always said 'the comrades with whom I play' when other boys said 'the fellers I play with'; whose trousers, though patched, were always clean; whose hair was always brushed back from his clean, bright young forehead; and whose blood always boiled over into Scripture texts and Jeremiads when he saw his misguided schoolmates hooking apples or shooting craps.

"There were 300 of these books in our Sunday school. This was the library. The children read them on Sunday for the same reason that the horse ate the moldy hay—because he was starving and could get no other. But the horse did not relish the hay, and it did not give him strength.

"Now it happened that one of my brothers, Will, and a young man named Basil Henderson came into office as the librarians. Although both were in good standing as 'very pious young men,' they somehow got the notion that the sad, draggled, unwilling atmosphere of the Sunday school might be improved by a more alluring class of books. As the present lot were in rags and the church coffer well filled, they had no difficulty in getting $200 to be expended in new books.

"So those two perfectly well-meaning young men, with the best intentions and perhaps a little push from their own personal choice, made a terrible mistake. They stocked up with Kingston's books for boys, Captain Mayne Reid, Fenimore Cooper, and a score of other glorious names.

"The children soon caught on to it, and a new interest in life developed. The whole school responded. Now no longer was it necessary to urge little Billy to 'get along to Sunday school or you'll be late.' Little Billy was there by this time, and in the clamoring crowd demanding 'libery books.' Boys who, thanks to their weak home government, seldom came, were now regular in their attendance, even if they did sneak out early. Never had there been such full houses, never such keen interest.

"The Sunday school was booming. This in itself caused faint surprise, but the ready explanation that it was the working of God's grace was very acceptable.

"Nothing definite happened until one Sunday afternoon in the respite hour, 5 to 6, I was devouring with eager intensity some thrilling pages in one of Kingston's *Tales of Adventure*, when Father came in. Probably made suspicious by my eager, wrapt aloofness, he said: 'What book is that you are reading, my son?'

"I was only twelve, but my instinct told me that a book in green and gold is, offhand, suspicious; a book that omits the good little boy is unorthodox; and a book that is wholly delightful must be sinful. Eager to meet any possible objections, I said nervously: 'It's a good book, Father. It's a Sunday school book, Father. I got it out of the Sunday school library, it's—a—good book.'

"'Let me see it.'

"Smelling disaster, I hurried up my biggest guns. 'It's a good

Sunday school book, Father. It's full of pious things. See, it's quite good. See here on page 25, it says: 'That wicked man was going plumb to Hell,' and there's more like that.'

"'What! Give me that book at once.'

"My arguments had all gone the wrong way; they had produced the reverse of the desired effect. That lovely, lovely book was taken away. A thorough investigation followed. The whole 200 books that had boomed the Sunday school were gathered up and shipped off to a jobber. Some nice books were put in their place—and the Sunday school fell back again to its dishwater flatness, varied only by little surface bubbles of smoldering wrath and rebellion."

The Dawn of Sex

In Seton's early days there was no acknowledged science of psychology. Yet, in his teaching he was an inherent practical natural guide and instructor with the most modern methods of education.

A number of memories of his boyhood are at hand. I give them as nearly as possible in his own words.

"I was 4 years old when I discovered that girls were not fashioned like boys; and before we left England (when I was 5) I had acquired the vernacular names for all the bodily parts in question. I was but 5 when I made a careful study of the male organs of a small dog that had strayed into our yard. I wanted only to compare notes and see how much he and I were alike; so was deeply resentful when he halted my biological investigations by snapping at me.

"I was not yet 6 when we lived for a couple of weeks in a rented house at Lindsay, Ontario. Next door was a 7-year-old girl who, one day, invited me into the hayloft and there gave me full instructions in copulation, with laboratory demonstrations. I did my best to respond, but alas! I was not old enough to profit fully by the opportunity.

"My thoughts, however, were turned that way; so that within another year, after seeing the animal life on the farm, I had a very fair outline of the whole process of procreation.

"It was the daily Bible reading in our family worship that completed my round of knowledge, by showing that man was subject to exactly the same laws as the animals, and was multiplied in precisely the same way.

"During the epoch of Elizabeth Street School, 1870–72, there was no aspect of human sex biology that was not the subject of daily discussion, as well as of common knowledge. Copulation was the accepted amusement of the bigger boys and girls; and hardly any attempt was made at concealment. The merits, charms, and availability of this or that girl were often and openly discussed. The tone and topics of conversation might well have belonged to the smoking room of a French club.

"Most of the older boys seemed to have assumed that such pleasures were as natural to their time of life as eating and drinking; and any boy not so minded was reckoned a sissy, to be scorned. The places of meeting were the park, the picnic grounds, the island, and above all the haylofts over the stables that were frequent in town.

"More than once I heard 15-year-old boys discussing the kind and amount of certain drugs one must give an unwilling girl to incline her to grant her favors.

"Now I must confess that, although I did not join their ranks, I had just as much desire as any of these young rakes; and the only reason why I was not into it as deeply as any of them was that I did not know how to make an opportunity; or, if an opportunity presented itself, as I now know was often the case, I did not recognize it, or know how to avail myself of it.

"Masturbation, on the other hand, seemed very rare; indeed, I saw nothing of it at that school, and it was only at Victoria Street School that I met with a group that practiced it daily. I must say that they were looked down on by the rest of the boys, and left much to themselves.

"With a full equipment of such knowledge at 10, including a perfect understanding of Lot's, David's, and Solomon's exploits, as set forth in the Holy Scriptures, imagine my surprise when, as I neared my nineteenth birthday, my father called me into his study and, in the most awkward, stammering, embarrassed fashion, 'felt it to be his duty to acquaint me with certain facts of sex'; and, by way of lesson number one (and the last as it happened), very

painfully conveyed to me the crudest fragments of information I
had fully possessed when I was 7 years of age.

"I could only reply: 'If you intended to do me any good by such
instruction, you should have begun 15 years ago.'"

His Deathbed

Juvenile reactions, as understood by modern child psychologists,
were in the realm of unexplored science in the days when Ernest
was growing up.

But the following incident, as he told it to me one evening when
I was feeling very sorry for myself over a sense of injustice, touches
a familiar chord in each person who hears it. We have every one of
us experienced the same emotions in some similar crisis, and can
understand and sympathize with all the feelings referred to.

"When my father," he said, "was in doubt as to the culprit in a
given case, he took no chances—he spanked us all so he could be
sure he got the right one.

"It was when I was about nine. I received a slight spanking for
something that, in this case, I certainly did not do. I went off to my
room, weeping over my wrongs. As I lay on the bed, I could not
help thinking: 'They'll feel sorry when I'm dead; I'll bet you they'll
be sorry!'

"That thought was so pleasing that I hastened to develop it. I
pictured myself moaning on a bed of sickness, my white, thin
hands together clasped in prayer; my sorrowing relatives crowding
eagerly and conscience-stricken about me—kneeling, contrite, sighing
with trembling voices: 'Forgive us! Oh, forgive us!'

"I could hear myself, in Christlike tones, reply: 'I forgive you.
You didn't know how wicked you were, or how good I've been.
But I'll forgive you. I have always been slighted, painted a naughty,
naughty boy, when I was spotless, a truly noble little fellow.'

"Then, as between their sobs they demanded what they could do
by way of penance, or to atone for the wrongs they had done me,
their conspiracy against innocent me, I heard myself, in sweet but
faltering childish accents: 'Just one thing.'

"Here my voice failed me, but I murmured: 'Water! Water! Moisten my pallid lips.'

"Then I resumed: 'Bring the Bible, and put it under my head. I want to die on the Bible, supported in death by the Bible, that erstwhile comforted and guided me while yet alive.'

"Then, when everyone rushed to get Bibles, and to comply with the request that I think grew out of a certain Sunday school book, I lay softly moaning.

"'What else can we do?' they hoarsely whispered.

"'Only flowers,' I replied. 'Deck my dying bed eftsoons with flowers, pure and innocent as I; and put a garland on my marble brow.' I had seen a picture somewhere with this treatment, and I liked the motif, as well as the phrase 'marble brow.'

"No sooner was this boon granted than, to their eager and contrite 'What next? Oh, tell us, tell us what we can do to atone?' I turned my pleading eyes toward them; and faintly smiling a wan but heavenly smile, I answered in a low sweet voice:

"'There is but one thing more I wish. Carve upon the stone that decks my final resting place one word—one single word that tells the story of my young and pure but blighted life. This single word alone carve thereupon: 'MISUNDERSTOOD.'

"Then I died.

"Oh, it was delicious! It was almost worth dying for; to be the hero of such a touching, lovely, lovely scene!

"My, if it only could be!

"I'll bet I'd make those folks sorry they licked me!

"Then I wept some more."

The Teacher's Pet

Speaking of the Victoria Street School, where the four youngest boys went for a time, and of the difficulties he and his brothers encountered there, Seton says:

"The Teacher's Pet—that was what they scornfully called me after being eighteen months in that fiery furnace—and there were some reasons for it. Though a small potato in the playground, I was head of the highest form; and as the teacher, Mr. Robert McCausland, told my mother, I was the brightest scholar in the school—which was not saying much.

"Then a curious thing occurred. One of the boys brought a lump of pitch to school. With true and scholarly ingenuity, I showed him how to bend a pin just so, embed it in the pitch, and set it on the chair of one's dearest friend. As soon as said friend landed on said pin, he naturally jumped up and shifted to another place, whence he could inspect the chair to discover his enemy. But the pin moved too. The pitch held the pin to his pants, and the second seat he landed on was worse than the first. In some cases, the victim got three deadly jabs before solving the mystery. You can have no idea, till you try it, of the pure joy of getting three loud squeals with one little pin.

"The whole head form entered merrily and wholeheartedly into this new and exhilarating indoor sport. The stir grew into a racket. Finally, the teacher dragged out a couple of the noisy ones and made them tell what they knew.

"The whole thing was out. Soon all was known, except the author of the scheme. The teacher easily picked out the guilty ones—every boy with pitch on his fingers was clearly in the plot. He did not look at my hands—I was his model boy, head of the class, beyond suspicion. But he lined up a dozen of the class, then produced his rawhide whip, a 'gad' as it was called in Canada. Every boy with a tarry hand got a fierce cut across each palm with that dread instrument of torture.

"I was virtuously sitting in my seat behind the row of the condemned, when it occurred to me that if I made haste I could have a pitch pin on the seat of each of my friends to welcome him home when he retired to his seat after the execution.

"I quickly set to work and had a number of the surprises ready just as our burly teacher was lashing the last of my friends. He was laying it on well. I was interested in his technique—too much so, for I heedlessly raised my fingers, busy with the pitch, just one inch too high. Across the top of my desk his quick eye took it in. He fairly gasped.

"'Wh—wh—Ernest, what, you? The last boy in the school I should have suspected! The most astounding impudence I ever heard of!

You—you—I'll make an example of you. . . . I'll give you a dozen on each hand. *Come out here!*

"Now one of the culprits, Piggy Craig, had fought me, licked me, blackened my eye, and sworn eternal friendship just one month before. He was an adept at dodging the lash punishment. As I marched out, Piggy whispered: 'Hold yer hand nigh yer shoulder. Jerk it away each time. He'll think he hit yer, it'll swish just the same.'

"'Hold your hand out straight!' thundered the teacher. 'I'll give you three and three about.' So I got three cuts on the right and three cuts on the left.

"'Will you have the rest now or at noon?' the executioner demanded.

"'Now,' I said sullenly, for I wanted to be through with it.

"But just behind me was my friend, the expert. 'Naw, naw' he loudly whispered. 'Take them at noon. He'll forget.'

"An hour later Tom Sanderson rang the noon bell. I rose and marched out with the rest, unchallenged.

"Piggy, my mentor, walked so as to hide me as we went; then, safely outside, said: 'Now, I told yer he'd ferget.' And chuckled in triumph over having saved me.

"As I look back now, I know the teacher *did not forget*—he did something that begins to spell the same way [forgive]."

Mibs Is Off

Incidents of his school days Seton recalled at various times. The sight of some boys at play would bring back with utmost clarity a memory which, though often in itself unimportant, was always an index to his character and gave an insight into the psychological development which resulted in his type of manhood.

His absolute frankness and sincerity often put him in the wrong, but one easily lost sight of the fact that he was telling of himself; it was a case history, and most of his reminiscences have real value in these days of research into motives and reactions of the human ego.

"At Victoria Street School," he told me one day, "I got into one very serious row.

"The periodicity of child games is a puzzling, inscrutable, but well-known phenomenon. Certain games are played at certain seasons and end at others with regularity, year after year. The games have little relation to season or weather; they come and go each year at the same time.

"Marbles, tops, baseball, football, mumblypeg—each had its place on the calendar; and no right-minded boy would think of playing it at any other time.

"Marbles, or 'mibs' as we called them, came in late March, while yet it was too cold for the fingers to function properly; and ended about May first when, by reasonable expectation, it should have begun. But no, it ended, and must end, May first; and any boy having the temerity to continue after it was called off was in for some trouble. It was the custom for some bigger boy to rush at any wrong-time marble players, shouting, 'Mibs is off'; then throw a large stone down to crush and, if possible, utterly destroy the unlawful marbles.

"My brother Walter was a wild and prankish boy; and, very ready to express and enforce the unwritten law, went about on May first, shouting, 'Mibs is off.' With a large stone, he helped to break up a number of games. But he soon got into trouble.

"Coming on a group at the contraband pastime, he yelled: 'Mibs is off,' and threw a rock down on the nest, just as one of the youngsters, Kid Campbell, reached out to rescue his marbles, and so received the rock with crushing force on his hand.

"His yells brought his big brother to the scene; many others at once joined in. My brother was plucky and could have taken care of himself against fair odds; but soon there was a mob, all sympathizing with the injured kid.

"Walter fled, pursued by the crowd and battered by many who could run as fast as he.

"'Ernest! Ernest!' he yelled as he saw his chance of escape grow less. I was indoors at the time; but some friend shouted: 'You better come; they're half killing your little brother!'

"I rushed to the rescue and tried to do some fist work. But they were 20 or 30 to us two, and they were now mob-crazy.

"Big Campbell, much older and stronger than myself, was leading them. He knocked me down on the first round; but I quickly jumped to my feet and retreated into a corner where the fence protected me on three sides.

"The mob shouted: 'Soak 'em! Smash 'em!'

"Then I surely did see red. What my friends called my 'awful look' came over me. I whipped out my long-bladed knife and yelled: 'Come on, I'll kill you all!'

"Campbell too jerked out his knife and madly retorted: 'I'll get you first.'

"Now anyone who knows knife play uses the knife like a short sword, the blade pointing forward from the thumb side of the hand. A man without knowledge holds the blade pointing down from the little-finger side. I had learned the art and held my knife the first way; Campbell held his the second.

"As we fenced for a chance, I led. The straight thrust brought him within my range long before his 'crooked thrust' could reach me. But he threw up his arm in time.

"As the cold steel touched his flesh, he gave a yell; the rest sprang back. I rushed among them, mad and reckless, slashing right and left. They scattered, and the row was over.

"As I stood there, glaring and defiant, I noticed the upper windows open, and as many girls as could look out, waving their hands, some shouting, 'Good boy!' some weeping hysterically.

"One girl I heard exclaim: 'Oh, I want to see! I want to see! I have always wanted to see somebody stabbed!'

"They let me alone after that, and I never heard any more of the affair; so I suppose the wound was not very deep."

The First Swear

"In spite of the unholy atmosphere of the school we attended and its daily dirty language, I do not think that one of us four youngsters ever swore, lied, or spoke a foul word during the two years we were in the midst of it; so much for the power of our home training.

"My little brother Alan was a bright-eyed, 6-year-old innocent, full of winsome good nature. One day I saw a much bigger boy named Tom Peacock knocking him around very roughly. I flew to the rescue, defeated the villain, and drove him afar to his own home.

"As he ran, I shouted after him, in the fury of warfare: 'If you ever lay finger on him again, I'll knock the stuffin's out of you!'

"My little brother was horrified. 'Oh—oh—oh! Swearing! I'll tell Pa!'

"All the gratitude for his rescue was wiped out in the horror of my blasphemy. He was going right now to tell Pa that 'Ernest was swearing.'

"I felt that I was lost. But, though young in years, I had learned some guile; I knew that every man had his price. I set diplomatically about it.

"By careful questioning, I found that my little brother's price was 'two mibs'; so, with two marbles, I bought him off.

"True to promise, he honorably kept the bargain; and, until this day, no one knows the dark secret but my brother and my guilty self."

The Toronto Fair

The Farmers' Annual Fair at Toronto was a big event in those days of 1872. It was primarily agricultural, and that had no special message for Ernest.

But that particular year the advertising said that there were several unusual attractions. For instance, there was to be a collection of Canadian birds artistically mounted in natural surroundings, and on each a label giving the name and something about the habits of the species; and, still more alluring, an exhibit of all the wild animals of Canada, *alive*, fully named, each in a spacious cage where its habits and manners could be observed.

At any price, Ernest had to go! This was the very breath of his nostrils.

But the entrance fee was 25 cents, and this was not within the bounds of reasonable sight.

Determined, however, to see at least the outside of the building, and trusting to luck to get a glimpse of the animals, he set out alone, on foot, taking with him his sketchbook and color box.

He was eleven years old, a slight small boy—never strong in his childhood, but with a determination that justified any attempt.

He knew the exhibit was on Queen Street some miles away, and marked by a big glass dome.

He left his home on Mutual Street soon after midday dinner and tramped southward until he came to Queen Street. He was not sure whether to turn eastward or westward, and was too shy of strangers to ask. But he had a dim memory of someone saying it was to the east, so he turned in that direction and went on at his best pace.

After what seemed some miles—and he was used to walking—he came to the Don River, crossed by the bridge, and strode along Kingston Road till he began to tire out. He had gone past the Nipissing railroad crossing and far into what was then the village of Leslieville on Ashbridge's Bay.

There was still no glass dome in sight, and finally he ventured to ask of a passer-by how much farther it was to the Fair Grounds.

The stranger replied in amazement: "Why, sonny, you are going the wrong way. It is way out on Queen Street West, near the Asylum."

This was a disheartening blow; but the boy turned about, doggedly resolved to at least find the place.

It was now about 3:00 P.M. He was weary and hungry. However, he set out rather sullenly now, trudged back to the Don, then along Queen Street into the heart of the city, and a little frightened, on and on, to the westward.

The sun was just about setting as he sighted the dome of the Fair building, a little glinted in the colored rays.

He was dog-tired, but slowly walked up to the door and read the sign: "Toronto Fair, 25¢ admission."

That was all that he had vowed to himself to do. He stood for a moment to gather himself together; then footsore, weary, and hungry, and prepared to face some humiliating paternal discipline for being out late, he turned on his long, long homeward tramp—eleven miles altogether.

Years afterward, when he referred to this episode in the presence of his mother, her eyes glistened with tears as she said: "Yes, we knew of it, and it wrenched my heart. But we could not send you without also sending the other three little ones. And the dollar was more than we could spare."

PART THREE

THE BLAZE OF YOUTH

YOUNG MANHOOD

The Cabin on the Don

One of the most poignant experiences in Seton's life occurred back in his boyhood days. It was 1874. He was fourteen years old. With all his innate longings to be with the wild things ignored—nay, even condemned—he lived his hopes and his dreams in building his cabin on the Don. He had no help from companions, he had no tools except the crude ones he made from what he could find in the woods. He carried every log and every scoop of sand and water on his own weak back, sometimes from miles away where he could find what he needed and could use without benefit of ax or saw. It took him months to complete it, since Saturdays were the only days he could devote to his secret project.

But eventually it was finished. It was but 5 feet high, 6 feet long, and 6 feet wide. It was dirty and uncomfortable. But it was his secret, his own property, his own desires made manifest, and in the heart of a little glade, hidden from view, and beautiful beyond words. He named it Glenyan, and rejoiced in spending every available minute in it. It was the one spot on earth where he could satisfy the yearning that was in him.

Then one day, after a cruel beating from his father, he sneaked away from the house and sped to his cabin where alone he could find peace.

As he neared the place he heard men's voices coming from the spot. The vulgar tones and the blasphemous phrases smote on his heart. When he was within sight, he gazed with horror on the group drinking from a bottle and playing cards. He looked with all the life gone out of him until they finally left, after defiling with unspeakable filth the floor of the cabin and even the little well that he had made to capture the water of the spring.

During all the years of Seton's life, he could not speak of those long-gone days without a break in his voice and a tear in his eye.

A more detailed description of the building of the cabin and the joy he found in it can be read in his *Two Little Savages,* as also in a slightly different form in his autobiography, now out of print.

But a much later memory he told to me. It was when first I visited Toronto with him. One of my objectives was to see Glenyan, the secret refuge where he had found unmeasured happiness.

As we made our way there—with hesitation on the part of both of us, fearing the emotions it would recall—he told me:

"During the late seventies my lovely ravine was known to be frequented by a band of robbers called the Brooks' Gang. They carried on many a campaign of thievery—highway and lowway—they burgled and they blackmailed. They even kidnapped men and held them for ransom. Mr. Michie, of the well-known firm of Fulton and Michie, was one of the victims; and another whom they tried to trap and hold was the Hon. George Brown, owner and editor of *The Globe.*

"But the strong hand of the law was on them; and finally the gang was rounded up to spend the rest of their years behind bars.

"In Toronto, during the nineties, there was a fine old gentleman named Alderman John Hallam. He had a great belief in the future of Toronto real estate; and was laughed at when he invested heavily in land beyond Rosedale Ravine—an investment, by the way, which yielded him tenfold in the after years.

"One day in 1892 he told me that on his new purchase, hidden in a dark corner of the ravine, he had unearthed what he believed to be the headquarters of the notorious Brooks' Gang. He took me to see it—a cabin, cut halfway into the hill. There it was, the cedar logs yet good, but the roof destroyed, the timbers scattered. There it was still, the graveyard of a hope—my own dear cabin."

Those of Toronto who so wish may see the site of the cabin at the foot of the hill on which Government House now stands. It is on the floor of the ravine on the westerly side, just north of the Mansion.

The Lynx of Cudmore's Hill

In December 1876, Ernest had a memorable experience in the ravine of Mud Creek just south of Cudmore's Hill near Toronto.

He had been very ill for some months, and for a period of recuperation had spent the summer in the country with the Blackwells. Now back home again, he was once more on his feet, strong in the legs, and eager as ever for glimpses of wild life.

The snow was deep in the woods, but a friend had loaned him a pair of snowshoes. With these on his back, and followed by his elder brother's big brown water spaniel Grip, he set out after noon meal one Saturday to scout through the wintry woods.

Leaving their house on Pembroke Street, he went at a 5-mile gait up to Bloor Street, then down the winding drive at the head of Parliament Street onto the Don flats.

There he tied on his snowshoes, for at this point the deep unbroken snow began. Up the familiar ravine he went. With a sigh, he passed the desolated site of his shanty, destroyed and desecrated as narrated, and on into the beautiful stretch of primitive woods that covered all the banks of Mud Creek and its hinterland far away northwest into the unknown.

Suddenly he found a fresh remarkable track. Each footprint was 4 or 5 inches across, the spaces between the tracks were from a foot to two feet; but the creature had jumped up onto a fallen tree and followed that. At places, it had leaped 6 or 8 feet in the snow for no obvious reason.

He followed it fast and eagerly. The dog sniffed at it, and growled angrily, but made no effort to pursue the thing that had made the tracks.

For a quarter of a mile Ernest trailed. Then far off he heard a strange caterwauling sound such as might have been made by a gigantic tomcat. The dog woofed and took refuge up against his master's legs.

The boy got a stout branch for a club and followed the trail swiftly but cautiously, peering ever for a glimpse of the creature.

The yowling grew louder, YOW YOW HOWL-L, YOW WOW HOWL-L, till it seemed like the yelling of a tiger. But he saw nothing of the yowler. Then, as he crept on, the sounds appeared to come from some high place, probably the top of a tree.

He pressed on cautiously. The dog cowered behind him, and grew distinctly embarrassing as it trod on his snowshoes and even got between his legs. Then he heard the sound of scratching, and realized that the creature was coming down from the tree, and was not far ahead.

The scratching ceased, and a terrific YOWL came from that direction. The dog was terror-stricken; he let off a yelp, disgorged his dinner; and leaving on a wild run, set off at a gallop on his backtrack.

"I did not get a single glimpse of the creature," said Seton in telling the story. "But I was sure it was a lynx, and that it was coming at me. I had no weapon but the stick. The example of the thoroughly scared dog affected me so that I too turned and ran as fast as I could on my snowshoes, following the line of retreat.

"Half a mile away, the woods ended; and here in the opening, cowering in terror, was that valiant dog.

"I got home as fast as I could, and sought my big brother Arthur, who was free on Saturday afternoon and had a gun. But before I could find him, it was near six o'clock and already dark. So I had to give it up for that day.

"Sunday was out of the question for hunting. A whole week passed before I could again go to the place, with my brother and a gun now. We saw nothing of the animal except the dim tracks. I might have thought myself mistaken, but that the following Monday, as I walked down Church Street near Shuter, I met a man carrying on his shoulders an enormous dead lynx. It was so recently killed that its yellow eyes looked still alive, bright and shiny.

"I was thrilled; and, going eagerly up to him, asked: 'Would you mind telling me where you got that?'

"'Sure, sonny. I shot him in the ravine this side Cudmore's Hill— Mud Creek, you know. He's been prowling around there for a couple of weeks, and killed a lot of lambs and chickens.'

"So my guess was right after all. But alas, I had missed the chance of a really thrilling adventure."

Toronto Marsh

In November of 1930, Seton had a letter from James L. Baillie, Jr., of the Royal Ontario Museum of Zoology. Baillie stated that he was preparing a history and natural history of Toronto Marsh and Island,

and that Seton's boyhood impressions of that area and the bird life found there then would be "exceedingly valuable" to him.

Seton's reply was characteristic of not only his willingness to be of help but also the clarity of memory concerning the things of his boyhood. He wrote:

"Toronto Marsh in its prime was a bird paradise. My earliest acquaintance with it was in the summer of 1870. It was then in its very finest primitive condition. From memory, I have drawn a map as I remember it, without any documentary assistance in making the same.

"You will notice that at that time there was no eastern gap. If I remember aright, the storm first broke through that narrow neck in '72 or '73.

"There were two hotels on the island—Mead's in the center, and Hanlon's at the west side of the bay. Old man Hanlon had two children, the boy Ed and a younger sister. Young Ed, at the age of 10, began to row his sister and himself to school every day, and back in the evening. It was thus he developed his powers as the world's greatest rower some 10 years later.

"The lagoon in the center of the island was a completely land-locked body of water, some 20 degrees warmer than the lake water, and was inhabited by swarms of peculiar life forms—insects and water snails.

"At the extreme southwest of the island was a long high bluff of gravelly sand. As near as I recall, it was 8 or 10 feet high, and a couple of hundred yards long. In its southern face, thousands of bank swallows had made their nests.

"We children did most of our bathing in the inlet called Gibraltar Bay. An artist named Armstrong had a painting cabin at the south end of this bay. There were a great many stumps of trees and old antlered trunks stranded along the banks; and any of these that looked at all like a human being, this man Armstrong embellished with paint and additional pieces of wood nailed on. So that, at all times, around this bay there seemed to be a dozen or more gaudily dressed men and women standing at pose.

"At one time, the point called Gibraltar was said to be only 100 yards from the main shore at Fort Rouille. But the process of the lake has continually reduced the size of the island and of its points. From all I can learn, a hundred years ago, the island was twice as large as at present. The most obvious erosions in my memory were those which took away a section of the eastern part and made the eastern gap. Also, on the southwestern point, the whole swallow bluff has been undermined and submerged by the waves.

"There was a little steamboat called the *Boquet*, that plied all summer long from the foot of Yonge Street to Hanlon's dock and to Mead's dock, for 10 cents a trip.

"The island was an uninhabited waste of sand, sprinkled with coarse wiry grass; but at the part east of the lagoon were a lot of old cottonwood trees, most of them down—the remains of the forest which was said formerly to decorate the whole island, and which gave to the bay its Iroquois name *Toronto*, meaning Trees-in-the-Water, because, approaching from the lake side, these trees seemed actually to rise out of the lake.

"Ashbridge's Bay was better known to me. Catfish Joe's island, as indicated, was some 3 or 4 feet above high-water level, and was the home of the wild recluse called Catfish Joe. He did some shooting but was more of a fisherman; and always in case of shortage he could drop a line in the right place to land a mess of catfish. He had a few hens on this island. A friend of his from the old country was visiting him once, and intended to stay a couple of days; but was very soon nauseated by the bill of fare. Everything smelled and tasted of fish. Finally Old Joe, noticing his unrelish, said, 'How would you like a couple of aigs?' 'Sure thing,' said his friend, delighted at the chance to get a change from the fish taste. But, alas, when the eggs were served, they were the eggs of hens that were fed chiefly on fish scraps, and those eggs were just as strong as rank old catfish could make them.

"You will notice that in those days the mouth of the Don came out at Catfish Joe's island. About 1866, I am told, a number of market gunners had bought houses on the lower Don. It occurred to them one day that very little effort would make a boat canal across the neck of land that divided the lower Don from the open bay. This would save them going all the way round by Catfish Joe's island, and would be useful to those men since they made frequent trips to Gooderham's Distillery, whose product was good and in high favor. This ditch was made easily. My impression is that it needed less than a 50-yard channel, and only a foot deep. But the angle of the river was such that the spring floods greatly widened it, and eventually, about 1870, this became the main channel. If I am not wrong, the men who did this were Bill Loane, Charley Pickering, and a couple of their pals; also old man Gooderham himself. I think the present George Gooderham could give you more accurate information. Dr. Scadding, the historian, I presume, has long gone over the Divide.

"By 1880, the old channel leading down to Catfish Joe's island was pretty well silted and grown up with weeds. It was simply a deep part of the marsh.

"It was, in a sense, an island; and from this island, in the summer of 1875, my father and myself had the pleasure of rescuing a young man named Skinner, son of the deputy sheriff Skinner. His grandfather had given him a gun for his birthday; and, though only about 12 years of age, he went a-gunning along the shore. Some rowdies in a boat volunteered to take him to some good shooting ground. They landed him on this island, took his gun, and sailed away, leaving him marooned. However, when they found out who he was and the position held by his father, they took alarm. They went back to find him. Failing to do so, they went to the Skinner house that night, restored the gun, and offered humble apologies.

"About 1886, David S. Keith, the plumber, built a dry dock on this island. It was a small affair, and was postulated on the success of Mayor Howland's Don straightening scheme. The latter, of course, was wasted money, and the dry dock equally a failure.

"Going farther east, we come to Leslieville on Ashbridge's Bay. This place I knew very well. Old man Leslie was one of the original settlers. His nursery and market garden along the shore of this bay made him famous in his day, and comfortably well off; but, of course, when his children cut it up into town lots about 1886 or 1887, they were made rich. It was a glorious place for birds. The variety of trees furnished by the nursery, and the food opportunities, as well as the protection, made it a sort of sanctuary the year round."

THE BIRDS

"I did not begin to keep a journal of the natural history of the region till 1881. My earliest and most important entries were made chiefly around Ashbridge's Bay, although the Don and the Humber also contributed.

"I do not know how minutely you wish these things rendered.

"Tuesday, Nov. 15, 1881, I tramped to Ashbridge's Bay; and there received from William Lang, the gunner, a Greater Yellowshanks, female, shot the day before on the marsh. In the upper part of its throat was a small fish, 2⅛ inches long, head downwards. In its stomach was another, partly digested, and the remains of a third reduced to a pulp.

"There was, of course, much open water at this time, but November is very late for the Yellowlegs.

"Nov. 22. I received from William Lang three adult Bonaparte Gulls in winter plumage, shot on Ashbridge's Bay; also a common Snipe, whose stomach was full of tiny spiral shells, the legs of some small crustacean, and the green cotyledons of some plant.

"Dec. 3. I went collecting with J. MacPherson Ross, superintendent of Leslie's Nurseries, an old art school friend of mine, who is still living in Toronto. We collected some Tree Sparrows. Later, I went to Lang's cottage on the shore, borrowed his telescope, and studied the sandy bar on Ward's Island. There were several hundred Gulls, a few of them Saddlebacks; and, sitting on the ice, a very large bird which turned out to be a fine Golden Eagle.

"Dec. 6. I went again. The weather was still open; there was very little ice. William Lang and a friend, J. Crowther, and I went out in 2 boats; collected a Coween and a belated Marsh Blackbird or Redwing. We saw several Coweens, some Swallows, and a Black Duck, many Gulls, one Eagle, and a Shrike.

"Dec. 8. Went again with Lang. Collected 6 Snow Buntings.

"Dec. 10. Went out with Lang. Collected a Chickadee.

"Dec. 12. Received from Lang a Star-nosed Mole, which had been caught under the ice of Ashbridge's Bay.

"Dec. 24. Went up the Humber River on foot, with George Malcolm. Collected a Downy Woodpecker and a Chickadee; also many Gulls.

"Dec. 29. Went out on the open water. Met a gunner coming back with a young female Red-throated Diver, a Big-billed Gull, and a Herring Gull. These I bought from him for 60¢.

"Jan. 10, 1882. On Mutual Street near Gold, found lying on the ground a dead Pileated Woodpecker which I took home and skinned.

"Jan. 11. I saw in the market a female Pileated Woodpecker, shot near Kingston.

"Jan. 18. Went on foot to the marsh with William Brodie, son of Dr. Brodie. We saw a Shrike, a number of Snowbirds, and many Gulls, one Coween, and a Meadow Lark. The last was at the Woodbine Race Ground. Bill Loane told me that several Meadow Larks had been shot recently around the Woodbine track. On our return, we started three of them, but did not get one.

"Jan. 20. Went to the marsh with Dr. William Brodie. Saw an Eagle, some Sheldrake, numbers of Gulls, and Snowbirds. Made the acquaintance of Sam Humphreys, the market gunner.

"Jan. 22. Up Yonge Street saw 36 Crows flying west in low straggling companies.

"Jan. 23. Went with William Brodie to the marsh. The bay was covered with an inch of water on the ice. Shot a couple of Tree Sparrows among the reeds. Saw a Saddleback devouring a Duck frozen in the ice. Saw 5 Ducks, also plenty of Gulls and Snowbirds.

"Jan. 27. Made a hide on the west end of Ward's Island, lay in this for some time waiting for Gulls to come to a fish bait; but none came.

"Jan. 28. Went up the Don with William Brodie. Shot a Nuthatch (white-breasted), a Chickadee, a Downy Woodpecker, and a Creeper. Saw a Ruffed Grouse and a Muskrat.

"Bill Loane was a very well-known character among the gunners of those days, and in most respects far above his class—a very fine man. During the last half of winter when there was no gunning on the Bay, Loane used to trap Snowbirds for the Gun Club. These birds were then shot as trap birds by the numerous members of the Gun Club, who wished to practice wing-shooting without the uncertainty and toil of a long tramp in the woods. These shoots usually took place on the Don flats, opposite the end of Wilton Avenue. Snowbirds (*nivalis*) were mostly used. I saw many of these shoots during the winters of 1874, '75, and '76, as many as a couple of hundred birds being used up on each occasion. Their bodies were taken home to make into potpies.

"On Jan. 31, 1882, I went to Ward's Island early in the day, and found Bill Loane putting out his nets for the Snowbirds. He showed me the whole operation. The net was 10 feet by 30, made of very fine twine, each mesh being ¼ inch each way. The net was staked on the bank, which was plentifully sprinkled with bird seed. At one side was a living Snowbird in a cage, to whistle and decoy the others. Around the bank were 3 or 4 other decoys; these, however, were not alive, but stuffed and mounted. The trapper was in a hide to one side. When the proper moment came, he pulled a rope and the trap was sprung. Loane had been at this business for many years. He was the only one practicing it in Toronto.

"He related many strange experiences in his trapping. When one or two Snowbirds came on the bank, he never pulled the net. He wanted them to be well fed, then go away and tell the others. On one occasion, he got 470 Snowbirds at one pull; on another 365 Marsh Blackbirds. In a single afternoon he had once caught 1000 Snowbirds. For these, he got five cents apiece from the Gun Club.

"He always knew when the Snowbird hordes were about to come by seeing Shrikes about the day before. On one occasion he saw a Shrike trying to drag the decoy Snowbird through the cage bars; so Loane took the cage and put it on the seed bank. Presently the Shrike came back, and was easily netted alive. But it made such desperate resistance and bit so fiercely that Loane broke its neck and sent it to the taxidermist. This specimen I saw; it was a common *borealis*, a young male in first plumage.

"Nearly every day I saw one or more Eagles and an occasional Fish Hawk. Loane said that Eagles used to be very common about here, preying on dead fish and crippled Ducks that had escaped from the gunner.

"He noticed that at Scarborough Heights, just east of Ashbridge's Bay, there was a solitary pine at the water's edge, where a long ravine came in from the north. This was a favorite perch with the Eagles. So Loane made a hide at the foot of it, and left this hide for a month or so till the birds got accustomed to it. Then before daylight one day, when there was a northwest gale, he hid inside with his gun and waited. Presently an Eagle alighted. Loane poked out his gun and dropped the bird, but continued in hiding. Before that day was over, he had killed 7 Eagles. All were White-heads but one, which was a Golden.

"He also told me of a young man who stalked an Eagle on a tree at Scarborough. The Eagle was winged and fell down the bank. The man descended and incautiously approached. The Eagle seized his thigh with the talons of both his powerful feet, and held on despite the man's most desperate struggles. In the morning his anxious friends found him dead, the Eagle still holding on, and his claws driven deep into the femoral artery; while, all around, the blood and marks showed how the gunner had struggled for his life.

"On another occasion, on coming home to dinner, Loane's wife said to him that the Eagles had been making an awful noise in the adjoining woods. He went out with his gun and found two fighting. Every time one made a swoop from above, the other turned on his back to receive him, and struck upwards with his talons. Loane watched his opportunity, and fired. The lower, a Bald-head, he killed dead. The other, a Golden, he just grazed on the wing, so that it fell; but immediately, instead of skulking and trying to avoid the gunner, the Eagle started off in pursuit. Loane ran, dodging about everywhere for some time, and the Eagle hopped after him over logs and trees. But at last the Eagle was left behind and Loane had time to reload. Turning now, he found the Eagle on a log, peering about for his adversary. He got a long pole and, advancing, he held it out. Immediately the Eagle clutched it revengefully in both his feet. At the end of this pole the Eagle hung; and Loane carried it home in that way, with the pole across his shoulder. He pitched both pole and Eagle into a closed shed. In the morning the royal bird was still holding on like a vise. Loane put the pole in a wagon, so that it projected out behind, with the Eagle hanging down from the outermost end. During that five-mile drive, the Eagle held on. Arrived in Toronto, he went to Passmore's taxidermist shop on Yonge Street, where he handed over the living Eagle with the pole to which it was so much attached. In Passmore's possession, the Eagle lived and throve for several years afterwards.

"The area around Gooderham's cow barn was not purely marsh; it was, I should think, a couple of feet above high-water level. But it was overgrown with the rankest kind of sedge and offered a home for thousands, maybe millions, of Meadow Mice. I never saw them so abundant in any other part of the world. Every board you turned over had two or three under it. Their little runways netted the whole of the surface. They were popping in and out all day long, and much more so in the twilight hours. Hawks, Owls, and Butcher Birds were continually hovering about to catch and feed on them. If one stood still in one spot for ten minutes, he was sure to see half a dozen. Whether it was so in all years, I am not sure. But this certainly was a favorite feeding ground for all creatures that reckon Meadow Mice a staple. . . .

"In the bird world, of course, the star performer of Toronto Marsh was Cory's Bittern. This dying species apparently had its last stronghold in that marsh. In those days we did not distinguish it from the Little Bittern, and doubtless specimens may still be found in Toronto bird cases, bearing the label of the Common Bittern, but really belonging to the vanishing *Coryi*.

"I could discourse on other mammals and many other birds of the great marsh. It was a tremendously important migratory bird station. Apparently hosts came from the south, up the Niagara River, crossed the lake with a great bend to the west, so as to keep in sight of Hamilton; then made Toronto Marsh their grand rendezvous and feeding ground before crossing the height of land toward Lake Simcoe and the far North.

"As you go over the viaduct that continues Bloor Street eastward over the Rosedale Ravine, look down on the south side of that ravine, and you will see a huge glacial boulder about 7 feet across, within 30 yards of the bridge. Old Silverspot, the hero Crow of my story, was killed by the Owl just 10 feet south of this boulder. Of course, it was then in the deep woods.

"There must be many of the old-timers in Toronto yet who can correct and supplement my memories. Dr. Brodie's daughters are living; also Oliver Spanner, the taxidermist. I suppose old Alderman Hallam is dead; but it was Hallam who gave me the history of Anthony Gapper, the naturalist. The Gooderham family knew the Bay and the Marsh as well as anyone. My old friend, Inspector James Hughes of the Education Department, was intimately acquainted with every part of Toronto. He was living and clearheaded when I last saw him 18 months ago.

"Of course, I have plenty more. But this may not be the line you wish to follow."

The Development of the Animal Story

I find among Seton's unpublished manuscripts the following article which expresses his lifelong conviction in this area of thought:

"There is a time in the life of a nation when it is delighted with the fairy tale and its near kinsman, the romantic animal story.

"There is a time in the life of a man when these are the favorite literature. It is in both cases coexistent with the epoch of growth, the period of intensest activity, physical and mental.

"Both the nation and the man outgrow these stories. They find pleasure in something more demonstrable. Worn-out Rome, like worn-out man, scoffs at the impossible tales that were fountains of happiness in youth.

"And yet there are some among these romances that never lose their charm. In all the countless fairy tales that have been offered to the public, in the volumes of animal stories that have been told—and for the most part forgot—there are a few that have come to stay, a very few that never lose their hold on old and young.

"An examination of these few will always show that their strength lies in this: THEY ARE TRUE. They may be mixed with error, they may be disguised by the fanciful and the ill-understood. They may stretch the facts at times, and garble the details. But still, in the main they are true. Each in succession was a better insight into animal life; and though more or less a fairy tale, it is true in sentiment, and leavened with observations that are evidently just throughout.

"They are glimpses into personalities, lovingly told by those who had the gift of seeing and of telling. As with all lasting work, they are the truth from the heart through the head of a man of genius.

"It is a singular fact that children have a keener intuition for this truth than most grownups. A collection made instinctively by several generations of children will be more likely to stand the test of time and bear the stamp of truth than would a collection made by a jury of men of letters, too apt to be swayed by the letter itself.

"Each successive age has produced a vast number of these stories; and when the erosive touchstones of time and telling were applied, the softer parts were worn away by the attrition of use, or the baser stuff dissolved by that subtle alchemy which none but the noblest metal can resist. And there were left only one or two tales complete, tales that the world is not willing to let die.

"It is a trite saying that every masterpiece of thought is the product, not of one man, but of the age he lives in. The man whose name it bears was merely the mouthpiece of his time. In all these lasting tales, therefore, we find a reflex of the time that created them.

"Man's earliest occupation was hunting. This engendered close study of the animals as beasts of the chase. This we see in the stories which stem from that period in the world. Those which treat of animals present them simply as creatures to be hated, feared, and killed, and resulted in the lowest type of animal story.

"A better acquaintance with the animals led to keener discrimination of their individual characters. A knowledge of their ways of life became the common property of the people. The courage, strength, and prowess of the lion, the parasitism of the jackal, the rapacity of the wolf, the cunning of the fox, were familiar in byword and illustration long before Aesop appeared to godfather the Fables, none of which it is likely originated with him. And yet we are right in calling them Aesop's Fables, for he was the mouthpiece of the public mood that made them.

"There were two elements of truth in these Fables—truth about the animals, and moral truth for man. But the untruth about them is in humanizing the animals in order that they may exemplify this moral truth—perhaps proper under the circumstances, but creating a false picture on the whole.

"La Fontaine, the French fabulist, occupied the same relation to his time as did Aesop to his. But between these two, there appeared a long, notable fable—possibly the longest and most notable of the animal fables—*Reynard the Fox,* a story of doubtful authorship, but of remarkable, instant, and lasting popularity. Its influence was so great that it actually changed the accepted names of some animals in several languages; and to this day it seems to be the authority on natural history for many nature writers.

"But an entirely new note was struck at the end of the twelfth century by St. Francis of Assisi, who chose to accept literally a certain Scripture text: 'Go ye forth and preach the gospel to every creature,' and thenceforth taught that the animals were meant to share with man in the benefits of Christian charity.

"About the middle of the nineteenth century there came a new school of philosophers, the Evolutionists, who preached that the animals are not simply our spiritual brethren but actually are our blood kin. The public acceptance of this idea has naturally resulted in hitherto undreamed-of consideration for the animals, and in the concession to them of a determinate and important legal status.

"Following this, and evidencing the same trend, there began to appear animal stories of a new type. They differed from the fable chiefly in this: they contained the element of sympathy for the creature. The stories had an animal hero, more or less humanized and unreal, but still an animal. This marked a step nearer the truth. To this class belong the *Jungle Tales, Black Beauty, Le Loup Garou,* etc.

"With this, there has grown up a parallel and distinctive literature of two kinds—the purely scientific study of the animal's life history, and the sympathetic expression of that history in the biographical form, with as little humanizing as is possible in preparing it for human understanding. Of the latter class are Warner's *Hunting of the Deer,* Brown's *Rab,* and so far as I could make them, my own stories.

"We think that in all this we are getting nearer to an understanding of the animal's nature. Doubtless we are, but we must realize that we are still a long way off. Our darkness in matters of *human* psychology is scarcely broken as yet. In *animal* psychology it is even more obscure. We must achieve much before even partly dispelling it; and it will be long after that before we really comprehend the spirit of the animals.

"Yet there are many good men at work. They are feeling their way, they are honestly seeking for the light, they are guided by pure reason; well-meaning, trembling, earthy, slow, but on the whole safe.

"Sometimes, however, reason does well to be guided by instinct. At times the men of reason may wisely follow the lead of a creature of instinct. The instinct of a child has again and again proved wise with the animals; the child is always the first to find the way to the heart of a dog.

"It has been said that a dog never bites a child. It is reported that a ferocious mastiff broke loose and dashed down the main street of a certain village, spreading terror as he went. Another dog attacked him and was killed by the brute. A man with a pitchfork had to take refuge up a tree. Other men were torn by the furious animal. Even his master dared not face him. But a little child, only six years of age, ran out and slapped the mastiff's face with his chubby hand, saying: 'You naughty doggy. Do into your tennel.' And the huge brute submitted, turned round, and walked back to his kennel, to be tied up by that child.

"Who can explain this authentic story? Certainly not those philosophers who consider the animal a mere automaton. Certainly not that eminent writer who said: 'If you seek to explain the dog by putting yourself in his place, you are lost.' So far, our little brothers have proved inscrutable mysteries to all these wise men; but not to the children, for they have kept on instinctively, unquestioningly, accepting the animal as a creature of like passions with themselves.

"While the philosophers follow the automaton theory further into the darkness, they hope for the light. They feel that soon there must come a leader to show them that light. They have no idea who he may be, or whence he may come. They look no doubt for another great savant.

"But is it not possible that here, as on another important zoological occasion when the wise and the mighty were guided aright to a new epoch, 'a little child shall lead them'?"

A Defense

Many times the question has been asked: "Are Seton's animal stories true?" The answer is probably "yes and no." He has said:

"In the story one has greater leeway than in the scientific treatise. The following I consider to be three allowable liberties in a popular story of an animal:

"First, one may select an unusual individual.

"Second, one may ascribe to him the adventures and attributes of several of his race.

"Third, one may make him do things which his species never was known to do, because never observed under these conditions, provided that the presented case is completely hedged about by probabilities. That is, one may assume the probable as proven.

"This last is the only one of these postulates that is ever opposed; but the objection is usually abstract, and disappears when an example is given.

"Thus, I never actually knew a red squirrel to follow and scold a bear, but have known them to do so to cat, dog, lynx, and man. Or again, I never really knew a wild wolf to store food, but have known foxes, coyotes, dogs, huskies, and half-bred wolves to do so. Therefore I have always felt that no great violence was done in making the red squirrel scold and follow a bear, or a wolf to store his food.

"Some incidents have been questioned in stories written in my very early days when I felt more strongly that liberties might be taken than I do now. No zoological authority has made adverse criticism on my more recent stories such as 'Jacky Warhorse,' 'The Slum Cat,' etc. I have no difficulty whatever in getting the dog man to accept my dog story or the wolf hunter my wolf story. The difficulty is to get the dog man to believe the wolf story or the wolf man to believe the dog story. Indeed each in his own field is so impressed with his animal's powers that he inclines to think me too conservative.

"Some will say, however, that even granting the truth of all details, I have added an atmosphere, a feeling of human sensibility, that conveys a wrong notion of the animal's way of life. To this I reply: 'The subject of my first book, and indeed of all my books, was the *personality* of the individual animal. No man can write of another personality without adding a suggestion of his own. The personal touch may be the poison of science, but may also be the making of literature, and is *absolutely inevitable.*'

"Which then is better? That which would reduce not only all animal traits but all human kindness also to a mere mathematical problem of reflex quantities and oscillating energies, or one which by the warming touch of sympathy brings the animal nearer to us, makes clear our kinship, and commends the study to the hearts of all mankind?

"Finally I maintain that my stories do convey a true notion of the ways of the animals, their troubles, their trials, their matings, their friendships, and their foes; the lives they live and the deaths they die."

Let me give a couple of examples of Seton's simple animal stories, hitherto unpublished, which demonstrate his approach to this principle.

Dabbles, the Coon

There were a pretty lot of roly-poly youngsters that the mother Coon led down to the water for the first time that bright moonlight night. They had had many little surprises on the road from their home tree, along the log fence. But when they got to the edge of the stream, the wonderful, soft bright uncatchable water was the greatest surprise of all.

Mother Coon had brought them down, not to frolic, but for serious business. This was mainly by example. The youngsters had an inborn notion of hunting that made it easy and natural to do as their mother did. So they prowled along the shore, raking in the mud with their claws, or looking about at each slight sound, in imitation of her.

Of course, some were quicker to learn than others, and each had a taste of his own. One preferred to keep well up the bank, another stayed close by his mother, two fought over a perfectly worthless old bone, and one independent little chap got off by himself and dabbled in the mud just as his mother did.

He had the luck to catch a baby frog very soon, and was greatly delighted with himself. He at once planned a much more important undertaking farther up the creek; but his mother stopped that, for she knew the dangers of the place, while his bravery was all born of ignorance. He decided to try it again as soon as he could escape his mother's watchful eye.

This was the beginning of his willfulness. The others did as their mother wished, and so she was able to take care of them. But Dabbles' head was turned by his first success. He became possessed of the idea that he was a very wise little Coon.

At last one night he saw his chance. He quietly left the nest in the hollow tree and went alone to the creek. He heard his mother calling, but he hurried on without answering, and traveled a long way down the creek.

That very day, Indian Pete had set a muskrat trap on a rat landing above the outlet. The trap was of course set in the water, and hidden. Dabbles came along flushed with triumph, for had he not already caught two frogs?

He saw this likely-looking place and proceeded to grope in the mud with his paws, ready to grab at anything that he could feel wriggling. But alas for him, he groped right into the lurking trap!

Snap it went, and Dabbles was a prisoner. Though firmly held, he was not much hurt, only frightened; and he squealed the long Coon whicker which would have brought his mother to help him had he not run so far from home that she could not hear. So Dabbles cried himself weak and hoarse with no good result.

Next morning Indian Pete came around to look at his muskrat trap; and there to his surprise was a little Coon, nearly dead with cold and fright, and so weak that it could not bite. He took it out of the trap and put it in his pocket, not knowing just what he would do with it.

On his way home he passed by the Pigott homestead and showed his little prisoner to the children.

Dabbles was still cold and miserable; and when put into the arms of the oldest girl, he snuggled in so contentedly that he won her heart, and she coaxed their father into buying the little creature from Indian Pete, to be a pet and plaything for the children.

This marked Chapter Two of Dabbles' history. He was so well taken care of now that in a few days he was all right again. He had the children to play with instead of brothers and sisters, and many curious things to eat instead of frogs. But still he loved to dabble his brown hands in the mud or anything wet whenever he could get the chance. He did not eat milk and bread like a cat or other well-behaved creature; he always put in his paws to fish out the bread, bit by bit, and commonly ended by spilling the milk.

As he grew stronger he became very mischievous. He seemed half monkey, half kitten, full of fun, always delighted to be petted and always hungry. Whenever a stranger came to the house, Dabbles would gravely climb up his legs and seek in all his pockets for something to eat. On one occasion he got into the preserve closet and made himself very ill before he was found.

As time went on he became even more mischievous. One day Mrs. Pigott set a hen with thirteen eggs. The next day Dabbles was missing. As they went about calling "Dabbles, Dabbles," they heard a faint reply from the henhouse, the gentle whicker that he usually gave in answer; and on going there, they found Dabbles sprawling on his back in the hen's nest, perfectly gorged; and the remains of the thirteen eggs told that he was responsible for a piece of dreadful destruction.

Mr. Pigott bore with Dabbles for a long time because the children were so fond of the little rascal. But the capsheaf was added one day when Dabbles, left alone in the house, discovered the ink bottle. First he drew the cork and spilled the ink about, then he dabbled his hands in it after his usual manner, and found a new pleasure in laying the inky paws on any white thing that would take a good paw mark. At first he made the marks on the table, then he found that the children's schoolbooks were just the thing, and gave much better results. He paw-marked them inside and out, carefully re-inking his paws when the marks got poor.

The family Bible came next, then the wallpaper seemed to need stamping. This led to the window curtains and the girls' dresses. And then, as the bedroom door was open, Dabbles ran and jumped on the bed. It was just beautiful the way that snow-white coverlet took the dear little paw marks as Dabbles galloped over it in great glee.

He was several hours alone, and he used up all the ink. When the children came in from school, it looked as though a thousand little Coons had been running all over the place and leaving black paw marks.

Poor Mrs. Pigott actually cried when she saw her beautiful bed, the pride of her heart. But she laughed when Dabbles came running, holding out his inky arm and whining, "errrr errrr," to be taken up and petted as though he were the best little Coon in the world.

But this was too much, as even the children allowed when they saw their white dresses; and sentence of banishment was passed on the culprit.

It wasn't easy, however, to find anyone willing to take the Coon, that is, anyone who would be kind to him.

The difficulty was solved at last by sending him to the famous New York Zoo in the Bronx Park. There you may still see Dabbles; if he is not sleeping in the sun or teasing one of his companions, he is sure to be dabbling in the water bowl, exactly as he did on that beautiful moonlit night long ago when his mother brought him and his brothers to the water, and where first he learned the pleasures of dabbling in the mud.

Two Sides of the Coin

Seton was a strange combination of exact scientist and imaginative romancer. When he was in the field, every detail of size, color, movement, sound, and action were recorded by him on the spot with an accuracy of observation that has never been excelled by any other naturalist. But often, after such an experience, he would fall into another world of approach. In this, we find pure inspiration, poetic presentation, with scarce a change of word or phrase in his manuscripts; something no longer a mental operation, but an expression of the heart, of the inner man that harbored the real love of nature.

I know of no one else who has shown in such degree these two facets of thinking and writing. To me it seems manifest that this is the secret of the success of all his published stories. With the utmost authenticity of facts, he has presented his animal heroes with the love for them that was the innermost core of his being.

The following extracts from his manuscripts show both sides of this coin. It is a joy to be able to lose oneself with him in a flight of poetic expression, and then to have the assurance that the most apparently trifling record may be accepted without question.

The Story of Undine

"There was naught but the silent forest, only it in its stillness." Again and again recurred these words—and I know not where I read them—as I traversed the primitive woods of southern Muskoka. The pine trees were standing thick in giant groves along the banks of the winding Black River. It was afternoon, and the birds were hushed on all sides. There was no wind and no sound in the tallest trees. There was naught but the silent forest.

On every side were the pines rearing their mighty pillars above the topmost boughs of the oaks and maples before they even began to branch; and doubling this dizzy height before, at length, they ceased to ascend, each ended its column in a broad uplifted crown of green.

No one who has not been alone for long in these primitive woods can fully understand the solemnity that seems born of their shades. And with the silence, the feeling grew until at length it became oppressive, and I was glad to turn from contemplating the grandeur of the scene, and notice some of its prettiness in a more open place where a few of the familiar flowers of the hardwood bush had sprung up to enliven the line of the needle-strewn earth with their simple contrasts of white and green. I gathered some, of course, for no one can ever see wild flowers without gathering them, even though it be but to throw them away a few minutes later; and I am not quite sure that the incentive feeling is on this account to be entirely condemned.

I, however, had other objects in view. I was, like Dr. Syntax, in search of the picturesque to some extent; and as I sat and sketched my simple prizes, I found pleasure in remembering the various fancies and legendary stories that have already begun to gather about our Canadian wild flowers and birds.

First of our spring wood flowers to catch the eye is the great white Trillium or Wake-robin—so called, I have heard, because its appearance marks the advent or awakening of the great bird host returning homeward from the south. Closely following the Trillium is the Star-of-Bethlehem, so familiar in the nosegays of sportive children in the woods; and not far away I found also the Solomon's Seal, the fancied associate of the Veery Thrush.

To quote from an old diary of my own: "This [the Solomon's Seal] I have always connected with the Veery by a sort of fantasy that is not entirely uninteresting or baseless, for it always springs up when the Veery comes, and blooms when its song is at the full. So it is pleasant to think of them together, for this surely is among flowers what the bird is among *its* kind. 'Simple as the curve' is the Veery's song, a simple curve is this slender Lily. The Veery's life blooms into his silver note, and the life aim of the Lily is finished in the simple silver-frilled bloom on its brow. Born together in the shade, their graceful lives are side by side until at last, when the summer wanes, the Veery flies away and the Lily dies."

But the afternoon had passed, and once more I returned to the path by the river. I had now left the pine woods and was again among the mixed timber. Suddenly my path was crossed by two animals that were worthy of a lengthy notice from their completely contrasting diversity. A slight rustling in the woods just ahead had chanced to catch my ear; and almost immediately afterwards, there stepped into full view a splendid red Stag. His antlers were not yet grown, but the proud erect head, the sinewy limbs, and the winged heels were there in their beauty to receive the meed of worship. For a moment he stood and gazed; but taking alarm, he trotted off a few steps and then took flight, skimming lightly over fallen trees, soaring over bushes until he disappeared in the woods.

I was able to see his snowy white tail long after I had lost sight of the Deer. When I pressed forward to watch this banneret as it twinkled through the woods, I almost stepped over a Porcupine that resented my intrusion at once by raising his spines and looking stupid. When I poked him with a stick, he grunted peevishly and proceeded slowly to shuffle away towards a small hemlock; and having climbed some six feet up this, he ensconced himself in a convenient crotch and tried to forget my invasion in a sound slumber.

I did not attempt to sketch him, for he looked like nothing in particular but a woolly black ball in the crotch of the tree. Besides, it was becoming late, and the remembrance of several miles of forest still lying between me and my shelter for the night was sufficient to spoil the Porcupine's chances of both immortality and further annoyance.

The heat of the day was over now; and many of the voices of the woods were beginning to awaken and salute the ear on every side, especially when at length the path trended downward and along by the river, here running "with an inner voice" among the towering elm trees. These rose like columns, to spring out in groined and pointed arches when at length each had attained the appointed height of the green vault.

If indeed mason or monkish builder ever gathered from tree aught of towering form or pointed arch to plan a chancel or to grace a noble hall, he surely studied nowhere but in such an elm tree grove. For this is the real forest cathedral; and here by the deep-voiced water, when the time of vespers has come and when the setting sun has drawn overhead the purple and scarlet curtains of the sanctuary, is heard the noblest voice of the woodlands, for here sings the Hermit Thrush, the forest angel. Here with voice of sublime power and sweetness, himself unseen but felt on every side, he seems to cry: "Oh, holy, holy forest; come, weary, weary." And as we pause to hear the invocation, comes again the echoing cry, "Oh, shadow holy, rest in solemnity."

The voice of the water seems to blend with his, and the echoing aisles of elm trees still repeat the liquid strain. The Veery catches up the spirit of the hymn, and from his station seems to call and call again: "Oh, weary, weary, weary," moving, melting with their sweet seductive strains, inviting and leading the weary one to rest, and tempting the heartsore to forgetfulness.

What happiness the naturalist can find in these lone places none but the naturalist can know. But the measure of his joy is equaled by the sorrow of the thought that in a little while every one of these glorious trees must be cut down and burnt; and all that goes to make the place what it is must be destroyed for the sake of clearing the land, which is, after all, of but little value.

It is not wise to lament the inevitable fate of all that stands in the way of progress; nevertheless it is a sad pity that so much destruction is deemed necessary. For in truth the pioneers seem to conceive a hatred of trees, and never rest content while a single living shelter is left upon their land.

It is only too well known now what mischief has been wrought in America by this strange mania; what droughts, what changes of a once genial climate, and what frightful loss of property and life have been brought about by a tree-denuded soil. Yet the work goes on, and the evil becomes worse. Again and again have I seen in Canada a piece of useless woods on a piece of rough useless land, totally destroyed, not apparently for the sake of either, but rather to gratify the arboricidal madness of a sometime pioneer.

Well do I remember the fate of such a spot. It was a quiet shady glen near my early home. Here silver birch and somber hemlock had united, and covenanted with the Veery, the Hermit, and the purest of running water, to form an "Eden once again upon the weary earth." Alone, I went there for years, till I loved the place as my own—thought it was my own, and was happy. Then came a change in my affairs which for long prevented my visits. At length, however, I returned; and at the first opportunity hastened away to my old haunt. But what a sight! Bare and bald now was the once shady glen but for a few stumps and brush piles; gone was the golden haze that had streamed through the roof leaves; gone the Hermit Thrush and the Veery; and the water sullied, and drying up in the sun.

Then I felt "the glory and the loveliness are gone away from earth." I was a boy then. I sat down on the bare muddy bank and cried. That was the death of my first love. I am afraid to form another. I am afraid even to go where I may again learn to delight in the spirit of some shady glen. The shadow of sure bereavement follows me, and now I care no more to see the place I had known so well. And whence my lamentation.

A Count of Quills

To illustrate the meticulous attention that Seton paid to his observations, we quote:

* "A large male porcupine, taken at Berlin, Rensselaer Co., N.Y., Jan. 14, 1924 (No. 67892 Am. Mus.), on careful examination by G. G. Goodwin and myself, gave the following as conservative results of a count:

Head (armoured part)	12½ sq. in.,		100 quills per sq. in.						1,250
Body	"	"	240	"	"	140	"	" " "	33,600
Tail	"	"	100	"	"	100	"	" " "	1,600
									36,450

The Flicker and the Stub

"Oct. 27, 1882. While examining an old stub in the woods to the north of Carberry, I met with an excellent illustration of the aptitude of the Spanish name for the woodpecker, 'El Carpintero'; I mean in the sense of being a worker in wood, and house provider for others.

"As far as circumstantial evidence revealed it, the history of the case is briefly this: First came the hard-working flicker and excavated the hole, perhaps while yet the stub was sound; and in the years that followed, we know not how many young flickers cracked their glasslike shells in this narrow chamber.

"After the flickers came no more, it was taken by some bird— a grackle perhaps—that, like the 'foolish man,' founded its nest upon sand and mud, finishing its superstructure with sticks and straw.

* *Lives of Game Animals,* Vol. IV, p. 620.

"Then, it seems, came a new possessor, who built a strong, shapely nest of moss and mud. But for the situation, it might have been the nest of a robin.

"Lastly, this many-storied tenement house became the eyrie of a kestrel, whose household furniture of straw and moss reached half-way up to the doorway.

"A strange tale of a hole surely.

"But there was more yet to be learned from the old stub; and allowing fullest weight to circumstantial evidence, and accepting the suppositions as fact proven, I may be allowed to relate as a matter of established history that, on a certain day, Sir Falco Sparverius brought home to his brood a tiny shrew of the species yclept by scientists the *Sorex cooperi.*

"Now it chanced that the young hopefuls of the robber baron were not just then very hungry—oh, marvelous chance!—so that the *Sorex cooperi,* being left to his own devices, set about to escape. He so far succeeded that he burrowed down through the home effects of the kestrel and the moss-builder. But when so far, the hard mud floor barred further progress, and the poor little captive, weary and wounded, soon died in the buried nest.

"There I found him, like Ginevra in the oaken chest, when, long afterwards, I broke open the rotten timber and made it disclose a tragic tale that, maybe, never happened at all."

The Mother Bear

"The proudest moment in the life of an animal keeper is when he can show a happy healthy family born and rearing among the creatures in his charge.

"Today, W. H. Blackburn of Washington Zoo took me to see the new family of Bears there—four little cubs born to one Russian Bear. They are now nine weeks old, and just beginning to go about with their mother. She moved her ponderous limbs and body with the utmost caution to avoid crushing the active heedless little Teddy Bears that seemed to swarm about her.

"They kept up a continual whimpering, and tried by every means to reach her body, and nurse. They stood on their hind legs, they

1. Rear view of Seton house in ruins, Scotland, 1790

2. Seton at two years of age,
with father and mother

3. The house where he was born,
South Shields, England

4. The Elms, the house
Seton's father built in 1866
in Lindsay, Canada

5. Old Ellen, the nurse, with her mo

6. Seton at easel, aged 14

7. Seton, aged 17

8. Brother Arthur and Ernest, 1881

9. Family photo, 1889 (Ernest in middle, rear row)

10. Seton, 1896

11. Seton, 1901

12. Seton, 1903

13. Seton, 1912

clung to her limbs, they tugged at her coat, and tumbled snarling and wrestling about on the floor. They louder and louder wailed in good and ursine terms: 'We are hungry, Mamma, Mamma; we are hungry.'

"At last she consented, slowly, cautiously, selecting a spot not littered over with cubs. She squatted, made a lap into which all rushed. Then she leaned slowly backward, till her broad shoulders touched the floor. The litter of little woolly pigs snarled and quarreled with each other, slapped each other's faces, boxed each other's ears, nipped each other's behinds, shrieked: 'Here, this is my place. I found it first.'

"''Tisn't, it's mine; get a place of your own.' They whimpered even when each was attached to a nipple. But all got places. One who had the two groin teats kept changing from one to the other in his greedy mumbling eagerness. The other three fastened on her breast where there are four nipples. They eagerly worked for their sustenance.

"Their whimpers died away as they contentedly snuggled and fed, while Mother Bear looked on with a wondrous beatific expression of joy. The only sound she uttered was a soft long 'sigh' from time to time, a sound of joy, I think—for the grim old animal visage it came from was lighted up with a wonderful something—the blessed holy light of a deep, a conscious, a joyful maternity."

PART FOUR

THE GOLDEN DAYS

LIFE IN MANITOBA

Willie Brodie

In his Toronto days, his early manhood, Seton had one most congenial friend. This was William G. A. Brodie, three years younger than himself.

It was Willie's father, the dentist, who kept the rattlesnakes that were so dramatically killed by Seton's rats.* He it was also who went back in 1885 to visit with Seton the country about Toronto Marsh when he was in search of—and found—the Florida Gallinule, said to be rare north of Lake Erie.

The son Willie inherited his father's natural history interests. When, in 1882, Seton set out from his father's house in Toronto for his brother's shanty in Manitoba, Willie went with him.

On one occasion Seton, in speaking of this boyhood companion of those days, said to me: "His superior knowledge of insects was of continual value to me, and our united efforts resulted in ever increasing light on the wonders and beauties of the new world we were exploring together."

Willie took up a claim in the primitive country of Manitoba and settled down to the life of a pioneer farmer. Then, for May 31, 1883, I find this entry in Seton's journal:

"Today received the sad news that my old friend, Willie G. A. Brodie of Toronto, was dead, drowned in the spring flood of the Upper Assiniboine."

As we spoke of the incident one night, he elaborated:

"Alas, poor Will, the most congenial friend of all that went with our crowd to the far Northwest, a young man of the highest moral character, of joyous outlook, gifted with a brilliant intellect; and, thanks to his talented father, equipped not only with an education that was up to date and modern, but better still, with vision, for his spiritual side was not forgotten.

"His father had planned for him a career as naturalist to one

* See Seton's *Great Historic Animals.*

of the coming provinces in the Northwest, and saw to it that his biological training was of the best. But it seemed to both father and son that a wise chapter in his development would be to live for three or four years the life of a prairie pioneer and farmer.

"It was for this that he came with me; and, after various frontier experiences, had staked out a claim among the settlers of the Upper Assiniboine.

"He was the only son in a family of seven children. He was his father's hope and his mother's darling, the idol of her heart. Handsome of face and tall of form, manly and athletic, a born naturalist, he was the hope and pride of the whole family.

"Why, oh, why should he have been selected for the sacrifice? What is the meaning back of the Mosaic injunction that the sacrificial lamb must be the flower of the flock, the perfect one, none else?

"Wholly broken by the blow were both parents. The father wrote me some months afterward: 'I am sitting in the dust and ashes of my fondest hopes. I have nothing to live for now.'

"Who can explain why he was taken? At twenty years of age, in the first flush of young manhood, in the morning glow of promise. Maybe someday light will come, and with it understanding, wisdom, and patience. But, looking on as now, we can only say in mutters of rebellion: 'It was not right! It was not right! Are those the rulings of a God of Love?'

"On the fourteenth of October that same year, I was camped in the nearby region. There I met Langley, one of Brodie's friends; and from him received Brodie's rifle, the last sad relic. I returned it to his people in Toronto.

"I also met Scott, who was Brodie's fellow settler; and from him got the details of that sad canoe upset in the ice-cold freshet of the spring, and learned how the body was recovered next day and buried on a knoll looking down on the raging guilty river."

The Journals

In an annex to our Main Library at Seton Village is a room, small in area, dominated by a portrait* of Seton finished shortly before

---

* This portrait was made and presented to Seton Foundation by Winifred Scutt, noted painter of many famous men of the West.

his death, and flanked by some twenty metal museum cases containing our bird and mammal study-skins. On one side of the portrait is a bookcase holding the first copies off the press of Seton's books; and on the other until recently a case displaying the fifty-odd fat journals of his natural history observations, begun in 1879 and continued day by day until two weeks before the end of his life in 1946. These diaries are handwritten, scribbled in pencil, ink—anything. They are profusely illustrated by his pen, and many of them water-colored. They are smirched with the blood of victims sacrificed on the altar of the knowledge-hunger. They are burned with sparks of the campfire; greasy with handling by unwashed, hasty eager hands. They are at times badly written, badly illustrated with hasty sketches—hasty but meaningful.

There are careful entries for every day of that long period, in which he never missed an opportunity to note in permanent form the little events which to him were the very breath of life. They represent more than anything else nearly seventy years of his life and thought, his stirrings and his joy.

These journals have been the basis for all his stories as well as his scientific books.

When Seton was first leaving his home in Canada to go off on his own, it was Dr. Brodie who told him to "keep a full journal of everything you see and hear."

"I did not at the time see just why," Seton later mused, "but I had faith enough in him to begin. He did not tell me, probably did not know, what good purpose was to be served, but it came to me gradually as the years went by.

"The older I grow, the more I see and realize the value of the daily note of the truth; the simple fact, bald, untooled, perhaps incomplete, but honestly given as it was found.

"The entries must be made *daily*—not from faded memory a month later. They should be fully embellished with diagrams, sketches, or photographs when these can help more fully to set forth the facts. The student may wonder at the time what good it all is. One answers that, first, it is always useful to have a record of one's doings; but, more important, writing a fact makes one observe it better.

"Surely all past experience proves it to be a wise thing—how wise and how precious one may not learn for years, may never learn at all. But we do know that it is always good to follow the trail in this way, for its own sake; it always pays in the end. There never yet was a sincere full record made of the testimony of the senses that did not finally prove a priceless treasury of fact.

"*The Journal of a Citizen of Paris,* the *Pepys's Diary,* Harmon's *Journal,* Lewis and Clark's *Journals* are familiar examples. These men wrote down the simple doings of the time, without intent to do anything but tell the truth, and without any suspicion that they were doing a great feat. These same journals are today among the most treasured sources in the world of authentic history.

"Scornful critics ask: 'Are there not enough commonplace records of commonplace things? Why should you set a new army of scribblers to work?'

"To such I reply: 'No man can daily write the simple truth of what he sees in nature or human nature and leave a commonplace record. It will, of course, be limited by his own limitation; but everyone soon or late gets a chance to observe something that no one else has in any way recorded—an opportunity that comes but once in an age. And the occasion is not lost if he has the habit of record.'

"Let me finish with a parable:

"There was once a vast and priceless mosaic inscription that contained the Truth, the one guide to human fulfillment. By accident— or divine purpose perhaps—it was shattered to a million pieces and scattered to the corners of creation. The pieces themselves are imperishable, but human happiness depends on the reconstruction of the inscription.

"Everyone who finds a little fact, however small, finds a scrap of that mosaic. If he honestly brings it, just as he found it, to those in charge, he is helping by that much. If he attempts to chisel the fact to make it fit into one or two others that he has found, he is by that much hindering the ultimate restoration of the lost inscription.

"When enough are brought together, no matter how ragged and incomplete some may be, they will fit each other. The right ones always fit—the wrong ones never do. And when they are all assembled, they will surely spell TRUTH.

"Now it is given to everyone who uses his eyes to find some of these fragments, and the only way to preserve them untooled is in a sincere daily journal.

"Those who made such records a hundred years ago were really providing the material for Darwin, for Pasteur, for Einstein, making possible the accomplishments of these men. Each of them took the accumulated fragments, put them together, and restored for us a section of the great mosaic. Those who make honest entries today are in like manner preparing the way for some other prophet whose message to mankind is sure to be yet more important; for the latest restored part will be the most significant because it is that much nearer to the whole design.

"No one knows, or can know, who the new prophet is to be, or when he is to come. But we do know that his work must be founded on the daily observations of all those who came before, and will be great in proportion to the plodding persistence and the steadfast sincerity of the obscure, apparently insignificant workers who believed in the larger good of nature itself—in the TRUTH as it will evolve when the time is ripe, when our eyes are strong enough to stand the white light of the only ultimate end of philosophy and religion."

The Hermit Thrush

During his days on his brother's farm in Manitoba, the period that he called his Golden Days, Seton made many notes on the birds particularly. While these entries are sincere detailed records of his observations, there is often a poetic quality about the telling that impresses the facts on the mind of the reader more deeply than could the bare information imparted.

I give several of these.

Speaking of the Hermit Thrush he says:

"This species returns to its summer haunts about the last of April in Manitoba, two or three days earlier in southern Ontario.

"It appears to be the first of its subgenus to return, which fact accords with its northerly distribution, when compared with that of most of its near congeners.

"About the fifth of May, the main body usually is seen in the Carberry woods, appearing so suddenly, in such numbers, as to warrant the statement that it arrives in large flocks. During early May, it continues to be common even in the opener country, and among the little scrubby copses that are found here and there, through the barren Sandhills. But as the month ages, it becomes more scarce; and by June is to be found in the woods only, and then is more often heard than seen.

"Its favorite haunts are among the timber which is too dense to permit the growth of underbrush, weeds, or any but the delicate flowers that characterize the deeper woods. Here, among the lower branches of the trees, it lives and builds, and sings its sweet song in the golden forest twilight that changes only to yield to the deeper shades of night.

"My Ontarian observations on this species do not lead to precisely the same general conclusions as those made in Manitoba, regarding the period that elapses between the date of arrival and the beginning of the song period; for I find a note made at Toronto on April 30, which records both events as having taken place together.

"Throughout the country between Lakes Ontario and Simcoe and farther northeast to Haliburton, I found the Hermit very abundant, being second in numbers only to the Veery among the Wood Thrushes. The statements relative to its being found even in isolated exposed copses in early spring, while later on it must be sought in the woods, apply to its migration apparently everywhere.

"The song of this bird is one of the noblest in our woods. It is no easy matter to describe it well, and it is still more difficult to distinguish it in the woods from the songs of the Wood Thrush and Olive-backed. Yet it is different from, and superior to, both. The beauty of the music, I think, lies less in the notes than in the quality. I have tried in vain to imitate with a piccolo some bars from the Hermit's hymn when I heard a thoughtful woodman compare the bird's voice to an echo from over the water. With this idea in my mind, I stood before a barn on a smooth stretch of prairie, after night, so as to secure a good echo; and found that a short, quick stave was always returned so unchanged in its timbre as to be deceptively like the familiar voice of the forest."

The Upland Plover or Quaily

"The upland plover, or quaily, as it is called in Manitoba, is a rather anomalous member of the family. As Mr. R. M. Christy observes: 'Surely no bird ever differed more completely from the generality of its relatives than this. It is a sandpiper which does not appear to frequent marshes, which breeds habitually on the dry open prairies, and which is frequently to be seen perched among the branches of the trees. Its tameness is excessive. Often when driving over the prairie, I have seen it remain within three yards of the passing vehicle, without the slightest concern. When on the wing, it offers a shot so temptingly easy that few can resist.'

"The note of this species is very peculiar. It is usually begun when the bird is sailing in the air, with a prolonged rattling whistle repeated two or three times in succession, and these run off into a long smooth slur which rises through half an octave and falls through nearly two; the effect is as mournful as can well be from a creature that is evidently expressing its delight in the joys of life and liberty. For a few seconds after alighting, the bird stands like a statue with its long wings stretched straight over its back, as though to display the beautiful markings of the underside, then suddenly it folds them and proceeds to walk about and pick up insects, keeping on nodding incessantly much after the manner of the barn fowl or gallinule.

"The nest is on the dry prairie, for the bird, so far as I have seen, manifests no more inclination to visit the water than does a barnyard chicken. The eggs are, as usual with the family, four in number, and are remarkably large for the size of the bird. The nests are so abundant on the Big Plain that I have frequently found two or three in a walk of less than an hour's duration.

"When her treasure is discovered, the grief of the quaily mother is most touching. She throws herself at your feet and beats her gentle breast on the earth, and sobs and wails in a manner that generally appeals effectually to the heart of the humane intruder. The Western farmers seldom molest the bird; indeed, I have more than once seen a plowman disfigure his new field by leaving in the center a tiny island of green sod, a yard across, because a quaily had her nest there; and the brave little bird never fails, but sticks to her task and brings out her young in spite of the desolating changes going on about her.

"The earliest nest that I noted was found on June first; it then contained 4 eggs. A week afterwards, I saw numbers of young ones. On July 12th I found a nest with 3 fresh eggs. Young ones seen July 23rd were half grown, but still in the down. On August

8th I took from a Swainson's buzzard a young quaily not half grown. These represent the extremes of laying and hatching; so that I should accept their testimony as indicating but one brood per season.

"During the breeding season, it is very rare to see a single quaily; they are nearly always in pairs, and if one is shot, the other generally waits to share its fate. But often both are killed at a single discharge, so closely do they keep together.

"On June 2, 1884, I counted those I passed in a journey of a few hours; there were 5 pairs, each bird keeping within a few feet of its mate, and only one which had no mate very near to it."

The Wren

"The first thing a wren does when he finds a hole suitable for nesting is to block up the entrance with the biggest sticks he can carry, until none but himself can get into the tiny doorway.

"If you look along any snake fence that has a few big rails in it, you are sure to find some of them hollow, and perhaps a few twigs sticking out. If so, that is a wren nest.

"When a boy, I used to carry a spoon in my pocket to lift out these eggs. On one occasion, the introduction of the spoon was followed by a sudden buzz-z-z; and I fled in consternation, finding I was trying to ladle out a nest of wasps that had taken possession of an old wren's nest.

"Mr. Kennicott ascertained that a single pair of wrens carried to their young about 1000 insects in a single day (Baird).

"I think that in southern and warm climates they lay more eggs than in colder ones. About Lake Ontario, I found 8 to 12 eggs, but as far north as 40° latitude, 4 to 6 were the common numbers."

Spring on Riding Mountain

"It's spring on the Riding Mountain now, there's flame in the grey-green brush, but not the withering prairie fire that kills and blasts as it goes. 'Tis a fire that is life to the woods and to me.

"After the flood on the earth, it is said a remaining family were dying of cold, but God sent a black-winged flake of heavenly flame that fired a bush. Men were warmed and saved.

"Since then, the Indians have not let the fire die; but drifting about in the woods is the winged flame, ready should it chance that all fires be quenched. And this is the flame in the grey-green brush when the spring's on the Riding Mountain."

The Prairie and the Flying Voice

It is no wonder that Seton, all the rest of his life, looked back on his Manitoban days with deep nostalgia. He was young, in robust health, alert to every sign and sound in the world of nature; and though working strenuously at day-by-day physical chores, was doing exactly what his life's dream encompassed.

These were days of bliss unspeakable; and with the recollections of that period immemorial, he lived a life apart from everyday commonplaces for the rest of his long life, with all the force they carried at the time of their happening.

On a Canadian lecture tour in the 1930s, he and I drove across much of the country that he had known in his young manhood during the early eighties. Memories of his adventures came tumbling into our car as we went; and as usual the emotions he had experienced back in those days thrilled and tormented him now as they had in the first instance.

Across our vision one bright October day, the flight of a golden-winged song lark, the Indian Chewesson, blacked out all the intervening years; and he was back in a timeless interval of longing; and the pain that comes of unsatisfied knowledge-hunger.

"I was very young then," he murmured. "Twenty-one snows I had seen in the woods, but my heart was sixteen.

"Oh, Father Time, steamroller, huge impulverizer, what would I not suffer to see it all again as I saw it then! The eager heart, the tireless limb, the unclouded eye, the unburdenedness of a manhood late arriving.

"Now I see it all in a distant purple mist that hides the stinging vermin, singing or crawling; lights up the trees.

"The long flat grey-gold stretch in spring, the blistering wind, not wholly gone, the snowbanks in the hollows, the prairie chickens marching insouciantly on the whiteness of the hillocks, draping them over with accurately constructed toe marks, all spaced and measured, somewhat overdone around that stiff rough prairie rose that swung its last red drupes aloft—food, food, held for the hardy ones that had braved it and bested the winter. Good kind old snow that hid these rubies showing now at sun-call.

"Gone is the wind-sting, the Buffalo Wind is blowing. Oh, how soft, how influential, running like an uptide in the backways and bays of one's being. Ozonic, tingling. Opium is that way, they say. And birds back responding; each morning more birds responding. The ducks and the cranes come responding, great angle-wing hawks in the sky are responding, black speckling flocks of the redwingèd blackbird, crek-crek-creking, increasing in numbers, skittering blots, gnats in the offing, smoke on the sky line, rising, whirring, wheeling, and shraying like mill wheels, like white combers on a pebbly mile of shore, their wing beats are shraying.

"Creking like voiceless things seeking expression, and the cranes on their eight-foot wings come croaking and trumpeting up in the blueness, croaking and seeking expression.

"Oh, how lovely and soft is the south wind, O gladmaker Shah-wandaysee, the lover, the loved of the prairie, moaning a little.

"How all things respond, how the brown prairie ridges respond, all a-greening—how the marshes respond, with their greening, and the myriad quack of the frog-folk that splutter as seeking expression; and burnt prairie ridges, refulge with an army, burst forth with the wool-bearing crocus, the pale bluish flower of the sandbloom—rising and opening and straining—seeking expression. Who can see and ever forget that sandbloom? I sought not to crush them, I walked as one in a garden; but they were everywhere, bursting, blooming, straining, looking, longing—I know it—that blue host was seeking expression. And I flung myself down on a willow knoll, a prairie bump made up of happenings, where died a buffalo long ago. Face down, unspeaking, I gasped as one whose thoughts are hurting him. Bursting was my full-grown childish heart, incomprehensibly suffocating, the very wind of God in my lungs, yet choking, urge-mad for expression. Shall I ever forget that hard-breathing time?

"Then a low sweet 'ting' vocal away in the wind's eye. Oh, soft it sounded tinklingly and offing dimmed.

"'I am the golden Chewesson!
I am the flute of the prairie!
The mellow wind-rider,
I am the bearer of tidings.'

"The striped gopher chittered insolently in my face, stopped, caught a creeper in his own groin, held a grass cane as one holds a piccolo and chewed and snickered, and bit in twain an early inedible pith weevil, then chittered and rushed and raced, as one who is mad for expression.

"The blessed voice wind-riding came:
'I am the child of the dawning,
The voice of the Prairie;
I am the Golden Chewesson.'

"Oh, silly mad jack rabbits racing—dumb racing. Oh, weasel white, measuring in three vast hops that long fallen tree by the sloughside. Oh, blackbird hosts spieling a-craiking. Oh, whistle-wing ducks flying, angling, changing. Oh, host of small birds, sneaking, dodging, flittering. Oh, billion blue bloom of the crocus. Oh, tinkling of chill melting snow mats, ye are mere vernalizations. Ye are no better than myself, corroding with love that lacks voicing.

"My lips are parched and my mouth is gummy. My heart is a-burst with a love pain. I am shaken as when I stand on the runway of an unfed buzz saw, or on the poop of an ocean liner whose propeller heaves out and is churning the air. Yes, as a thresher mill shakes and roars when ye choke it with frozen sheafs. My eyes with their tears are scalding. If only I could blast it out aloud, and race and shout like an angel!

"And ever that rich and rounded ringing:
'Hear me, ho ye winter-withered,
Hear me, all ye hunger-hounded;
Waken up, O Manessigan,
The high red sun, your lover, comes.

Wake, sweet sleeping prairie,
Waken, teeming mother prairie;
I am the bringer of tidings,
I myself am my own tidings,
I am the blue of the crocus,
And the green of the slough-rush,
The joy of the frog-pond,
The child of the morning,
The son of the dawning—
I am the Golden Chewesson!'

"Oh, blessed bird of the prairies, now understand I your coming, the cool sweet wind is blowing in my heart, I am no more a winged thing in a net. I am shouting in your shouting.

"Soiled was my face with the muck of the prairie, clogged my teeth with chewed-up willow twigs, gritty and bitter. Bleeding my lips. Trembling with cold and damp my body, but never again will I so happy be as now.

"For my heart has burst the strangle hold.
My soul has sloughed its pupa case.
My song has broke the stifle gag.
A voice, a voice, I have found; a voice expression found.
Oh, vibrant shining Chewesson!
A voice that with the sons of God might sound,
Rejoicing, singing as archangels joy and sing;
To sing and ring the secrets of the soul
That in itself has vocalized the spring."

Bingo

Ye franclynys dogge leapt over a style
    And yey clept hym lyttle Bingo
BINGO and yey clept hym lyttle Bingo

Ye franclynys wyfe brewed nutte browne ayle
    And yey clept itte rare goode stingo
STINGO and ye clept itte rare goode stingo

Now is not thys a prettie rime
I thynke itte ys, by Jingo
JINGO I thynke itte ys by Jingo

(Old Ballad)

"I had finished my breakfast [Nov. 25, 1882], and was lolling back on the hinder legs of my chair after the manner of our ancient and honorable family. The above antiquated rhyme was galloping up and down and in and out of numerous vacant corridors of my brain, disturbing nothing but echoes and clouds of three-year-old dust to remind me that, in '79, I was an art student in London.

"My eyes meanwhile rested on that portion of our cowshed which was visible through a clear space on the frosted pane, when the career of the rhyme was abruptly ended by the sight of a large gray animal that dashed across my clear space of glass, into the cowshed, closely followed by a smaller black-and-white animal.

"'A wolf!' I exclaimed as I sprang to my feet and dashed out with a rifle to help the dog; not our own, I should say, but the collie of our next neighbor.

"By the time I was outside, the two animals had left the stable and were running over the snow, not towards the wilderness but in the direction of the settlement. But soon it was apparent that, while the wolf was straining every nerve to head for the woods, the dog was working even harder, and contrived that each new rush should be towards the farm of his owner.

"About every hundred yards, the dog closed in and seized the galloping wolf by the haunch, then at once retreated to avoid the counter-chop of the latter. The chase continued for half a mile before I came up. Then the pair were close to the door of the dog's owner.

"As soon as he saw me near, the dog knew he would have help, and at once closed in for the death struggle. In a few seconds, the whirling ball of two struggling animals resolved itself into a wolf writhing on the ground with a bleeding collie gripping his throat; and now it was easy for me to come quite close and end the fight, by sending a ball through the wolf's head.

"As soon as he saw that his foe was dead, this dog of marvelous wind went off at full gallop across the prairies to the house of a farm four miles away where he had left his master when first he started the wolf. I never saw a finer dog; for the wolf, though of the small or prairie kind, was larger than the dog himself. He had run it down in the snow, and undoubtedly would have killed it alone, as I learned he had several times done already with coyotes as well as foxes.

"I was so enamored of his prowess that I took the earliest opportunity of securing one of his alleged progeny; that is to say, a son of his wife. This probable offspring of an illustrious sire was a roly-poly little ball of fur, as black and woolly as a bear cub, and almost indistinguishable from the same excepting by his bushy tail, his tan forelegs, and the ring of pure white that he always wore about his muzzle.

"After securing possession of his person, the next thing in proper order was his formal christening.

"What should I call him? Surely the riddle is already read. The rhyme of the Franklin's dog had not haunted me without a prescience, and with all adequate pomp I clept him Little Bingo.

"Early next spring I set about seriously giving Bingo his education. After much trouble and great pains, I got him taught to go over the prairie in quest of our old yellow cow and bring her home to be milked. Having once learned his business, he grew only too fond of it. Not once or twice, but ten or a dozen times a day, this energetic cowherd would of his own free will sally forth, and a few minutes later return driving the unhappy yellow cow at full gallop before him. Of course, this kept her from getting lost, but then it prevented her feeding. She began to get thin and to give less milk. In fact, she got 'into training,' but so did the dog; and soon it became the sole aim, pleasure, and pursuit in life of my black collie to bring our yellow cow at full gallop into the stable. This was going too far, the cow's life was becoming a burden to her; and at length, seeing that Little Bingo knew not enough to be temperate in his pleasures, I compelled him to become a total abstainer.

"Little Bingo, I called him, but he wasn't so by any means. He was now much larger than any of his near relatives, was in fact the largest collie in the settlement; and before he was two years old he had in fair fight conquered his famous sire. Yet I must confess that, although larger and stronger, he never had the amount of 'grit' and 'bottom' that was characteristic of his immediate ancestor. He was a farmer's dog in every particular. He would never leave the team. Where the horses were, Bingo was, and nothing seemed able to keep them apart by day or by night. This interesting assumption of ownership on his part lent the greater significance to the circumstance that I shall now narrate.

"I am not superstitious. Up to this time, I had had no faith in omens. But I was now profoundly impressed by a strange occurrence in which Bingo took a leading part.

"One morning my brother Arthur set out for Boggy Creek for a load of hay. It was a long day's journey there and back, and he started betimes.

"Strange to tell, Bingo for once in his life did not follow the wagon. Arthur called him, but still he stood at a safe distance; and eying the team askance, he refused to stir. Presently he raised his nose in the air and gave vent to a prolonged melancholy howl. He watched the wagon out of sight, and even followed it a hundred yards or so, raising his voice from time to time in the most awful howlings.

"All that day he stayed about the barn, the only time in his life when he was willingly separated from the team; and at intervals howled a very death dirge.

"I was alone, and the dog's behavior inspired me with an awful foreboding of calamity that weighed on me more and more as the hours passed away.

"About six o'clock his howlings became simply unbearable; so that, for lack of a better thought, I threw something at him and ordered him away. But, oh, the feeling of horror that filled me! Why did I let my brother go away alone? Should I ever again see him alive? I might have known by the dog's behavior that something dreadful was about to happen.

"At length, the hour for his return arrived, and there was Arthur on his load. I took charge of the horses, vastly relieved, and with an air of assumed unconcern asked: 'All right?'

"'Right' was the laconic answer.

"Who says there is nothing in omens?

"During the winter of 1884-85 our house on De Winton Farm was deserted. Arthur and I both went eastward, and Bingo was transferred to the establishment of Mr. Wright, our most intimate neighbor.

And so well satisfied was the dog with the change that he refused to return to his old quarters when we came back to the farm.

"In the fall of 1886 he was still a member of their household, and I had been away from the Province. I thought he would have forgotten me after two years' absence, but not so.

"One day early in the winter, after having been lost for forty-eight hours, he crawled home to Wright's with a wolf trap and a clog fast on one foot, and the foot frozen to stony hardness. No one could approach him to help him, he was so savage. But I, the stranger now, stooped down and laid hold of the trap with one hand and the leg with the other. Instantly he seized my wrist in his teeth.

"Without stirring, I said: 'Bingo, don't you know me?'

"He had not broken the skin, and at once he quit his hold. After that he offered no resistance, although he whined a good deal while I was removing the trap. You see, he still acknowledged me his master.

"He was lame the rest of that winter, but recovered minus two toes which mortified and dropped off.

"Bingo lived with the Wrights till 1889 when he was poisoned by a malicious neighbor.

"How sorry we are for the sufferings of the poor dog, and how little we care for the equally great sufferings of the equally intelligent and conscience-clear wolf that the trap was meant for!

"Before leaving the subject of Bingo, I should have related the last, and I may say only, incident in his public career.

"The fall came about, and with it the Carberry Farmers' Fair. One of the prizes offered was for the best collie in training. At the suggestion of Gordon Wright, I entered my dog; and setting off early in the day to the town with both dog and cow, I stationed Old Yellow out on the prairie close to the town, for I knew that Bingo would not perform with a strange animal.

"When the time came and the eyes of Europe were upon us, I gave the signal: 'Go and fetch that cow here,' and Bingo set out like a rocket in the direction of our cow. Both animals had learned well their parts. The dog knew that it was his business to take that cow home, and the cow knew that it was milking time when the dog came. So away they went at full speed, heading for the

Thompson homestead, till they faded out of sight over the prairie. That was the last that judge or jury ever saw of my collie in training, and the prize was awarded to the only other entry."

A Lament

When Seton went to London in the June of 1879 he wished to study at the Royal Academy. It was necessary to pass a competitive examination to be admitted. A large drawing of an antique figure was required. To do this study, he worked each day from 9 to 4 at the British Museum.

Here, next to his easel, was that of a young girl about his own age who, being a Londoner, and in touch with the world of arts and letters, was a great help to him. Throughout his life he never ceased to be grateful to Miss H. H. Hatten for her understanding of the young ill-dressed boy who felt so out of place in this new way of life.

They kept up a more or less desultory correspondence. One letter, the nearest approach to a personal expression of his feelings, I find among his papers.

Even this, however, with its close note of friendliness, veers to his natural history ideas and ideals rather than to what might be considered a note of information about incidents in his everyday life.

"New York life goes hard against the grain with me; in fact, it is not life at all in my estimation. Life is feeling one's limbs and the blood in your veins, knowing you are alive.

"But I had resolved to work steadily for one year. This I did; then once again turned my face towards the boundless glorious woods. And here I am on the shores of the great mysterious Lake of the Woods, the Lake of Ten Thousand Islands, the Ultima Thule of Champlain's most extended exploration, a lake whose strange recent origin is still attested to by the unique nature of its form, surroundings, and outlet.

"This is the land of the Ojibways or Chippewas, Hiawatha's people; and to this day, the birch-bark wigwams and canoes are the most familiar evidences of human presence along the banks and shores. The campfires still burn brightly among the solemn pines and glitter on the ripples of the fish-frequented lake. The young Indians, armed with tiny bows, range the woods about the camping ground and strengthen their limbs and deepen their woodcraft for the day when, not the squirrel and blackbird, but the moose and bear shall be the objects of their chase, just as in the day when first the hardy French voyageurs reached this inland archipelago.

"But a change is at hand here also. Last night I stood on a rocky headland overlooking the vast expanse of water with its endless dotting of pine-clad islands, and in the blue bay below me the Indian squaws were paddling their canoes or fishing for their evening meal. On the land, the brown-limbed children were playing around the campfires; and purpling the waters and firing the pine tops was the red sun as it rolled down into the lake. It was a sight to make me glad. But the words of a settler were in my ears.

"'You see yon hills,' he said. 'They are solid iron, and their valleys and rivers are full of gold. These islands are copper and a hundred other precious minerals.'

"Then the whistle of the locomotive sounded through the tamaracs behind me, and assured me that yet a little while and all these things must change and old things pass away.

"It is not long since first the railroad touched these shores; and at but a single round of the last bay at the extremest north point of the lake does it meet the waters. But what a touch! What havoc it means! Soon these vast mines will be opened, and the rush of commerce will begin. Soon the last of the great pines will be felled for the sawmills, and soon the last of the Chippewas will quietly disappear from the lake, and its aspect and its beauty are gone forever.

"Well, it's no use lamenting. The beauty of barbarism must pass away and give place to the higher beauties of civilization and art.

"I mistrust myself even while I lament, for I know my words are wild. But still to see one of our grand old pines come crashing down to lay its many-wintered pillar on the earth, and to have its leafy crown shorn off and burnt for rubbish, is to me one of the saddest of familiar frontier scenes. I never feel disposed to sketch a tree until I learn that it is doomed, and that soon an unsightly stump will be the sole remembrance of its grand old column."

PART FIVE

CAMPFIRES AT EVENING
IN THE WEST

Government Naturalist to Manitoba

For long I did not know how Seton had been appointed Government Naturalist to Manitoba. In reply to my query one day, he told:

"After my summer in and about Carberry in 1892, I went for a few days to Winnipeg to see old friends and gather what I could of natural history happenings, arriving September 12.

"Through the firm of Hine and Co., taxidermists, I met W. Scott, the government advertising and immigration agent. His special job just then was preparing the Manitoba Exhibit for the great six-months fair to be opened at Chicago, June 1, 1893.

"Of course I was intensely interested; and when he asked my help, we went first to the Government Museum, where were a lot of mounted birds and beasts—all, however, without labels. Calvin Hine, with Scott and myself, set about naming them. I supplied the names, Hine the date and locality. Then we planned a fine natural history exhibit for the Chicago Fair.

"But there were many gaps that should be filled. So, equipped with government funds, we spent a couple of days among the taxidermists of Winnipeg—W. R. Hine, George Grieves, A. Calder, E. W. Darbey, W. F. White—and picked up much desirable stuff at fair prices.

"After drawing up a definite plan with Scott, I left for Toronto on September 15. At that time the Hon. Thomas Greenway, Premier of Manitoba, was staying at the Queen's Hotel in Toronto.

"Accordingly, I called on Mr. Greenway. This was on September 19, 1892. I found him kindly but strangely unconversational. Most of the time, he stared at the carpet and twiddled his fingers in silence.

"I went at once to the business in hand, and said: 'First, appoint me official naturalist to the government of Manitoba. This is to be without salary, except when on specially appointed missions, at which times I am to have $5 a day and expenses. I will undertake to assemble and display in Chicago a natural history collection that will be new in its methods and tremendous in its advertising value. I must, of course, have a fund in accountable checks to make the necessary purchases. Several States,' I added, 'have made such appointments.'

"The Premier continued to twiddle his fingers in silence, stared at the carpet for five minutes, then said coldly: 'I accept.'

"Thus it was that I became the Government Naturalist of Manitoba.

"After making many purchases in Toronto from the taxidermists William Cross, George Dippie, O. Spanner, etc., I went to Chicago to arrange the exhibit on April 22, 1893.

"Meanwhile a new situation had developed. Mr. Greenway, dissatisfied with the meager space allotted to Manitoba by the management of the Chicago Fair, had decided to build adequate quarters of his own at the main gateway of the Fair, but outside. He put one of his subordinates in charge. This man had appointed Calvin Hine taxidermist to the present exhibition, and Hine refused to take orders from me, or even to consult me.

"To avoid a deadlock, the said officer divided the duties: Seton was to be in charge of the buying; Hine to have charge of the taxidermy; both responsible to the director. In other words, the arrangement was out of my hands. The result is best forgotten."

"How long," I asked, "did you remain Government Naturalist?"

"When I was appointed," Seton answered, "no limit was set on the term of office. The charter has never been revoked, so I guess I am still an official of the Canadian Government," and there was a note of pride in his voice.

Field Notes on Birds of New Mexico

The following notes were made between October 22, 1893, and February 2, 1894. During the whole of this time Seton was riding the range, hunting and trapping for wolves, coyotes, and bobcats. Bird-collecting was a side issue; which, with the fact that it was wintertime, accounts in part for the poverty of the list. All were made in Union County, New Mexico. The numbers in parentheses are the specimen numbers in the bird collection at Seton Village.

The record herewith will be of particular interest to those who, some seventy-five years later, are observing the bird population.

Common Mallard Duck. Perico, Nov. 15, 1893. Collected a female Mallard out of a small flock. The species is common here, as well as at Clapham; wherever, indeed, there is a sufficiency of water.

Perico, Dec. 26. Shot a fine male Mallard out of a bunch of 7. It weighed 4 lbs., and was 24½ inches long.

Green-winged Teal. Clayton, Oct. 23. Saw about 20 Teal; collected 1. The species is well known here wherever there is water.

Shoveler. Clayton, Oct. 23. Saw a small flock of Shovelers—less than a dozen.

Redhead. Clapham, Oct. 26. Collected a Redhead Duck out of a small flock on a prairie pond.

Wilson Snipe. Pinabetitos Creek, west of Clapham, Nov. 25. Saw a specimen of Wilson's Snipe.

Killdeer. The species was abundant about the little lake or mud pond in Clayton, back of the hotel, Oct. 22, 1893. By abundant, I mean there were 20 or 30 there.

Blue or Scaled Quail. At Clapham, Oct. 25, 1893, saw a flock of about 20 Blue Quail. They are said to be abundant here. At Brooks' Ranch, 4 miles north of Clapham, Oct. 30, I noted many of these Quail running about. On this ranch, Nov. 9, I found a fine male Quail, lying dead, killed probably by a poison bait (1937).

Perico, Jan. 3, 1894, collected 10 out of a bevy of 20 Quail (1943 to 1946).

Common Dove. First noted at Clapham, Oct. 24; later seen in many places. One of the most abundant and generally distributed species.

Vulture. Oct. 25. Saw a Vulture (*aura?*). Nov. 3, saw another; it flapped and sailed alternately every 20 yards, and looked to me much like the Black Vulture, although I expected to see only the Turkey Buzzard here.

Nov. 5, saw several Vultures (Black, I think); they are common here.

Marsh Hawk. Near Clapham, Oct. 27, saw a Marsh Hawk. They are quite common here, and seen every day (1935).

Nov. 5, saw several at this place. At Perico, Nov. 18, saw a fine adult in full blue plumage.

Perico, Jan. 3, 1894. Found a Marsh Hawk dead near one of my wolf baits, evidently killed by poison (1947).

Perico, Dec. 28. A Marsh Hawk figured in a curious incident of wolf trapping. I had buried a bait, and a few feet away on each side had hidden three large wolf traps, carefully set and concealed. As a final touch, I scattered a few scraps of meat over and near each trap. A Marsh Hawk, sailing near, came down to get the meat scraps and was caught by the foot. He was still fluttering there at dusk when a prowling she-wolf came by. Attracted by the sight of the fluttering Hawk, the wolf came forward heedlessly, and was caught in both of the other traps, one on a forefoot, one on a hind.

She was unable to move these with the drags, but broke a spring in each trap. This freed her from one drag but left her no better off; for the broken trap became hooked and entangled in the other, and thus bound her hind and front feet together.

In the morning, when I arrived, she was foaming with rage. She had torn the Marsh Hawk to little bits, and would have served me in the same way, had she been able to get at me. She had chopped her own limbs in her rage, and even bitten off her own tail. I ended her troubles with a rifle shot.

She was a very small lobo wolf, and weighed only 75 pounds.

Rough-legged Hawk or Featherleg. Pinabetitos, Nov. 25. Saw a Featherleg eating on a burro that we had killed for wolf bait.

Perico, Dec. 11. The Roughleg is quite common here, and feeds much on carrion.

At Pinabetitos, near Clapham, Dec. 25, I laid a drag with 20 poison baits; of these, as shown by the tracks, 3 were taken by Hawks, but none of the birds was found.

Golden or War Eagle. Eagles are common, and occasionally kill antelope. They are said to be destructive to jack rabbits also. When the jack rabbit is out on the open prairie, the Eagle can get him with something like certainty; but when under a bush, no matter how small, he is safe; for the Eagle will not swoop at the rabbit. The fear of cactus and bayonet is ever on these birds.

Nov. 11. At Clapham, saw 2 Eagles feeding on a skunk that had been killed by a poison bait. One flew, but the other stayed till I was within 50 yards. Tried my new rifle on him—missed.

Nov. 5. Had 3 shots at a War Eagle on a tree—missed (fault of the rifle, sure!). These birds are numerous in this region; saw several today.

Perico, Nov. 14. Saw 2 Eagles. They do much damage to the pelts of coyotes that have been killed by poison, so are not in favor with the hunters. No one considers them a menace to calves or to sheep under guard.

Nov. 24. At the Callis Ranch, 25 miles south of Clapham, saw a Golden Eagle eating on a dead sheep.

Nov. 27. Saw a large dark Eagle hovering near my wolf baits. Saw another Dec. 3.

White-headed or Bald Eagle. Less common than the War Eagle, but found throughout the region. The two species are much alike in habits here.

Clapham, Dec. 6, 1893. Saw a fine big Bald Eagle in full plumage, and made a sketch of him.

Duck Hawk (?). At Clapham, Oct. 25. I saw what I took for a Duck Hawk or Falcon. At Perico, Nov. 18, I saw another, and next day at the same place had a close view of one. If it is not *anatum*, I don't know what it is.

Pigeon Falcon. At Clapham, Oct. 27. I saw a small Falcon that I took for this species.

Kestrel or Merlin. At Perico, Nov. 20. I saw a light-colored Falcon among the trees by the water hole, and secured the specimen. It was the first time I ever saw Richardson's Kestrel alive. It proved to be a female. Its stomach contained a Longspur (*mccowni?*); its abdomen was much infested with worms.

Sparrow Hawk. At Clapham, Oct. 26. I saw 2 of the common Sparrow Hawks; next day at the same place I saw another, and on Oct. 5, several. After this, none were seen; no doubt, the above were in migration.

Short-eared Owl. Perico, Dec. 20. After sunset, on the trail home, I put up a pair of Short-eared Owls. They were resting on the prairie close together. They circled about each other in the air, uttering once or twice a short screech or scream.

Paisano or Road Runner. At Clapham, Oct. 29. I collected a Ground Cuckoo or Road Runner (1934). Brooks calls it a Mexican Peacock; and Mexicans call it *Paisano.* On the ground, it runs, and looks much like an English Pheasant. Its stomach was full of insects, including grasshoppers.

Nov. 1, at the same place, I collected another (1936). It came running around the ranch house, behaving much like a Magpie, pumping its long tail, behaving, as Coues says, "like half magpie, half chicken."

Yesterday another came and enlivened the place, alternately as alert as a Robin, then as posed as an Owl. It hopped 10 feet up onto the roof, apparently without effort or reason.

Perico, Dec. 19. William Allen came home, bringing me another *Paisano.* This he shot with his revolver, "creasing it," that is, shaving off a thin slice of its occiput as it ran about—so that it was uninjured as a specimen (these cowboys can shoot). He says it strutted all around his noon camp, with head and tail up like a Rooster. Then it "walked up" an upright tree, using its wings as it climbed.

This was, without exception, the fattest bird I ever saw. When skinned, there was no red meat visible on the body—nothing but solid yellow fat; on the belly, this was an inch thick. The stomach was crammed with grasshoppers. He must have worked hard to find them, for the winter cold and hard, though snowless, is on us.

Kingfisher. At Clapham, Oct. 26. Saw a Kingfisher on the stream. The species is not uncommon here.

Downy Woodpecker. At Clapham, Dec. 8. Among the cottonwoods by the creek, I saw a pair of Downy Woodpeckers, the first I have seen in the region—doubtless because my time is spent chiefly on the plains.

Texan Woodpecker or Ladderback. Clayton, Oct. 22, 1893. On the street is a solitary cottonwood, the only tree in town up to date. Working away on the trunk of this today was a Texan Woodpecker, and stalking it from all directions were all the cats in the town.

Clapham, Oct. 31. I collected a specimen (1934).

Perico, Nov. 16. I saw several of this species, and at Clapham, Dec. 8, a number more. It is quite common wherever there is timber.

Perico, Dec. 30. Three days ago William Allen collected for me a Texan Woodpecker, L. 7½″ (1942).

Red Flicker. On Dec. 7, near Clapham, I saw 2 Flickers. At Perico, Dec. 18, I saw 2 others, had a close view. They were certainly red-shafted. It is noteworthy that in both cases it was a pair, apparently keeping together.

Currumpaw, Jan. 8, 1894. Saw a Flicker.

Shore Lark. Clayton, Oct. 22. Fifty yards back of the hotel is a small muddy pond. Around this all day are flocks of Shore Larks. These birds abound everywhere on the prairie. As they fly overhead, they are clearly distinguished by their long dark wings, black tail, white body, dark head and neck, and their occasional call "chee chup," which happens to be given as an Indian name of the bird in the north.

Clayton, Oct. 23. Collected a pair of Shore Larks (1931–32).

Perico, Nov. 19. Near one of my poisoned baits, picked up a Shore Lark, apparently killed by the poison (1938). The house dog also was gathered to his fathers at the same time, and by the same means.

Pinyon Jay. Jan. 27, 1894. In the pine-clad hills, 10 miles north of Currumpaw, saw a number of Jays apparently of this species. These hills are also known as the Brakes of the Cimarron.

Raven. Clapham, Nov. 2. Saw 2 Ravens flying up the Arroyo Leone near here. These birds are found in small numbers throughout the region.

Brewer Blackbird. Abundant about the town of Clayton during my stay, Oct. 22, 1893.

Lap Longspur. Perico, Nov. 19. A new species of Longspur has arrived in vast numbers. It seems to be the Lap, and is evidently migrating southward.

Mccowni Longspur or White-tailed Longspur. Clayton, Oct. 22. Fifty yards back of the palatial hotel is a muddy pond on the tin-be-

decked prairie. Around this all day, the bird life is swarming. There
are dozens of Killdeers, scores of Brewer Blackbirds, hundreds of
Shore Larks, and thousands of White-tailed Longspurs. No doubt
they are somewhat concentrated here on account of the water—a
scarce opportunity in this land—but on the prairie they are almost as
abundant.

Oct. 23, collected some Longspurs, by the help of a wild cowboy
who, thanks to his prairie pony, was able to retrieve my specimens
that fell on the gumbo flat. All were *mccowni* (1925–30).

Clapham, Oct. 20. As I take my daily ride, I see countless multi-
tudes of these Longspurs. They are by far the most abundant bird
of the region. At each 100 yards, on the prairie, a flock of 50 or 100
rises and flies over, usually going southward, displaying their white
tails as they go overhead, and announcing their identity by a little
Chirrup chirrup.

Tree Sparrow. The familiar Tree Sparrow did not appear till mid-
winter—if such a word can be applied to the cool, bright, snowless
January of the foothills.

Currumpaw, Jan. 17, 1894. Saw my first flock of Tree Sparrows;
collected 4 (1953–56).

Jan. 19, same place. Tree Sparrows in flocks about the ranch and
sheltered ravines.

Junco (*oregonus*). Currumpaw, Jan. 15, 1894. Saw a number of
Juncos. Collected one (1950), Jan. 17; at the same place, collected
another (1952), Jan. 27. In the cedar brakes south of the Cimarron,
saw a flock of Juncos.

Canyon Towhee. Currumpaw, Jan. 15, 1894. Saw several Canyon
Towhees, and collected one (*P. f. mesoleucus*).

Shrike (species?). Saw one near Clapham, Oct. 27, and another at
Brooks' Ranch 4 miles north of Clapham, Nov. 27. At the same
place, Dec. 6, I saw one in hot pursuit of a Sparrow for several
hundred yards. The birds were lost to sight in the bushes, but clearly
the Shrike would secure his victim soon or late. There can be little
doubt that a Shrike can capture a Sparrow any time he needs one,
at the expense of a little effort.

Canyon Wren. Currumpaw, Jan. 15, 1894. Up the canyon among the rocks, found several Canyon Wrens and collected one (*C. m. conspersus*) (1949).

At the same place, Jan. 19, collected another (1957). They are quite common here, and already beginning to utter the spring song.

Solitaire. Near Clapham, Oct. 24, 1893, collected a Solitaire (1933).
Oct. 26, at the same place, saw another; it was in full song.

Currumpaw, Jan. 19, 1894. Solitaires are quite common here, going in small straggling flocks, but ever solitary, each one flocking by himself. Collected one (1958).

Robin. Clapham, Nov. 5. Today, a common Robin was chirruping pleasantly on the cottonwood tree above our water hole in the Leone Canyon.

Currumpaw, Jan. 9, 1894. Saw a flock of Robins.

Currumpaw, Jan. 13. Collected a Robin (1948).

Same place, Jan. 15. Saw a large flock of Robins, at least 100. Collected another Jan. 17 (1951).

Same place, Jan. 19. Numbers of Robins about just now.

Same place, Jan. 21. Saw a large flock of Robins; it contained over 200.

Bluebird (species?). Perico, Nov. 15, saw a Bluebird today.

Four Months in New Mexico

Walking simply for the sake of a walk, or taking an outing for the sake of being out, never had any charm for Seton. It was too much like exercising with dumbbells. What he always craved was a definite object, to which the walking or the outing was merely incidental.

Thus it became his habit to announce a purpose, and to some extent arrange a program before commencing a trip.

I find among his unpublished notes, the following:

"When I set out for New Mexico in October 1893, seeking for a rest after overlong hours of study, I resolved that my first object should be to kill fifteen gray wolves; my second, to ascertain accurately the weight of all large animals killed, and thirdly, to sketch the tracks of all the quadrupeds of the region.

"The only game I saw between Chicago and the Rockies was a jack rabbit, which I sketched from the train.

"At Pueblo, I had my first view of real mountains. On the high prairies about this pretty little city, I first saw the characteristic plants of the region—the sagebrush, the various cacti, Spanish bayonet grass or soapweed, the ubiquitous cottonwood. The leaf stalks of this last are, as in others of this genus, so remarkably flattened laterally that they very much resemble a ribbon. This renders the leaves easily moved, so that in the slightest breeze they are continually fluttering when all other foliage is absolutely still. The advantage of this arrangement is probably to repel insects, and also to keep the leaves free from dust in these arid regions. Possibly also to throw off the rain and dewdrops before they act as burning glasses, and so prevent the leaves being blistered by the concentrated heat of the rays of the semitropical sun; for it is well known that even in our temperate climate many trees of stable foliage have their leaves injured for this very cause.

"I saw no wild animals about Pueblo. But on the road to Clayton, the terminus of my journey, I saw numbers of prairie dogs and cottontails, meadow larks and some magpies. These latter are characteristic of all foothill landscapes, wherever there is wood, and are conspicuous from afar by their pied livery. They are much disliked by the ranchmen on account of their habit of pecking at the backs of horses that have been injured by the saddle.

"Clayton is a promising prairie town of 400 inhabitants. Its interests are reflected in the talk of the inhabitants, who discuss only cattle and politics.

"It was at this place that I made the acquaintance of the remarkable bounding shrub called tumbleweed. The first one seen was jumping along at a great rate over the prairie half a mile away, and I took it for a fox. When, at length, it ran into a hollow and did not reappear, I went after it; and it was only after many examinations and repeated views at various distances that I satisfied myself that the supposed fox was none other than this bounding shrub. It is a low, thick, rounded plant which, in the fall, dries up stiffly into a globular form; and breaking off near the ground during a strong wind, it goes bounding o'er the plain before every varying breeze, continuing its career until some water hole or canyon receives the wanderer, and holds it till it decays.

"The balls are usually from 12 to 18 inches in diameter, but I have seen one 4 feet across. This large one, however, was but 18 inches through, much like a great cheese, so that, in traveling, it went wheelwise on its edge.

"On the second day I went down to the stockyards to see the sheep herded into cars. I had been told that goats were used for this purpose; were, indeed, an essential help, but I thought my informant was playing on my ignorance.

"I learned that day, however, that sheep are such hopeless fools that it is impossible to drive or direct them with success; their one idea is to follow the leader. But, by taking advantage of this peculiarity, they are easily put into the cars. A great number of the sheep, sufficient to fill one deck of the car, having been separated from the flock, the goat among them, one of the men shouted: 'Go on, Billy.' The goat, being thus admonished, mounted the gangway at once, but, looking around, he found that none of the sheep followed him. He therefore went back to the pen, walked through the sheep again; and remounting the gangway, was followed by a procession of the woolly imbeciles. Then, stepping aside, he returned to the pen, leaving the stream of sheep to pour into the car.

"Something, however, occurred to break the continuity of the influx before the car was loaded, and the sheep that were left rushed back to the far end of the pen. Billy was now quietly nibbling at a stick, when one of the herdsmen, observing the trouble, shouted: 'Go on, you lazybones, make a lead.'

"Billy immediately rejoined the flock and led them into the car as before. Thus, in a short time, the flock of 3000 sheep were successfully shipped in ten double-decked cars.

"I found out afterwards that it was usual for a few goats to be herded with the sheep; for, in case of sudden fright, the sheep gather round these, their intellectual superiors, and are thus prevented from stampeding or scattering.

"A flock of sheep on these ranches usually contains from 1500 to 3000, under one shepherd. As it would be impossible to count them each day, they detail one black sheep to every 40 or 50 white ones, and simply count the black ones, for it is evidently improbable that any great number could stray away without at least one black being missed.

"On the third day, I left Clayton to visit the ranches and the cowboys, driving with the mail carrier twenty-five miles toward the southwest. The whole region was open rolling prairie, and the only wild animals seen were prairie dogs. They abounded wherever there were level stretches of low prairie. They do not live in 'towns' in the sense that books would lead one to understand; i.e., with the mounds actually crowding each other, for it is really the exception when they are less than fifty feet apart.

"The prairie dogs are extremely shy, always running to the mouth of their burrows as soon as a possible danger is descried, even in the far distance. So, though you may fire at, and instantly kill, a prairie dog, he drops at once into the unknown depths and is lost. For this reason, and because I had not time to trap them, I got but three prairie dogs during my whole visit.

"In accordance with my program I list them:

Prairie dog   weight 2 lbs. 14 oz., shot
   "   "   "   2 "   14 ", trapped
   "   "   "   1 "   12 ", poisoned

"Occasionally burrows are seen with two entrances—one perpendicular, and one sloping. These correspond exactly to the stairs and drop hole of a fire hall, one being for easy ascent and descent, the other for dropping down when extreme haste is necessary.

"I have often heard of drowning out prairie dogs; but no one, so far as I know, has been able to achieve it. On one occasion I tried to do it but failed miserably in the attempt. I diverted an irrigation ditch into one of the holes, down which three prairie dogs had just disappeared. The stream was a foot in width and nearly an inch in depth. It ran at the rate of a mile per hour. Yet, although it ran from 3:00 P.M. until 7:00 the next morning, no prairie dogs came out. Neither was the hole filled. The same experiment was tried with two other holes in the same colony, and with no better result. Unless there was some outlet for the water, the first burrow must have held considerably over 3500 gallons, which would be equal to a 5-inch tunnel 4000 feet long—or four fifths of a mile!

"The extreme timidity of these rodents must often cause them to suffer considerably from hunger; for, if one be approached as it sits on its mound, it goes down with a few 'barks' and does not appear again that day. In some cases I satisfied myself that the frightened creature remained two or three days before it recovered from its fright sufficiently for it to reappear. Possibly, however, it may have had a store of food, on which it subsisted during the imaginary siege.

"The dog holes are also the homes of numerous cottontails, kit foxes, mice, owls, rattlesnakes, skunks, ferrets, and insects. The prairie dog is to the subterranean hosts just what the flicker is among birds, a universal house-provider.

"The enemies of the prairie dog are very numerous. Every carnivore in the country preys on him. And yet he lives and multiplies, in some regions actually becoming a pest. The badger is perhaps his most dangerous persecutor, because he can easily dig him out, and therefore makes him his staple diet. But the black-footed ferret is said to be nearly as destructive. I failed to secure, or even see, a single specimen of this animal, although I often heard it described under the name of 'marten.'"

General Report

Seton goes on in another manuscript:

"My wolf hunt in New Mexico began October 22, 1893, and ended February 5, 1894. The country abounded in wild life. There were small herds of antelope every eight or ten miles; there were a few deer in the brakes; there were badgers, coons, jack rabbits, cottontails, and prairie dogs. A few bears frequented the wooded hills, and bird life abounded.

"But I was there for wolves, and killed over a hundred coyotes, partly by poison, partly in traps. However, I got only five of the great gray wolves—the lobos, or 'loafers' of the cattleman; and all of these I got with steel traps—not one by poison.

"I made the minutest study of trappers' ways and tricks, of the animals' reactions to each and every smell and hint of human presence; and I discovered finally a combination of devices by which I can, if I wish, catch coyotes with something like certainty. Once I discovered it, I got one or two coyotes every night.

"But I do not propose to let anyone in on the secret. I have changed from a coyote killer to a coyote protector; and the devilish secret of destruction shall perish with me."

The Wolf Song

As usual, to the rhythm of his tread Seton one day composed the
following:

"The Currumpaw Cattle are sleeping,
The Red Moon is floating o'er us,
As the King of the land and his Wild Wolf Band
Are raising the hunting chorus.
And now is the time—ye-o-o-o
For the hunting chime ye-o-o-o
Ye-o-o-o-o-o-ow-o
Ye-o-o-o-o-o-ow-o

"The Storm Wind blows on the Currumpaw,
The Cattle are mad stampeding;
But the hunting is good for the King Wolf's brood,
And they hunt in the storm unheeding.
For now is the time, etc.

"The White Snows drift on the Currumpaw,
The cow-men are saving their Cattle;
But the Currumpaw pack on the Red War Track
Is raising its song of battle.
For now is the time, etc.

"In the rain and the snow on the Currumpaw,
In the storm and the silver night,
They slay and they feast on the flesh, red raw,
They live by the right of might.
For now is the time, etc."

Yellowstone Trip

On June 2, 1897, after living in New York for some time, Seton set out again for the West, with Yellowstone Park—or rather the animals there—as the immediate objective.

He went as the special correspondent for *Recreation Magazine.*

On June sixth at 6:15 A.M. he reached West Salem, Wisconsin, and was met at the station by Hamlin Garland, who drove him about for half a day, showing much of the local setting of his own famous stories.

Seton reached Mammoth Hot Springs in the Park on June ninth; and thanks to General E. M. B. Young and Captain George Anderson, was well received and provided for. An old friend, Elwood Hofer, turned up and acted as guide to Yancey's where arrangements were made for Seton to occupy a tumble-down log shanty near the main house, which was Yancey's Hotel.

This shanty Seton at once began to rebuild in order to make it a possible habitation. In a pile nearby were a number of old slabs and other lumber which had been discarded from other buildings; and with Yancey's permission, Seton used these for his renovation of the shack.

He was to eat at the hotel, and a price was agreed upon. When leaving the place about two months later, Seton found himself billed for the lumber, although it had been used on Yancey's own building, and was left for the use of others who would pay rent on it. This Seton laughingly passed off; but when he found a bill for nearly twice the price stipulated for meals, he went to the proprietor.

"Did we not, when I came, agree on a price for my meals while I was to be here?" he asked.

"Yep."

"Well, this bill puts the cost at twice what we agreed on. What is the reason?"

"Well, when I made the price, I did not know that you would stay so long," was the reply; and apparently he thought he was well justified.

Seton's journal and sketchbook of the time are crowded with drawings, photos, and observations on animals, especially of beaver, antelope, elk, etc. These, however, are fully set forth in *Recreation Magazine* for 1897 and 1898, as well in his own later *Life Histories of Northern Animals* and *Lives of Game Animals,* so need not be repeated here.

It was here that he met many old-timers, most of whom he recorded in his sketchbooks. But of Calamity Jane he says: "Jane wouldn't pose."

On August first, Seton left Yancey's, and in his journal for that date I find:

"Aunt Dinah made a crazy quilt, as crazy as a fad;
 It had no patch that did not match with some queer quirk she
  had.
Now I believe each one who lives is making such a quilt,
His daily life the fragments give, of which its breadth is built,
And oft looks back on some bright patch that conjures up fair
  fancies.
I wonder what we'll someday think of these past days at Yancey's."

The Teddy Bear

During the past week I have read an account of the origin of the toy teddy bears. It did not coincide with the story Seton told me. I have no way at this moment of checking the accuracy of either version; but, for the sake of record, I give the incident as he gave it to me long ago.

While Seton was at Yancey's in Yellowstone Park he saw much of wild life, but was disappointed at meeting no bears, for which he had been told the Park was famous.

He consulted various authorities and was assured that there were plenty of bears, but that they hung around the hotels, especially the Fountain Hotel near Old Faithful Geyser.

Accordingly, Seton set out for the Fountain; and within an hour of his arrival encountered, just back of the hotel, an old black bear mother and her two cubs. The cubs scrambled up a tree at their mother's command. It was near sunset so he could not photograph them, but I have the page of his journal with the sketch he made at the time.

It was the next day, August seventh, that Seton spent the whole day in and about the garbage heap, making dozens of sketches and photographs. Here it was that he made the acquaintance of Old Grumpy and Little Johnny, whose adventures he told later in his *Lives of the Hunted.*

In the winter of 1901, Seton lectured at Bryn Mawr College on the animals of the Yellowstone. He told the story of Little Johnny; and the mischievous imp made such a hit that the graduating class adopted him as their mascot. Then a representative for the class went to Schwarz's toy shop in New York and asked if a manufacturer could make a score of the little woolly bears. The toymaker gladly undertook the commission, and soon found that there was a ready sale for the shaggy bears in the trade.

Shortly after this Teddy Roosevelt, then President, went on his famous bear hunt into the Cane Brakes of Kentucky. This advertising possibility caused Schwarz to rename the toys "teddy bears," after which they had a great and growing boom—are indeed going yet.

Mrs. Custer

We have mentioned the fact that Seton harbored an absolutely unforgiving hatred toward General George A. Custer. He had consummate reason for his active antipathy; for, although he had never actually met the man himself, he had spent many months, many times, on his trail, and with those who had had the closest association, both Indians and Whites.

He considered Custer "the lowest scum of the earth," "a murderer of helpless women and children," and many other things which he could amply justify with historical records not at that time generally open to the public.

In 1897, after a stay at Mammoth Hot Springs, Seton spent some time at the Crow agency where he saw much of the Indian agent Barstow, E. A. Burbank, the artist, and the missionary Rev. Mr. Burgess.

On the hillside to the southeast was the battleground where Custer met the fate he so richly deserved. White stones sprinkled across the hill showed where each soldier fell.

There has seldom been a fight more discussed, and until recently more misrepresented, than this.

While there, Seton saw a resident storekeeper showing a party of tourists over the field. He heard the guide say that the brave and noble Custer, with 300 men, was peaceably camped on the hillside when a band of 12,000 bloodthirsty Sioux, armed with repeating rifles, crept up on him and massacred every White soldier in his sleep.

Seton got the true story from many of the contemporaries, among them Ohiyesa, better known by his White name, Dr. Charles A. Eastman. The tale was also given him by that student of the Indians of those days, E. A. Brininstool. Authorities have differed in minor details; but all the proven facts point to not only the perfidy of Custer in his attack on the Indians, but also his stupidity in the management of the campaign.

For years Seton, in his desire for fair play, longed to expose the disgraceful treachery of the man who was being held up as a hero to the boys of the nation. In private, many times he said what he thought and what he wished to publish. But, as in the cases of many other like-minded men, he was deterred by the fact that he knew Mrs. Custer and admired her exceedingly.

Seton had first met her in the East, and felt it a high honor that he entertained her in his studio a number of times.

She always spoke with apparently the deepest reverence for her husband. But we all suspected that a forced loyalty and a knowledge of the truth were behind her words. She called him her "hero," "the man I love," etc. Most of us do not voice our affection quite so obviously.

But she was a noble woman, and everyone loved her.

One day she came to Seton's studio for a visit and brought with her her autograph album. She asked him to write something original in it. As I remember it, this is what he wrote:

"A thousand times I've crossed your trail
    Where roams the prairie beast.
And never dreamed that we should meet
    In salons of the East.

"Now as I touch your gifted hand,
    I make this large request:
May we so hand-touch as we ride
    Some unborn day out West."

Adventures on the Crow Reservation

While at the Crow agency, Seton met many of the old-time Indians, some who have come down in history.

One of these was White-Swan (Min-a-te-us), one of Custer's scouts. He was a good sign-talker, and he and Seton spent many hours communicating in the sign talk of the Plains. Seton acknowledges with appreciation the help he received from this Indian for his *Sign Talk Dictionary* brought out in 1918.

White-Swan's experiences in the Custer campaign had been thrilling. When Custer realized how serious was his situation, he sent White-Swan with an urgent message to Reno. By disguising his Crow headdress, White-Swan got started, but the bullets were flying thick. One passed up through his right hand and out at his elbow, shattering the bones. An arrow went through his left thigh, and a Sioux war club smashed in his head, just as his horse fell dead. White-Swan's head and shoulders fell under the horse—which is the reason he was not scalped. Two days later, when Terry's burying party came, they found White-Swan still alive. In the hospital, he was revived. In time he partially recovered, but was always thereafter lame in one leg, crippled in the right arm; and he had lost the power of speech.

Although his health and strength were wrecked in the U. S. Army service, the government had always refused to pension him. But he was a clever pencil artist, and he eked out a scanty living making paintings and pictographs for sale. Seton was glad to buy all the drawings and pictographic records he had ready at the time of their association. These help to decorate the walls of Seton Castle today.

White-Swan died about 1910.

Another famous survivor was Curley, a Crow scout. It is understood that he left Custer with a message for Benteen before the fighting began. In any case, he escaped unscathed.

In September 1912, Seton was staying for some time in the Crow camp. He had been there several days and had not seen Curley. When he finally asked for him, he was told:

"Curley's sick in his lodge." Seton went at once to see him.

"Hello, Curley," he greeted him. "What's wrong with you?"

"Heap sick," was his answer.

"What's the matter?" Seton asked. Curley rolled over, pulled up his shirt behind, and showed a bad boil over his kidneys.

"I'll soon fix that," Seton said. With a little difficulty, he got hot towels and fomented the spot till it was white, fat, and puffy; then, with a sharp knife, made a quick, deep incision. The output was immediate and copious. The next day Curley mounted his horse again.

The story grew, and now they say in Montana that "Seton was the only man who ever stuck a knife into Curley and got away with it."

It was at this camp also that the wedding of Clifford White-Shirt and Lottie Jack-Knife was held up because the missionary insisted that the groom have his long plaits of hair cut off. But this story appears in my *Pulse of the Pueblo,* so will not be retold here.

Two other famous Indians Seton met there, and hobnobbed with. One was Sharpnose, whose wife, a fat jolly Indian woman named Lottie Shoe-string, offered to make Seton a war shirt for two dollars if he would supply the buckskin. This he was glad to do, and easily got it at the trader's store.

The woman took his measure thus: Standing behind him, she glanced up and down, then said: "You are high—you are not wide."

That was enough, and the result was a beaded war shirt that fitted perfectly. It is now in the Seton Museum at Santa Fe.

While working at it, she often looked up at Seton with a twinkle in her eye and a little giggle. Finally she said:

"You know General Miles?"

"Yes."

"You see his war shirt?"

"No."

"Well, I make him dat, a good one, and he say, 'I want scalp locks on it.' I no savvy where I get scalp locks; so when he not looking I cut scalp locks here, my own head, and sew dem on. He no savvy. He tink dey come from dead Sioux scalp," and she giggled convulsively for a minute.

While Lottie was working on the war shirt, Seton painted a portrait of Sharpnose. This he did largely in the studio which E. A. Burbank had established there. The portrait hung for long in the Seton Gallery, but is now in the possession of Manly P. Hall of Los Angeles.

Another famous character was Hairy Wolf. One day, Seton learned, the soldiers from Fort Custer had surrounded Hairy Wolf's tepee and forcibly taken off his two children, ten and twelve years of age, to send them to the White school far away. This kind of treatment was always a matter for burning indignation. The Indians love their children as much as we do ours. They do not want them brought up in the White way; they wish them to be Indians.

The result was a meeting of protest by the Indians at the camp. A man named Rapaho did all he could to incite them to open rebellion. The Custer battlefield was in plain view from the camp. The little white monuments, one for each White soldier killed, could be clearly seen; and he pointed to these as evidence of what the Indians could do if they wished.

Seton, telling the story, remembered with deep sympathy Hairy Wolf's fiery denunciation of the Whites: "They have taken our lands, they have taken our buffalo, they are taking our guns. Now they want to take our children. How long are you going to stand it? Are you warriors or a lot of whimpering old women? If there be ten real men here who will join with me, we will go out and make a stand against this thing, and at least show that we are men, even if we leave our bones on the prairie to bleach with those of the buffalo."

But Plenty-Coups, the great war chief of the Crows, was there. He rose and calmed the meeting with a few words. "What you see at the Fort here is nothing. Rapaho has seen St. Paul; but I have seen Chicago, New York, and Washington. I know they can put a hundred warriors against our one. If we could not drive them back when they were a few, what hope have we now that they are increased a hundredfold?

"I do not like the new condition any more than you do. But I am sure we cannot change it by going backward. We must adapt ourselves to the new condition and make the best of it. We must learn to live by farming and ranching, as do the White settlers.

"I am too old for the warpath, too old for the plow; so I have opened a grocery store, and ask my people to come. At least I will sell you what I promise. They have not turned me into a White trader."

The Crows, though incensed, decided finally to follow the advice of Plenty-Coups; and peace was maintained, at least outwardly.

The next day Burbank and Seton went to Plenty-Coups' store. He showed them, among other things, his system of bookkeeping. Two sides of a long shoebox were covered with totems, one for each customer. Under each totem was a pencil stroke for each dollar the customer owed, and a long slanted stroke for the tenth dollar. When all were paid off, he used a rubber eraser to wipe it out.

Seton asked if he would sell his record. Plenty-Coups said: "No, that must be destroyed when the accounts are paid up."

"Then will you allow me to take it to my lodge?" Seton asked. The Indians trusted this White man, so that finally Plenty-Coups said: "Yes, if you do not tamper with it."

So Burbank and Seton got two shoebox sides exactly like those of the tally, and spent half the night copying it, grease spots and all. Next day they went back. Seton said: "See, Plenty-Coups, we have copied your tally. Ours is exactly the same as yours."

He inspected the two minutely, and agreed they were alike.

"Then," said Seton, "you keep mine and let me keep yours." This he finally agreed to, and now the Plenty-Coups ledger is in the Seton Museum at Santa Fe.

Here also, while riding across the Custer battlefield, Seton had a curious adventure that for long he kept to himself. A horned toad scrambled through the grass, and Seton easily caught and imprisoned it in a bag. Soon another darted under his horse. He leaped from the saddle and seized the horny. At once, it shot a stream of blood from its eye onto his middle finger. He had a very clear view of the whole performance and was careful to let the blood dry on, till, back in camp, he could get additional witnesses.

The whole thing seemed so fantastic and unnatural that he never dared to tell it until he found that Ditmars and several of the Smithsonian naturalists had had similar experiences.

The Indian Outbreak of 1897

Leek's Ranch in Jackson's Hole, where Seton arrived August 31, 1898, brought to mind years later the following story.

Seated around the fire that night, he heard the inside history of an Indian rising that had furnished the papers with many gory tales within the previous few months. It seems that the Fort Hall Indians, realizing that their own hunting grounds were no longer well stocked and that, furthermore, their people had always hunted in Jackson's Hole, organized a big hunt along the Snake River in the Hole.

The enterprising ranchmen of the region considered the game an important asset of their region, and resented the coming of the Indians, although there was nothing illegal in the expedition.

Nevertheless, some fifty of the ranchmen gathered at a point a mile from the Indian camp, hid their horses; then came under cover of darkness, each man with a Winchester and abundance of ammunition. At a long-range distance they surrounded the Indian camp. On a given signal, all opened fire on the Indians, who were sitting unconscious of danger around the campfire. Each White man blazed away as long as the cartridges in his repeater held out. Then they scattered and fled back to their horses.

Now, from the nearest telegraph office, they sent urgent requests for soldiers to come and suppress the "latest Indian rising."

The troops came and ordered the remainder of the Indians back to the reservation.

Such was the story Seton heard about the campfire, from the shameless White men who took part. "I bet," said one, with a laugh, "we left not less than fifty *good* Indians on the ground." No pretense of punishment was made against the Whites; and of course no White man was hurt or suffered any property loss. Yet this is called the Indian Outbreak of 1897.

Howard Eaton

On September 3, 1897, Seton left the Crow agency; and on September 6 arrived at the Eaton ranch where he found Howard Eaton awaiting him. He had arranged for a general hunt and a wolf hunt.

"Quite early in the day," records Seton, "we saw a demonstration that filled me with pleasure. Eaton had some thoroughbred greyhounds, really kept for running coyotes; and, granted an open level plain without cover, the greyhounds would catch a coyote within a mile.

"But in this case the game put up happened to be two buck antelope; and the calm way in which they sailed away on the level and left the greyhounds far behind dispelled all doubt as to the relative speeds of the two species.

"A still more thrilling experience was ahead," he continues. "I have more than once described the wonderful bounding of the mule deer or mountain blacktail. They seem to soar up 10 feet and come down 20 or 30 feet away each time. They float like birds. It looks easy, but we know that the bounding blacktail cannot run with the low coursing whitetail. The bounding is very laborious. Why, then, do they do it?

"I got my answer in the hills of the little Missouri.

"As we rode with our greyhounds, we came by chance on a prey we sought not—a blacktail mother with her twin young! Great-eyed, great-eared, they stood at gaze, all three. We tried to turn our pack aside, but the greyhounds sighted game; and off like arrows shot, they went. The blacktail turned for flight. We did our best to call the fleet hounds back, but who can turn a greyhound from a foe that runs?

"Off they went, and the blacktail sped away. How the memories of my youth came back as I watched them bounding along the level bottomlands—bounding—bounding—oh! it was beautiful, it was glorious! But it was sad! For, notwithstanding all their wondrous powers, their winged heels, the deer were losing ground. The greyhounds, far behind at first, were low skimming like prairie hawks, were making three yards to the blacktails' two, were gaining. They went faster yet, were winning, would surely win. Desperately, we tried to ride ahead to cut them off, to turn or call them back. Their speed, their mad impetuosity, grew only faster and fiercer. In spite of every effort, we knew that in a few minutes we should see three defenseless blacktail mangled by our hounds.

"On and on the chase. The little ones were suffering now, were weakening. It was a question of barely a quarter mile. Then we riders saw a thing that touched our hearts. That poor devoted mother, in despair, dropped back behind—deliberately, it seemed. She was sacrificing herself. At least her young should have a chance.

"My blood rushed hot. My hand sought the gun in reckless determination to stop those dogs. Only twenty-five yards ahead the mother now, when all at once an inspiration came. The Unseen Prompter whispered wisdom; and the mother turned aside, made for the rugged piling hills so near. She—all three—soon reached their base, and tapped with their toes, then rose in air to land some fifteen feet above; and tapped again—and tapped and tapped all three; and so they rose and sailed and soared. The greyhounds reached the rise, and there were lost. Their kingdom was the level plain; on the rugged hills they were helpless, balked, and left behind. But mother and her two went bounding, soaring like hill hawks. They sailed away till hidden in the heights, and rested safe at peace.

"That day I learned the meaning of the bounding. These are the deer of the broken lands; theirs is the way of the uplands; this pace is their gift, their power, and their hold on life."

The Passing of Four-Bears (*Mah-to-to-pah*)

Seton's sympathy with the Indian was deep and broad, and his indignation at the perfidious treatment of the Red Man by the White
was ever ready to burst forth. On July 21, 1939, at one of our summer
classes at Seton Institute, he had discussed the breaches of promise,
the breaking of faith, the disgraceful betrayal of one incident after
another in the early history of our country; and had finished with the
story of the agent who in 1848 deliberately distributed to the Indians
the smallpox-infected blankets during an epidemic.

He left the class, deeply moved, as he often was, by his own oratory.
He went over to his desk and wrote:

"Oh, God! my boy is gone!
  My boy, my beautiful boy is gone!
  The hope of our tribe is gone!

"He had the strength of a great war-chief;
  He had wisdom beyond his years.

"But now he is gone, and I am left
  Like a burnt stick standing alone in the trail of a prairie-fire.

"A measure of wisdom I have,
  But my strength is gone.
  I am no longer the great war-chief;
  I have no strength to hunt food for my people;
  I am no longer strong in service.
  My hope was in my boy, but he is gone.

"My boy! my boy, the hope of my people,
  The hope and joy of my old age.

"But he is gone.
  What profit have I in longer living?

"Oh, God, show me the way of wisdom,
Show me the way of courage!

"They have killed him, the Whitemen from the East,
Not in open battle, so he could die like a war-chief.
But they sent him a bundle of death blankets;
A present, they said, from the Great White Father;
Blankets, many blankets, in which had died of their own people,
Died in the black and spotted plague.
Death blankets they sent us,
Knowing that these would destroy us.
With soft words and holy names on their lips, they presented them.

"Now the black spotted death is raging in our village;
Many are down;
And my boy, my beautiful boy is gone!

"His manly face disfigured with the spotted death.
Would it had taken me.
What profit is my life to me now?
Better far that I seek the Shadow Land.

"I, Mah-to-to-pah, Four-Bears,
I, that in the days of my strength,
    killed four great bears
In one day by the power of my hands.

"Now all that I prize is taken from me.
It is better that I go.

"I mount my strong red pony.

"Far out on the plain are the black bands of buffalo;
Grunting, roaring, for this is midsummer,
The mad moon of the bulls,
When they will not run, but stand and fight.

"I mount and ride,
I leave by the river gate,
So none may see me.

"I urge my brave pony
Till we are among the bulls.

"Then I drop from the saddle—
So it shall afterwards be known—
And send an arrow into the pony's haunch
So he will run and leave me;
And, coming to our village,
They shall see the arrow
And know it for mine;
And so shall know the truth.

"Then, with knife in hand,
I rush upon the nearest bull
And stab and stab.
I invite his fighting rage,
And so we close.

"Yes, they will follow my trail,
And find my trampled and broken body
With vultures sailing over.

"It is well.

"It is better so.

"Oh my boy! my boy! my boy!"

The Tanager, 1885.

The Kingbird going to fight the Hawk.

Wild Geese, 1902.

Chipmunk from life, 1878.

Front of cabin in Glenyan near Toronto.

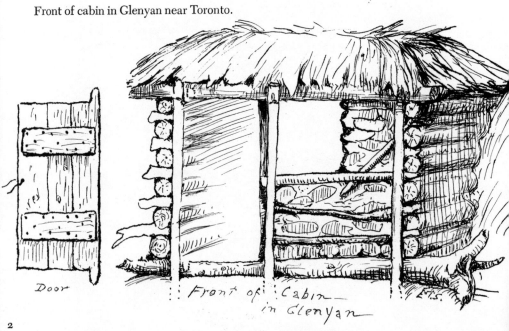

Lynx, 1902.

Toronto Id.

Swallow Bank

Gibraltar Bay

Hanlon's

Mead's Hotel

Lagoon

Lake Ontario

Here about 1872 a storm broke thru making the Eastern Gap

Catfish Jos. Id.

Marsh

Marsh Id.

Ashbridge Bay

Leslieville

Kingston Road

Cow Byres

Don River

Windmill Pt.

Canal

Gooderham's Distillery

City of Toronto

Western Gap

site of × Ft. Rouillé

York Block-house

Garrison Creek

S

N

Map of Toronto Island & Marsh in 1870. drawn from memory in 1930. by E.T. Seton.

about 5 Miles from East to West.

Map of Toronto Island in 1870.

4

Golden Eagle studies, 1887.

Fox, 1887.

Dabbles the Coon inspecting his handiwork.

Silverspot the Crow.

Solomon Seal and Veery.

Sleepy Porcupine, 1886.

Least Shrew, 1900.

Cactus Wren, 1885.

Meadowlark in song.

9

Barnyard and cowshed at De Winton.

Quail studies, 1894.

Marsh Hawk, 1890.

merlin, by
Ernest U... L... Seton
31 nov. 1891

Marlin, 1891.

Bull Calf's Teepee.

Bull Calf's Teepee

Evensong.

EVEN Song

John Yancey, 1897.

White Swan, the Crow.

Mule Deer head, 1887.

Turtle Dove, 1890.

English Sparrow.

The brave hunter and the mother Squirrel.

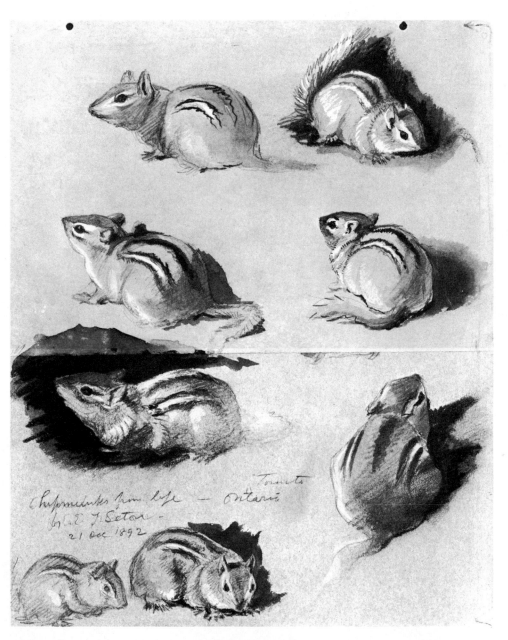

Poses of Chipmunk, 1892.

Buffalo head, 1894.

Juncos, 1881.

English Robins, 1890.

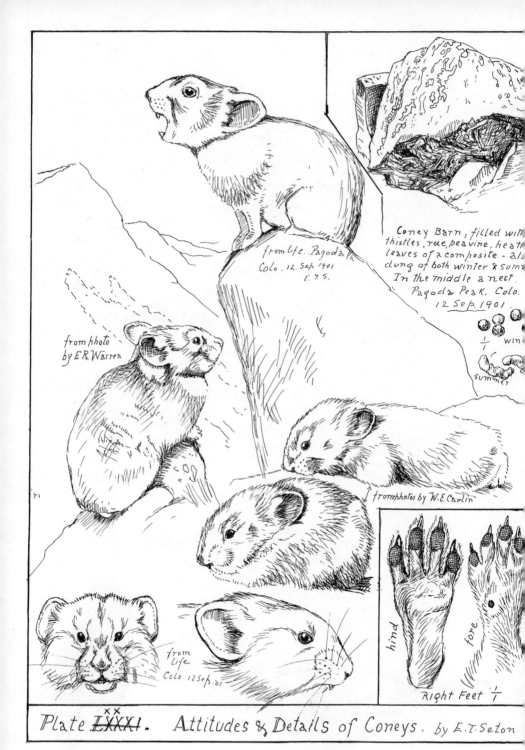

Coney Barn, filled with
thistles, rue, peavine, heath
leaves of a composite - al..
dung of both winter & summ..
In the middle a nest.
Pagoda Peak. Colo.
12 Sep. 1901

win..

summer

from life. Pagoda P..
Colo. 12. Sep. 1901
E. T. S.

from photo
by E.R. Warren

from photos by W.E. Carlin

from
life
Colo. 12 Sep. '01

hind

fore

Right Feet ¹⁄₁

Plate LXXXI. Attitudes & Details of Coneys. by E.T. Seton

Attitudes of Coneys.

De Winton farm houses, 1882.

E. T. Seton
at age of 22 – St Josephs Hospital
1883

Self portrait while in hospital, 1883.

Very early drawings, 1879.

Cougar and kits (an etching)

Mule Deer, for Century Dictionary.

Sleeping Wolf.

The Triumph of the Wolves, a canvas 5½ by 7 feet.

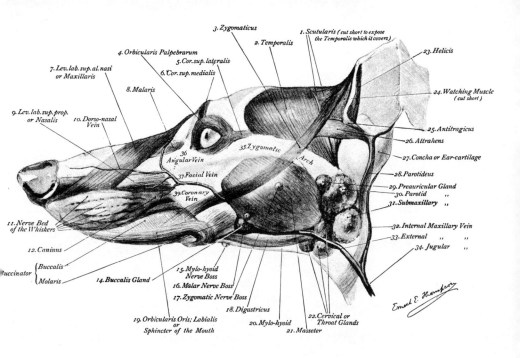

1. Scutularis (cut short to expose the Temporalis which it covers)
2. Temporalis
3. Zygomaticus
4. Orbicularis Palpebrarum
5. Cor. sup. lateralis
6. Cor. sup. medialis
7. Lev. lab. sup. al. nasi or Maxillaris
8. Malaris
9. Lev. lab. sup. prop. or Nasalis
10. Dorso-nasal Vein
11. Nerve Bed of the Whiskers
12. Caninus
Buccinator { Buccalis / Molaris }
14. Buccalis Gland
15. Mylo-hyoid Nerve Boss
16. Malar Nerve Boss
17. Zygomatic Nerve Boss
18. Digastricus
19. Orbicularis Oris; Labialis or Sphincter of the Mouth
20. Mylo-hyoid
21. Masseter
22. Cervical or Throat Glands
23. Helicis
24. Watching Muscle (cut short)
25. Antitragicus
26. Attrahens
27. Concha or Ear-cartilage
28. Parotideus
29. Preauricular Gland
30. Parotid ,,
31. Submaxillary ,,
32. Internal Maxillary Vein
33. External ,, ,,
34. Jugular ,,
35. Zygomatic Arch
36 Angular Vein
37. Facial Vein
39. Coronary Vein

Ernest E. Thompson

Ernest E. Thompson

Plates from Seton's Art Anatomy of Animals, 1895.

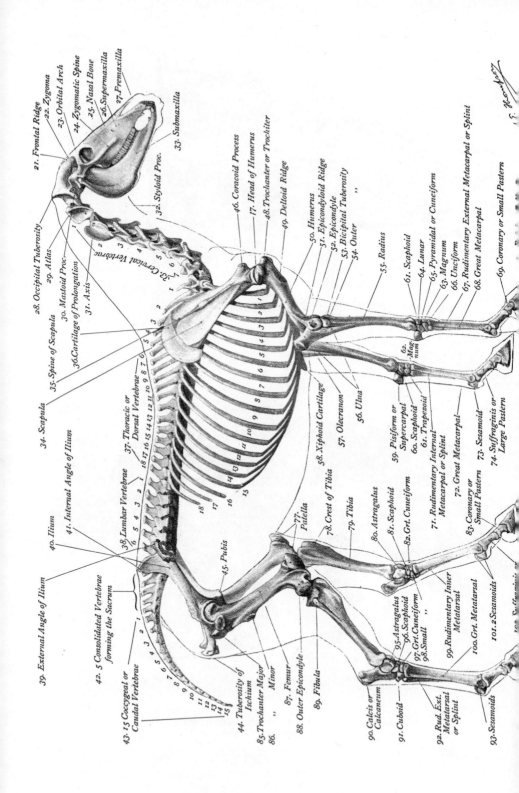

21. Frontal Ridge
22. Zygoma
23. Orbital Arch
24. Zygomatic Spine
25. Nasal Bone
26. Supermaxilla
27. Premaxilla
28. Occipital Tuberosity
29. Atlas
30. Mastoid Proc.
31. Axis
32. Styloid Proc.
33. Submaxilla
33. Cervical Vertebrae

34. Scapula
35. Spine of Scapula
36. Cartilage of Prolongation
37. Thoracic or Dorsal Vertebrae
38. Lumbar Vertebrae
39. External Angle of Ilium
40. Ilium
41. Internal Angle of Ilium
42. 5 Consolidated Vertebrae forming the Sacrum
43. 15 Coccygeal or Caudal Vertebrae

44. Tuberosity of Ischium
45. Pubis
46. Coracoid Process
47. Head of Humerus
48. Trochanter or Trochiter
49. Deltoid Ridge
50. Humerus
51. Epicondyloid Ridge
52. Epicondyle
53. Bicipital Tuberosity
54. Outer   ,,
55. Radius
56. Ulna
57. Olecranon
58. Xiphoid Cartilage
59. Pisiform or Supercarpal
60. Scaphoid
61. Trapezoid
61. Scaphoid
62. Magnum
63. Magnum
64. Lunar
65. Pyramidal or Cuneiform
66. Unciform
67. Rudimentary External Metacarpal or Splint
68. Great Metacarpal
69. Coronary or Small Pastern

71. Rudimentary Internal Metacarpal or Splint
72. Great Metacarpal
73. Sesamoid
74. Suffraginis or Large Pastern

77. Patella
78. Crest of Tibia
79. Tibia
80. Astragalus
81. Scaphoid
82. Grt. Cuneiform
83. Coronary or Small Pastern

85. Trochanter Major
86.   ,,   Minor
87. Femur
88. Outer Epicondyle
89. Fibula
90. Calcis or Calcaneum
91. Cuboid
92. Rud. Ext. Metatarsal or Splint
93. Sesamoids
95. Astragalus
96. Scaphoid
97. Grt. Cuneiform
98. Small   ,,
99. Rudimentary Inner Metatarsal
100. Grt. Metatarsal
101. 2 Sesamoids

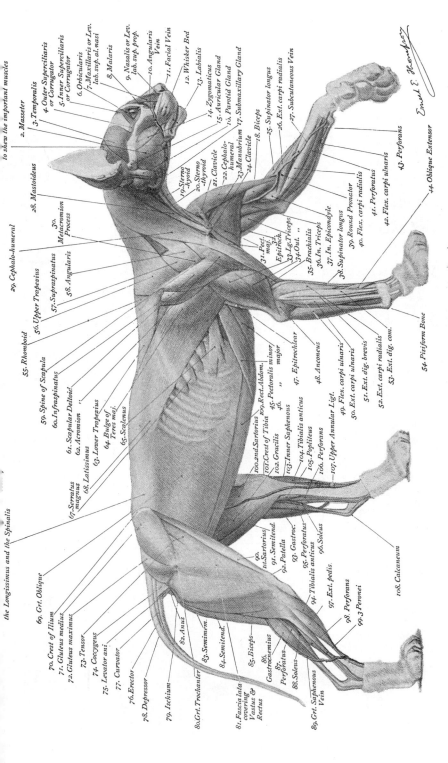

the Longissimus and the Spinalis

to shew the important muscles

2. Masseter
3. Temporalis
4. Outer Superciliaris or Corrugator
5. Inner Superciliaris or Corrugator
6. Orbicularis
7. Maxillaris or Lev. lab. sup. al. nasi
8. Malaris
9. Nasalis or Lev. lab. sup. prop.
10. Angularis Vein
11. Facial Vein
12. Whisker Bed
13. Labialis
14. Zygomaticus
15. Auricular Gland
16. Parotid Gland
17. Submaxillary Gland
18. Biceps
19. Sterno Hyoid
20. Sterno thyroid
21. Clavicle
22. Cephalo-humeral
23. Manubrium
24. Clavicle
25. Supinator longus
26. Ext. carpi radialis
27. Subcutaneous Vein
28. Mastoideus
29. Cephalo-humeral
30. Metacromion Process
31. Pect. maj.
32. Epitroch.
33. Lg.Triceps
34. Out. "
35. Brachialis
36. In. Triceps
37. In. Epicondyle
38. Supinator longus
39. Round Pronator
40. Flex. carpi radialis
41. Perforatus
42. Flex. carpi radialis
43. Perforans
44. Oblique Extensor
45. Pectoralis minor 46. major
47. Epitrochlear
48. Anconeus
49. Flex. carpi ulnaris
50. Ext. carpi ulnaris
51. Ext. dig. brevis
52. Ext. carpi radialis
53. Ext. dig. com.
54. Pisiform Bone
55. Rhomboid
56. Upper Trapezius
57. Supraspinatus
58. Angularis
59. Spine of Scapula
60. Infraspinatus
61. Scapular Deltoid
62. Acromion
63. Lower Trapezius
64. Bulge of Teres maj.
65. Scalenus
67. Serratus magnus
68. Latissimus
69. Grt. Oblique
70. Crest of Ilium
71. Gluteus medius
72. Gluteus maximus
73. Tensor
74. Coccygeus
75. Levator ani
76. Erector
77. Curvator
78. Depressor
79. Ischium
80. Grt. Trochanter
81. Fascia lata covering Vastus & Rectus
82. Anus
83. Semimem.
84. Semitend.
85. Biceps
86. Gastrocnemius
87. Perforatus
88. Soleus
89. Grt. Saphenous Vein
90. 2nd. Sartorius
91. Semitend.
92. Patella
93. Gastroc.
94. Tibialis anticus
95. Perforatus
96. Soleus
97. Ext. pedis.
98. Perforans
99. 3 Peronei
100. 2nd. Sartorius
101. Crest of Tibia
102. Gracilis
103. Inner Saphenous
104. Tibialis anticus
105. Poplieus
106. Perforans
107. Upper Annular Ligt.
108. Calcaneum
109. Rect. Abdom.
110. Sartorius
111. Sartorius

Ernest E. Thompson

Plates from Seton's Art Anatomy of Animals, 1895

29

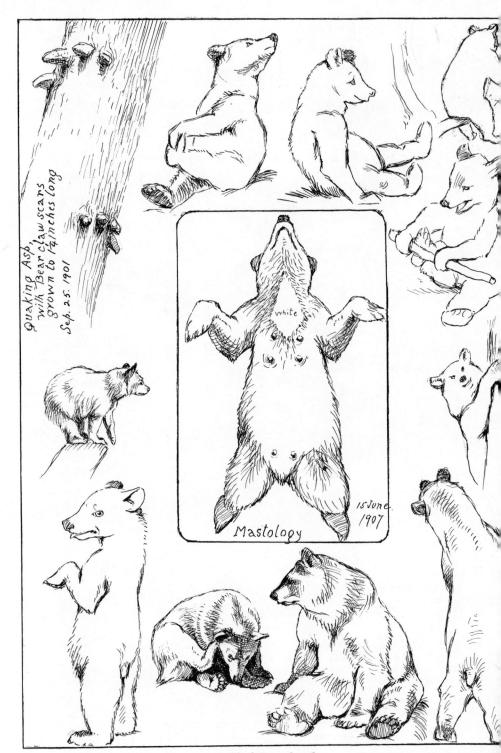

Quaking Asp, with Bear claw scars grown to 14 inches long Sep. 25. 1901

white

Mastology

15 June 1907

Black Bear details.

Seton Castle, a pencil sketch.

THE BUFFALO WIND

THE BUFFALO WIND

THE BUFFALO WIND IS BLOWING

PART SIX

TENDING THE FLAME

CONSERVATION

Teddy Roosevelt's Bird Skins

In the eighties, while Seton was still living in Manitoba and collecting specimens of the birds of that region, his friend, Dr. T. W. Gilbert, said to him: "Why don't you get in touch with the Smithsonian Institution? They are always glad to help young naturalists; and you can be of service to them by sending your specimens from this new region."

The result was that Seton wrote a long respectful letter to the Smithsonian Regents, telling what he was trying to do out on the prairies. An answer came from Professor S. F. Baird, then the head of the Smithsonian. It was most cordial and encouraging. He informed Seton that specimens of all the common birds, beasts, etc., from his region were greatly desired for their museum, and added that they could not pay cash for these, but could amply compensate him in books of science, "of which we have great store."

Seton sent numberless small collections of bird and mammal skins to the Smithsonian, and for some of these got in return desirable skins from other parts of the country. He was brought by correspondence into contact with other young naturalists, and swapped skins with them. The fact that it was done through the Smithsonian obviated any trouble with the Customs.

Among those whose skins he got by this exchange were those of a young man on Long Island, New York. They exchanged skins without any direct contact. It was many years later before Seton realized that that young man was Theodore Roosevelt.

Long after, when Roosevelt was the nation's ruler in the White House, Seton showed him some of those skins. He was delighted and said, "I remember the very day on which I collected those on Oyster Bay, Long Island." The skins were prepared by his own hands, and are proof of his carefulness in all things he undertook.

Citizenship

Seton, as we have seen, was born in England, and all through his life
he maintained the utmost loyalty to his mother country, although he
was only six years old when his family took him to Canada.

As he grew to manhood, in spite of this allegiance, he wished to
become an American citizen, and soon took out his first papers. While
awaiting the appointed time for the completion of the legal requisites,
he had been made official naturalist to the government of Manitoba.
It was not long after that he met Theodore Roosevelt. They found
much in common, had many pursuits to engage in together.

Then Roosevelt became President, and Seton's Canadian government position gave him new opportunities for usefulness. He acted
many times as unofficial ambassador between the White House and
Rideau Hall, Ottawa, where dwelt Lord Grey, the Governor General
of Canada, a close friend of Seton's and a statesman of farseeing
wisdom.

Seton's services were not of a political kind. His hopes and efforts
were all in the line of wild-life conservation; and a number of times
he found joy in acting as a link between the two nations, British and
American, and in promoting better understanding by his activities as
such.

A typical case was as follows:

President Roosevelt on one occasion said to Seton: "I wish you
would run up to Ottawa and find out what those people are willing
to do about an international game and timber reserve on the banks of
Rainy River."

Accordingly, Seton took the night train to Ottawa and drove to
Government House where he had a standing invitation to visit.

After the formalities, Lord Grey said: "Now what is back of this
visit?"

Seton told him in detail what was desired.

After a little thought, Lord Grey answered: "Very good. You must
have a talk with the Hon. Frank Oliver, Minister of the Interior. I'll
ask him to dinner tonight."

That night, after dinner, as they sat around sipping coffee, he told the Minister of Roosevelt's plan for an international game and timber reserve to extend for ten miles along Rainy River, and five miles back on each side, that is, five miles deep into Ontario.

Oliver was deeply interested. The plan was one for his department and, with Laurier's backing, he had full power. But he hesitated.

"I would be only too glad to do it; however, I would not dare."

"Why?"

"Because it would give my enemies a chance. They would say: 'Yes, another timber limit to reward some sturdy supporter, another plum for the obedient partisan of big service.'

"I can, and will, gladly set the region aside as a game sanctuary and wild-life haven. But I cannot mention the timber there. It is chiefly white pine, and worth millions as it stands."

Then Seton said: "If you establish a wild-life sanctuary, you must in some way have official wardens on the spot."

"Yes."

"And part of their work would be to fight forest fires."

"Certainly."

"Could you not instruct them to co-operate fully and continuously with the wardens of the Minnesota side?"

"It is quite essential that they should."

Equipped with this information, Seton hied him back to Washington and told President Roosevelt in full. The result was that the real United States Ambassador, Pinchot, went up to Ottawa and formally concluded the bargain for which Seton, as a scout, had prepared the way.

In matters like this, he was a link, an unofficial intermediary, and he treasured more than he could tell the privilege and honor of being a friendly ambassador, promoting understanding, kindness, and co-operation between the two great countries.

While he found himself in a position to be of such service, he felt it would be unwise to change his status as a British citizen, so allowed the time to go by in which he would have had to complete his naturalization.

Then he started the Boy Scouts, first in England with Baden-

Powell, then in America. He was Chief Scout here from the inception in 1910 until the First World War began in 1914. Questions of nationality of course were rife, and his position was peculiar. Attention was called to the fact that he was still a British subject, an official of the Canadian Government, and was therefore not properly qualified to head up a patriotic American organization. So, at the next Annual Meeting in 1915, he was not re-elected to the office he had held from the beginning.

He had indeed volunteered for active service at both Washington and Ottawa as well as in London. In each case he was turned down, chiefly on account of his age, then fifty-four.

At this point, Theodore Roosevelt took a hand in the controversy. His first exclamation was: "Why, I took it for granted that you *were* an American citizen!"

"No," Seton said. "I live in New York and am deeply in sympathy with the American ideal of government; but I am still an official of the Canadian Government, and as such have, as you know, the peculiar and happy acceptance as a trusted ambassador, agreeable to both great nations."

"There is something in what you say," answered Roosevelt. "Nevertheless, I think it is your duty to identify yourself with the country whose laws are protecting you.

"You live in New York, have made that your permanent address, and by all the rules of sound ethics, you should take out your papers as an American citizen.

"If my son Kermit were to go and live in Canada—as he may—I should insist on his taking out naturalization papers and becoming a subject of Great Britain."

That settled it. Again Seton took out his first papers. But at the appointed time, in spite of his efforts to change his arrangements, he was on a long lecture tour abroad, and again the period expired before his return.

Now, however, he was determined to go through with it. He made the project his first aim; and setting aside all other considerations, he finally, on November 6, 1931, in Santa Fe, New Mexico, became a full-fledged American.

Teddy's Obituary

The friendship between Seton and Teddy Roosevelt lasted throughout the remainder of the latter's life. At the time of Roosevelt's
death the following letter from Seton's pen was published in a local
newspaper.

"Over twenty years ago, when I first came to New York to live, I
was one evening dining at the Players' Club, and there met a strong
young man about my own age, who was interested in all the activities of each guest at the table. But he seemed to discover a special
interest in a series of observations I had made as a wolf hunter in
the West.

"That young man was Theodore Roosevelt.

"Some men knew him as a statesman, some as a sportsman, some
as a soldier, and some as a reformer. But I knew him as a naturalist;
and at each of our meetings, he talked on my subject as a master,
and as though, after all, natural history was the only thing really
worth while. That was one of his gifts—the wonderful breadth of
sympathy which made him enter into the individual activities of all
those about him.

"It is very difficult to appraise fairly the gifts of a man in the
highest possible place of power; but we whose business it is to learn,
and gather up the learning of the world of the outdoors, do not hesitate to give to Roosevelt a position in the front rank of naturalists.

"He and I have several times differed in matters of detail, but in
all large issues of my interests we have been at one; and I treasure
today among the best of the things I own, an autographed letter of
praise that he wrote in 1909, when my most ambitious book was
published (*Life Histories of Northern Animals*); just as I treasure
the memory of those early days when he was the first man of position
in New York to give me the hand of good fellowship as a naturalist.

"We can but sadly recall and paraphrase the words of the prophet
on another occasion of national bereavement: 'Know ye there is a
great man, and a Prince, fallen this day in our nation!'"

The Individual

Seton in his work was unconcerned about results in any worldly sense. He was impelled to act in his own way and direction, and then to reveal. He was driven from within. He was antagonistic to no laws laid down by others; he was simply unconscious of them—they had no existence.

Circumstances were for him just what he made them. He was silent but entirely indifferent to them, and somehow they seemed to shape themselves to fit his needs.

One might well wonder what Seton, with his woodcraft and naturalist background, found to help him in Paris. Certainly it was not the academic or the student life.

A brief extract from a letter written to a friend at the time reveals his attitude of growing aversion to the teachings, together with the realization of what he might still do.

"I have spent all the afternoon at the Louvre," he wrote, "and as I went from one great master to another, and saw all kinds of peculiarities and extremes, yet all resulting in great pictures, this is the lesson that impressed me more and more: that man who does immortal work develops *himself*. Here have I, living in Norway, been trying to grow a palm tree, because I saw that African palms were good. And each fresh frost cut down my poor, puny sprout. My wretched seedling had to contend with a great strong, frost-defying pine that kept springing up. It has only recently dawned on me that I must grow my pine. That is my timber. What a tree I might have had now had I realized this ten years ago!

"This, then, is my theory: I have something which no one else in the world has. It may be a little thing, but it is *me*. It is my pine tree, and I shall grow it, though it never exceed a foot in height. It will always be at least a living thing."

The Development of Young Canada Geese

"In the fall of 1902, I received a pair of Canada Geese that, though birds of the year, were said to be mated. At any rate, they always kept close together, and did not quarrel, a fully good sign in the goose world.

"Early in the month of March, they began to make a nest on an island in the main lake at Wyndygoul, my home. The chosen spot was on a high sharp ridge, and the geese began to lay before the nest was complete, so that two eggs rolled out and lay near the nest where they spoiled before I saw them. Five were left within the downy couch; it was scarcely a hollow.

"As nearly as I can tell, the bird began to sit on April tenth, the goose chiefly staying on the nest. The gander, known as Long Neck on account of his remarkable neck, swam around the island most of the day, patrolling it like a coast guard.

"Ducks of all kinds were allowed to feed near as usual, and to come on the island at their pleasure; indeed, a black duck nested within ten feet of the goose. But no geese were allowed anywhere near, no matter about the species; they were immediately chased away, and the gander that had bullied Long Neck all winter was at once routed and fled before his savage attack. Men and boys were similarly driven off.

"But one day I watched my chance, and landing on the island while he was on the other side, I walked up to the nest. The goose on the eggs hissed, and the gander came hissing, splashing over the water. He dashed up the slope. I was now sitting within four feet of the nest. He came at me in great haste and with much threatening, but I made no move. He waddled and fluttered around till he stopped between me and the nest. Then bolt upright he stood, hissing occasionally but not attacking me, and seemed content to know that at least I must 'go over his dead body' before I could touch his mate or nest.

"The goose left the eggs each day for twenty minutes about noon, carefully covering them with the down before quitting.

"On the tenth of May, twenty-eight days as nearly as I could tell,

I saw a little gosling put his head out from the mother's wing. Next day I saw the two old geese followed by four goslings swimming on the water. I landed on the island and found in the nest one egg, chipped, with the little one pipping loudly. I broke the egg partly open, but the gander came at me now so furiously that I dropped it and fled. He then took his place over it, brooding low, but not sitting, and threatening me as he made low snaky passes with his long neck over the nest.

"During the day the mother was three or four times on the water, always followed by the four young, then back on the nest. The gander brooded part of the time, and at length the little one came out. Later in the afternoon, I found it lying ten feet from the nest, cold and nearly dead, while the others were away swimming. I put it back in the nest, wrapped it up in the down, then fled before the gander, who came splashing on the lake at me. An hour later the mother was brooding it.

"On May twelfth this last little gosling, the runt, was swimming with the others, and running on the bank with them, but it was slow and evidently feebler than the others. It was last of the five, but never last of the procession; for the mother invariably led, and Long Neck always brought up the rear. Nothing could exceed the vigilance of that bird.

"I watched the brood for hours, and never once saw the gander eat except when the goose was on guard with her head aloft. I do not know how he managed to get enough food.

"There were doubtless many enemies about, as I lost a large number of young ducks that summer. But there were none apparently that dared to face old Long Neck; for day after day went by and still the brood continued, the runt gaining in strength so that he was now rarely far behind his brothers, and the procession was shortened thereby. The passing of any large bird overhead caused the father to begin a warning note; and if the assailant came near, he uttered his trumpet note and flew to do battle.

"The goose is only half a water bird. Part of the time I saw the family on the various lakes, but just as often I discovered them afar in the woods or in the fields half a mile from any water. They wandered fearlessly where they would; and wherever they went, I could see the long neck of that eternally vigilant and fearless old gander.

"The growth of the little ones was something extraordinary. In a month they were as large as mallards, and in two months their bodies seemed to be fully grown.

"According to my notebook, on July tenth they were as large as their mother, but with only one showing traces of the down of their youth. Their wings, however, were yet without quill feathers, still mere rudiments.

"In the middle of July the old ones had begun to molt, and I saw a singular case. The mother goose had had a wing clipped; and on the morning of the eighteenth, I stood within eight feet of her and saw her deliberately jerk out six secondary quill feathers, most of which had been cut. She tried a number of others without success. This shows that the process of molting is helped by the bird's deliberate act.

"During August the quills on the wings grew rapidly; and by the twentieth of the month all the young were strong on the wing, flying easily about the pond. The parents did not join them because they were pinioned.

"The gander continued to guard them as before.

"By September twelfth, they began to associate with the other geese; and a recent addition to the flock, a gray goose in full possession of her wing power, began to do her bit to lead the army south.

"With the wild geese, flight is not merely a mode of travel; it is a grand ceremony, as I saw many times. This wild goose would go swimming across the lake, throwing up her chin, and uttering a low quack, quack, quack, quack. As she swam, the others followed. She increased her speed as she saw them coming. Throwing up her beak more and more, her quack grew louder and louder till she broke full in the loud trumpet note. She rose easily from the water with little or no spattering, and flew away over the trees southward. The others tried to follow, but of course failed; and she, finding herself alone, circled back to the water and rejoined them.

"This I saw many scores of times, and the old goose always flew southward.

"In the spring I released eight snow geese on the north shore of the lake, and all dodged past me and made northward on foot through the woods. Whether this was a mere attempt to seek cover, or a distinct northward migration instinct, I cannot say, but all eight did it separately.

"By the thirtieth of September, the young Canada geese were quite indistinguishable from the old ones excepting by their voice. Ordinarily they have a piping treble note; but when they trumpet, it is like that of the old ones. The little runt grew with his brothers, and could not be told apart.

"These geese had more grass than any other food, and spent at least half of the time roaming the woods. During heavy rainstorms, they drifted about on the open lake, while the ducks sought the shelter of the lee shore.

"Eventually, of course, the young Canada geese followed the instinct of the race and flew south for the winter."

Nature Never Draws a Circle

"There is never a true circle in nature, never a straight line, never a true square. If you were exploring a cave, or a prairie, or a desert island, and found a perfect square or a perfect circle laid out in stones or other objects, you would know at once that a man had done this, for nature never deals in such things.

"It was a trifling experience that led me to this thought; and since then I have made countless observations that led to the same conclusion—there is never a true mathematical form in nature.

"Never a straight line? What about the horizon line of the sea? The answer is that it is not a straight line, but a fragment of an imperfect circle, the vast circle of the globe, broken by waves and warped by tides.

"The sun and moon are doubtless circles, but far from perfect if we are to believe the astronomers; and it seems that there is not an angle made by stars that is exactly a right angle, or a line of three or more stars that is a true straight line.

"Is not the ray of light from the setting sun through the trees a straight line? Not any more than the ray of light that is bent as it enters the clear pond. It is easy to show that, theoretically, nature's supposed straight lines, right angles, and perfect circles are not mathematically true.

"There are, however, a number of interesting things that get very near to the true forms. The old phrase 'straight as a reed' must fall to the ground, we learn, as soon as we approach a reed bed. But there are some pretty nearly straight lines in the work of a spider just beginning her web. The finished one yonder is so pulled and geared that its lines are more or less out; but the new ones, in mere sketch plan as yet, is made of a few lines long and tight, and of course straight—straight as a string.

"'Straight as an arrow' is an ancient saying referring, not to the flight (that is always curved), but to the arrow itself. The arrow must be straight in order to fly reliably. It is probable that an arrow was the first straight thing designedly made by man. To find slender shoots already straight enough to make good arrows has always been considered a piece of good luck among savage hunters; and in each country of the bow is found a tree that, producing such shoots, is known as 'arrowwood.'

"Seen among the tangled and twisted growths of the woods, our North American arrowwood (*Viburnum dentatum*) looks marvelously straight; and yet I never saw one of the shoots that did not need a lot of twisting and chewing before it would pass even among the imperfect shafts made by the Indians.

"Nature rarely attempts the right angle; and in the material world outside of crystals, I doubt if she ever succeeds. One may often find a nasturtium leaf in which the larger veins form right angles in the middle, and are subdivided into angles of 45° with an exactness that seems to form a surprising exception to the rule. But the straight edge of a proper instrument applied would soon spoil their claim.

"I once saw a remarkable thundercloud that had an immense right angle bitten out of its side. The legs of the angle were, perhaps, half a mile long. It was so wonderful that the country people took it for a sign that their community was 'right' though others said: 'No, it meant that there was nothing right in the country except this thundercloud.' I found that it exactly fitted the angle of the window sash as I stood indoors. Unfortunately, there was no camera near to perpetuate and prove the wonder.

"There is certainly one thing in the skies which exhibits four perfect right angles. I observed it many times during winters spent on the

Northern plains. That is the sundog. The air filled with crystals of ice repeated the sun's rays in such a way that a long perpendicular line through the sun was crossed by a horizontal one at the middle of the sun's disc.

"But these, it is claimed, have no real existence; they are tricks played on the eye by refraction.

"The search for the circle has a better chance of success. All can recall perfect circles discovered out of doors—the fairy ring in the grass, the cup that the acorn recently sat in, the orb of a bird's eye, the newly sprung toadstool. But the compass carefully applied discredits one after another.

"The globes of peas-in-a-row in the pod are nearly perfect, and yet some of them do not roll straight down a slightly inclined board; and this 'tabling' is the test that shotmakers put their shot through, rejecting all that do not roll off at the slightest canting.

"But yonder in that tree is something very like a perfect circle— the hole of a woodpecker. I wonder how he gets it so true? It is certainly not by hewing to any given line, for it is less of a circle when he begins it than at any other time. If he stood all around it to peck with his head into the center, we could understand it, but I have seen him do it and know that he completes the outer part of the hole from one standpoint. I imagine his test is that it must not be too tight a fit anywhere on his body as he enters, and his body happens to be nearly circular. Hence the hole.

"Yet another circle I have several times seen—a grass blade sharply bent in the middle, blown all day by a light, south-veering wind, and all the next day by a light northerly wind; so that its top, dragging in the sand about it, showed the outline of a perfect circle because the central point was fixed.

"It is easy to imagine how a circle of this kind sketched in the wet sand, then frozen and drifted over with a different soil, might become embedded, and appear at last as a true circle engraved on the rocks exposed by some geologist in the future. And this suggests the general proposition that a perfect circle cannot be made by growth, can be made only by the principle of rotation.

"A very fine example is afforded by the newly made nest of the robin. After each fresh layer, she smooths the mud by sitting in it and turning round and round. She is, in fact, making an earthen pot, but rotating the tool instead of the vessel. The result is a remarkably true ceramic of unbaked clay.

"Again we must look to the skies for perfection. It appears that the great ring around the moon on threatening nights is a true circle. Also that which is so often seen around the sundogs. But again the scientists aver that these absolute circles and lines have no more real existence than the mirage which often accompanies them. They are optical illusions.

"If we walk along the bed of a pebbly brook, we shall see among the thousands of stones some that seem to be perfectly round, till we take them up or test them. A boy's marble placed among such instantly catches the eye; it is something different.

"Instinctively one feels that this is human handiwork. It is too nearly round to be produced by the chance rubbing and rolling of the brook.

"This, then, is the mental attitude in all such discovery: there *may* be true circles, lines, and angles in the heavens; but on the ground or in the earth, with the possible exception of crystals, it is different. If we find there any object, be it block of stone, fragment of bone, piece of clay, wall of cliff, mound of earth, or arrangement of sticks with perfect mathematical lines in or on it, we should conclude instantly and safely that man has been here, that this is some of his handiwork."

The English Sparrow

The history of this stout hardy bird in America is much as follows:

"In 1858, a Mr. Debtors of Portland, Maine, conceived the idea of naturalizing the English Sparrow in America. He imported and set at large three pairs, which in time showed their perfect adaptability by rapid multiplication. Subsequently, several large importations were made by corporations, as well as by private parties. And now the original little band of six, which twenty-five years ago landed at Portland, their Plymouth Rock, is now represented by the teeming and ever spreading thousands that have already occupied all the Eastern States and pushed as far north in Canada probably as the climate will allow.

"Wherever he has made his appearance, the same story is told of the sparrow. Our native birds cannot stand before him. He has been selected and specialized by a long hard struggle for existence in the Old World, and been developed into an ideal of energy, dauntlessness, and hardihood. He is the exact type of the Saxon, his invasion is the precise epitome of the White man's occupation of America. He came a stranger, weak and living by suffrance, till, waxing strong, he turned about and proceeded to extend his territories by the most highhanded aggression.

"The hardihood of this bird precludes the necessity for migration; or perhaps it were more correct to say that, owing to their ability to obtain food all the year round, they have long ago lost the migratory instinct.

"Early in March, or late in February during mild seasons, the sparrows begin to show signs of arousing sexuality; and as the season advances, amusing courtship scenes are to be noted daily. It frequently happens that a single female is beset by two or more admirers, who, with drooping wings and oft-repeated 'chirrups,' hop about after and around her, hoping by persistence to obtain some concession. The female, so far from expressing any satisfaction, usually lays about her with a good will, plucking at the wings and head of the ardent suitors, and apparently doing all in her power to drive them away. It is noticeable, however, that if she does succeed, she immediately follows them, to again lead them into temptation. Dr. Brodie informs me that he once saw a female on the rain trough seize a male that was courting her, and, suspending him for a minute over the edge, let him drop. During this curious mark of attention, the male seemed to shut his eyes and resign himself with perfect satisfaction to the rough treatment accorded by the object of his affections.

"The ardor of his devotion to his little brown mistress is so very noticeable that when I read in Chaucer the passage 'Ye Sparowe Venus' son,' it strikes me as being the most concise description of his character ever written.

"Next in prominence after his master passion is his pugnacity. He seems to be the son of Mars as well as of Venus. Love and war take up the whole time of this troubadour; so entirely, indeed, that he is no troubadour at all, for of all his family, he alone makes no pretensions to being a songster; though in justice it must be added that frequently during early summer he may be heard uttering in rapid succession a series of rolling 'chirrups.' The result may be styled a song, as it is not unmusical, and is at least as successful as the notes of many of the smaller sparrows.

"A curious but not very surprising change appears to be going on in the plumage of the sparrows. After they had braved the Canadian winter a few times, a great number of the birds began to display white feathers in their wings and tail, as well as on various parts of the body. Latterly, however, this tendency has become less evident; but it is apparently represented by a general lightening of the whole plumage.

"Early one day in March my attention was directed to an unusually noisy riot among the sparrows; it proved, of course, a courtship with numerous suitors. A second glance showed that the hen who had broken this multitude of hearts and was just then doing her best to break as many heads was indeed a belle of unusual gifts— not a common brown little lady, but a rare beauty, as showy as a showbird, for she had *white wings and tail.*

"Someone (it sounds like Dr. Watts) has written: 'Birds in their little nests agree,' etc., and points them out as models for men. But it would appear that the present does not afford a happy illustration of the statement, for I once had the opportunity of observing a lively fight between a pair of newly mated English sparrows. The cause of dispute was feather beds. The birdhouse had been chosen, the previous tenants (bluebirds) evicted, and loads of rubbish and bric-a-brac carried up. Then the hen, who seemed to have rather luxurious ideas, proceeded to bundle in all the large feathers she could find. The male seemed to think she was carrying that sort of thing too far, and so proceeded to draw the line by ejecting the feathers en masse. She returned with another load, just in time to see the last float to the ground. She now carried up both loads to the nest, but only to have them speedily dragged out by her lord. She fluttered down and regathered them, then faced him with her heart full of indignation and her mouth full of feathers. Both were chattering their loudest and looking daggers. It was at last settled by the hen prudently giving in for the time. But, as usual with her sex, by giving in, she fully gained her point. The nest at last was stuffed full of the largest and softest feathers he could find for her.

"In Ontario, the sparrow appears to begin laying early in April

if not in March, and two or three broods are produced each season.
The young, when first fledged, are much like the female, but the
throat of the males usually shows a faint dusky patch. In August
when the second plumage is assumed, the black throat patch is
developed.

"The question at present regarding the sparrow is: what are we
to do with it? It has multiplied so enormously, and has stirred up so
many enemies by its aggression and by its granivorous tastes, that
considerable discussion is being excited as to the advisability of
making war on the species. Dr. Brodie and I have paid a good
deal of attention to this subject, and have collected a considerable
amount of evidence relative to the food of the bird.

"The conclusions that our experience points to are that the sparrow
is an omnivorous bird, though preferably granivorous. It feeds chiefly
on grain and buds in the winter and spring. During the breeding
season, it feeds itself largely, and its young perhaps entirely, on
insects, most of them noxious; that the young after they begin to
forage for themselves continue for some time to be chiefly insectiv-
orous, and they destroy an immense number of grasshoppers and
other pests. But as they grow older, they assume the granivorous
habits of the parents. Though, on the whole, the balance of evidence
is against the species, it is not yet convicted of serious crimes, while
further research may have the effect of reversing this partial judgment against it. And, finally, there is as yet no serious objection to the
sparrow if its numbers be *kept within reasonable limits.*"

Then and Now

In 1902, Seton wrote the following condemnation:
"Five years ago, when I camped by Jackson's Lake, the scene
was one of the liveliest description. Thousands of wild geese and
ducks were scattered in flocks on the broad surface of the water.
The shores were alive with bands of the snipe and plover kinds.
The margin of the lake and the small ponds were dotted everywhere
with wading birds; gulls winnowed on the tranquil surface, and
new flocks of migrants arriving kept the air a flutter of wings
wherever one looked. In air, on the land, or in the water were

hosts, thousands—yes, tens of thousands of harmless beautiful wild birds, their many cries creating a changing volume of sound that is delightful music to all who appreciate wild life.

"Last year I was at the same place at the corresponding season. But what a change! Two or three fish ducks and a loon were all that remained of the former bird population. The rest had been destroyed by man; and the dead fish and insect life that had constituted their food lay in stinking heaps along the shore.

"If any good was to be gained by this destruction, one might condone it. However, nothing but evil came of it—evil so far-reaching that the end is not yet."

A Dirge

Much in the same vein, he wrote the following dirge. Yet with his sane approach to all things, it ends on a note of optimism.

"This was a land of hope. Young men with their young wives were possessing the soil—hope bright in every eye. Older men, who had failed in the East, were here, with newborn hope. Every furrow struck, every fence post sunk, every sod house temporarily built, was prompted, planned, and made in hope.

"There was dirt and discomfort, yes, even hunger and want in these temporary shacks; there was what would have been misery and squalor in a big city. But every face was bright, every eye was radiant; for over, through, and dominating all, there was a magical something to turn the hardships into a passing joke and the squalor into freedom—a glamor and glorifying light, the light of a glowing faith. The sun came up and sank each day in a world of newborn hope.

"Gone are the buffalo and the antelope—going fast the badger and the quaily. The geese come not on their ancient airy trail.

"The young folks today do not know what a trail is. The summer-long procession of the flowers is gone. The grama grass, the avens, the salmon flower bloom no more. The barn cattle trample where the buffalo grazed, and roosters crow where the prairie fowl once danced their minuet.

"The prairie is gone—the land is one big farm. All things wild and sweet seem doomed in the lurid clouds.

"The end is as hopelessly sad as it was infinitely beautiful. But even as I lament, I stop and wonder if my 'words are wild,' for I know that the new order is better. It must be so.

"As I seek the saner view, I wonder, is it indeed the prairies I lament, or is it rather the prairie days of my youth gone by?"

Bring Back the Game

In 1924, Seton made a lecture tour through Canada. All of his programs were on natural history subjects; but that year he was particularly stressing the need for preservation of the game that still remained and the restocking of many species. He was in frequent conference with the Wild Life Branch of the Interior Department. Finally on November fifteenth, he addressed the Canadian Club at Château Laurier in Ottawa. A transcript of the talk, impromptu so far as composition goes, is as follows. The context, of course, was based on accumulated data made by him from many sources.

"Mr. President, and Gentlemen of the Canadian Club:

"I rejoice, for many reasons, in this large opportunity of striking at the ganglionic center of Canada. For many years I have been preaching a certain doctrine, doing it in diverse places and in small and devious ways. Now I seize on this, the most monumental occasion that ever has been opened to me, to proclaim the latest ideas on wild-life conservation—ideas which I hope will be acceptable to you, as I believe they will be helpful to those who follow after us.

"My home for many years has been on the outskirts of New York City. I live there among my American friends; I knew that my way was in America.

"However, though living in the United States, I have continued my official connection with the Manitoban government. I am still a British subject, and it overwhelms my powers of utterance to realize that I am come back to my own people, and find that they still hold for me a place in kindly remembrance.

"One bright sunny day last September, about one o'clock in the afternoon, sitting at my dining-room table with three young persons,

I suddenly saw, trotting up the drive, a great big, wild, beautiful red fox. I turned to my guests, gasping: 'Oh, look, look, look, look, look, look!' Why I whispered I do not know. There was no need for it, because we were indoors and the fox was three hundred yards away. The young folks looked to where I pointed, and exclaimed: 'Oh, oh, oh, look! Oh, isn't he beautiful! Oh, look at his white shirt front! Look at the black silk gloves he is wearing! Look at that beautiful tail! Oh, isn't he beautiful! Oh, I am so glad I saw him!'

"The expressions of joy elicited from those young people by the spectacle of that wonderful, beautiful, harmless example of wild life trotting up the drive exceeded anything I had ever heard from them. And these exclamations were real, they were spontaneous, they were hearty.

"Were these young men and women any different from others about us of our race? Certainly not! They did not differ from you men assembled. Every one of you would have experienced the same wonderful surge of joy on seeing that exquisite creature living its life before us, unafraid. We all found, and you would have found, and every child in Canada would have found, that very same joyful thrill.

"Now let me tell you what I used to see in my early days in Manitoba. In 1882, '83, and '84, I traveled over the plains north of Winnipeg, and west of Winnipeg—far west—and far north. I went with an ox team, whirling along at the giddy, record-breaking pace of nearly a mile an hour. It had this advantage: I had time to look about—plenty of time to observe the things about me. I could go up on a side trip, on foot, miles away, make a long curve, and again strike the ox team quite easily—no trouble at all.

"Down along the Souris plains, every slough was dotted with ducks, and there were far more sloughs than there are now. The shores were spotted over with shore birds: several different kinds of plover, two or three different kinds of sandpiper—willets, sanderlings, peetweets, snipe—all these species in numbers—and curlews, long flights of them. There were brown cranes, flying in flocks of fifty or sixty, sending out that wonderful—[here Seton gave an imitation of their call]—fairly thrilling you through and through with their joyous aliveness.

"Whooping cranes and pelicans were there in lesser numbers, four or five together, perhaps. There were swans occasionally, and abundance of Canada geese. These honkers, in long double lines, flying near the horizon, looked like the waves of the sea as they went.

"Sometimes the snow geese came down and whitened the plain till it looked like a fall of snow. There were prairie chickens in hundreds; and every mile or two we found a mound where they assembled in the mornings for their wonderful chicken dance.

"There was not a day when we did not see one or two foxes, not a day when we did not see three or four badgers, sunning themselves on the ridges. There were deer in the foothills of Turtle Mountain, or along Riding Mountain. In those days there were even a few buffalo. And every night, after we had camped and the sun went down, we were sung to sleep by the coyote's song. Oh, how I loved it! How I wish I could hear it now!

"Men of Canada, I traveled over that same region a month ago, this time in a motorcar. Through Ninette and Pilot Mound I went, and right on to Morden; and during that long journey of over fifty miles, *I did not see one wild living creature*—not one!

"Where have they gone? Maybe that is not a necessary question. We know *where* they have gone. But *why?* That rather is the question I wish to put before you now. *Why* have they gone? Was it necessary to agriculture to extirpate all these wonderful, beautiful wild things? Certainly not.

"The buffalo? Yes: the buffalo had to go, because he was not compatible with agriculture. But the badger was a harmless thing. The worst I ever heard imputed to a badger was that he dug post-holes where they were not wanted. But that happens so rarely—so very, very seldom.

"The coyote? Gone, gone, gone! Why? Well, they say he stole sheep, but you may be quite sure of this—that nine sheep out of ten that are killed are killed by dogs, not by coyotes. Nevertheless, if the coyote killed sheep at all, I bow my head and say: 'I am sorry, but he has to go.'

"But what about the prairie chickens? What about the wild geese? What about the cranes? What about the swans? What about the ducks? Were they inimical to agriculture? Absolutely not. On the contrary, they were helpful. Any of us who shot chickens during the summer, as we used to do in those early days, knows that grain was never found in their crops at that season. Perhaps in the fall, after the grain was on the ground, but they never molested standing grain. Their crops contained green leaves, berries, grasshoppers, bugs, and other harmful insects. These are what they fed on all summer long. They were absolutely helpful, beneficial, to agriculture, and not a menace in any sense. Now they are gone, gone.

"I came down on the National Railroad from Swan River to Gladstone the other day. On the train in the smoking room were four young men. Each of them was carrying in his hand one of those diabolically wicked, shameful things, a pump gun. They looked out of the window, two of them at one side and two at the other, watching for prairie chickens. Seventy miles they rode, watching for prairie chickens; they did not see one. Eventually they saw two ducks and got out. One remarked to the other, in my hearing: 'Funny we don't see no chickens. Why, last year, you mind, we got four hundred. Don't understand it.' Oh, the fools—the miserable, blind, bloody fools! They themselves got four hundred last year, and wonder where they are gone! Did they not realize? It was no use my saying anything; I could only make notes to spread before a more responsive audience.

"All over the West, all over Manitoba, I found that same story: gone, gone, gone, gone. And for this simple reason—that we brought in weapons of such destructive force, such virulence, that no wild life had any chance against them. The only reason we did not use poison gas was, we could not get and apply it.

"We have desolated our heritage, absolutely devastated these wonderful wilds. We have robbed our children. We have robbed our country. I have no language strong enough to picture this thing as it appears to me, and as I think it will appear to you when you are confronted by cold facts and figures.

"Why should we not have abundant harmless wild life about us all the time? Have we not the same right to see these things as we have to see beautiful pictures? Do they not give the same type of joy exactly; or, if anything, a little deeper and stronger, because, back of the wild creatures is the wonder, the mystery of life? It appeals to our ancestral memories and brings to us a message that the pictures cannot always give.

"With my peculiar status in the United States, known to be an Englishman, yet in close touch with all American activities related to outdoor life, and a personal friend of President Roosevelt, I have had many times the singular joyful position of being a secret, unofficial ambassador to Ottawa.

"Here, on one occasion, when I came to discuss the question of reserves, Sir Wilfred Laurier turned me over to Mr. Frank Oliver. The latter, after voicing his approval of the scheme, yet foreseeing difficulties in doing what I asked, went on:

"'Realize, first of all, the Americans never valued their game until it was gone. They never set about restocking until they had nothing left. Then they woke up to what they had lost. They had robbed their nation of a very large and valuable asset. They had robbed their children of their bounty.'

"A significant pause, then he continued: 'Now, I am sorry to say it, but my people must go through that same sad and shameful experience. They have to lose the game before they will ever bother about conserving it.'

"Remember that was twenty years ago or more.

"I believe that I have come back to that proposition at the right moment. I believe that you have gone through more or less of that shocking course of events. You have lost the game. Now I hope the time is ripe for the next step. I think the psychological moment has arrived when we may consider something else.

"First, I put before you the yearlong, lifelong pleasure of seeing beautiful, harmless wild life. This is the natural right of every one of us.

"The second use for the game is to furnish the young men with a few days' sport in the fall. Why not, as long as the game is not depleted by overshooting? It is the natural right of young men to go hunting in the fall and to bring back a reasonable bag—as much as the game supply will stand.

"Now, that is worth something. How much, it would be pretty hard to put down in figures—and in the figures you would put down, you would underestimate it. You have to take into account what is spent on your autumn hunting trip. Those who keep the amount within three figures are very few. The number of my American friends who get into the four figures with their hunting trip is much larger. You see, they are willing to spend money for it, and that is one means of gauging the value of game to the country.

"There are other methods of appraisal too. There is one that I do not dare to talk too much about. I might be charged with being a militarist if I emphasized the value of the training with the gun, the outdoor life, the development of manhood, self-reliance, courage, the power to go it alone. All these things have their worth, and we know these qualities are born in and nursed by outdoor sports.

"Then, the third and last consideration. This is the one with which I go fearlessly before parliamentary committees and before boards and assemblies at Washington: *It pays. It pays.*

"You know that Congress is extremely sensitive in its pocket nerve. (Of course, I know that Parliament is not.) In Washington, before one of those committees, we talk very freely, are usually quite frank and open, and I say to them, for example: 'Now, gentlemen, I personally care nothing about its money value; my concern is for the wild life. I haven't fired off a gun for twenty years and maybe never will again. I enjoy the wild things and I am willing to pay a large price for the enjoyment. That, however, I know does not appeal to you because it will not win you any votes; at least you think it will not. But what will win you votes, and may win consideration for the game, is the fact that from a monetary angle it pays.'

"Let me give you one or two concrete illustrations. The State of Pennsylvania went through the worst experience of any State for which I have details. They slaughtered their game in the most shameful fashion. I have heard of such diabolical wickedness as this—the whole of the settlers would gather in a drive, a roundup. All the boys and men, perhaps three or four hundred, with guns and tin pans and cowbells, would drive the woods, making a line covering a whole township or two, and sweep the game into a prepared enclosure. They would crowd it into the corral and slam the gates. Then all these brave men would get up on the walls and shoot, shoot, shoot, shoot, just for the exquisite pleasure of seeing these helpless creatures die—after which they left the bodies to rot in piles.

"Wasn't that noble? Wasn't that uplifting? Oh, splendid amusement! Yes, that is what they did, until they wiped out their game—absolutely desolated all Pennsylvania. I do not believe there were a hundred deer left in the whole State.

"Then they woke up—thank God for that! They woke up.

"And to their everlasting credit be it told: it was not the sentimentalists, it was not the economists who headed the campaign. It was the sportsmen who did it. They got together, raised a fund, secured about 150,000 acres of worthless land that had been denuded of timber and that had no game at all. They bought this for an average of about ten dollars an acre. They set to work to restock it. They managed to have good laws passed at Harrisburg to protect the project. They went about the matter in the one wise and successful way, the way that has always been demonstrated as sure to succeed.

"First of all, about half of the area in each region was set apart as a game refuge or sanctuary, in which there might never be an ax lifted or a gun fired. Nobody could go in there unless it was to stop a forest fire.

"In the rest of the area there was to be open shooting but only during the game season and under proper restrictions. No man could enter without a license unless he lived in the State; there was some special privilege for the resident.

"No settler was allowed to live in a game refuge. No, no: you do not want any settlers in there! Absolutely keep them out. It is the only safe way.

"Now, with this new organization and this new approach, and with common-sense consideration of the whole problem, what is the result today [1924]? They have probably 100,000 wild deer. At any rate, they kill about 5000 per annum without depleting the stock.

"They have carefully nursed the black bears, and now have abundance of them. We know very well, in spite of the terrible tales and foolish newspaper talk, that the black bear is a perfectly harmless animal. No black bear ever molested you when he could get away. If you corner one, of course it will fight—so will a rat or a chipmunk. I have met hundreds of black bears and never saw one that did not run or get away if you let it. These harmless animals are now appreciated in Pennsylvania as splendid game, to such an extent that each black bear is considered to be worth a thousand dollars to the State.

"The turkeys have come back; I do not know to what extent.

"Rabbits, coons, squirrels, grouse are in corresponding and increasing abundance, so that 600,000 sportsmen were able to enjoy the State Game Preserve in 1921. In other words, any resident of the State of Pennsylvania can count on going on an occasional hunting trip and on having fun in a legitimate way, conscious at the same time that he is not desolating the country, that he is not robbing the children.

"That region of useless land in Pennsylvania now yields a net revenue of some $400,000 per annum. With this fact, you can go before parliamentary committees, sure of a sympathetic hearing.

"The State of Maine is another case in point. I do not know the details so exactly. They had practically no game in that region; they were down again to pretty near the zero mark. What they did have was leaking in from New Brunswick and from Quebec.

"But they set to work to restore, restock, and take care of the game. Now, I am told, game furnishes to the State of Maine their third best revenue. Their first is timber; their second is shipping; their third is game, which is pouring millions each year into the coffers of the State. Whether that means into the treasury of the State of Maine or into the pockets of the farmers and other citizens who live there, I do not know; but that is the broad fact—it is their third best revenue. You see, *it pays.*

"Now here is the question that is put up to me at many places throughout Manitoba: 'How are we going to go about it here? It is pretty hard to establish public sentiment, in view of what has happened and what the conditions are.'

"There is an answer. In twenty places at least I have advocated this: establish a little sanctuary. If you can have only ten acres in town, or adjoining the town, set that apart as a wild-life sanctuary. That presupposes, I grant you, a fence. You must have a dogproof, catproof fence. However, that does not cost too much. Mine cost something like thirty or forty cents a running foot, the fence being seven and a half feet high. That is the first step.

"Now, what begins to happen? I have seen this over and over again. First of all, the wild birds find that, for some inexplicable reason, they are not molested in there, and they crowd in to nest. I saw in one little sanctuary of scarcely one acre forty-two robins' nests, and other birds in similar ratio. They congregate in that little area; they multiply and they keep on coming in. Species that would not otherwise come find that here is a safe place, and they too move in. Right here in Ottawa, with a sanctuary of ten acres, you might reckon on having spruce partridge and ruffed grouse, as well as sundry game birds which are being imported, such as the Hungarian partridge and the ring-necked pheasants. We have proved it over and over again. They would nest there, then gradually overflow, beginning to restock the surrounding country. From that they spread farther and ever farther.

"By the way, here was another question asked: 'In the case of these creatures that are brought up in a sanctuary, are they not so innocent that when they go outside they become the easy victims of the first gunner that comes along?' No, they don't. Not at all. How often have I seen it demonstrated otherwise!

"I went to Boston not long ago, and there in the sanctuary that has been established in one of the city parks I saw three hundred wild duck come in off the sea to be fed. I stood within ten feet of them, and the keeper fed them out of his hand; they came to him for their daily meal. They played around all day; but when nighttime came they went back out to sea, four or five miles away, and no one could get within a mile of them out there.

"I hope you have heard Jack Miner and know of the splendid work he is doing—the demonstration he is making of these things. Look at the wild geese on his place. They barely move out of your way when you walk among them. But once they are outside the sanctuary, no one can get within gunshot. They are safe in their wariness. You ask, how do they know? That is a mystery; we do not understand. Experience, of course, teaches them in part; the example of leaders helps, and they are wonderfully quick to learn.

"In Yellowstone Park, I could get within twenty feet of the big mountain rams; but outside of that sanctuary, you could not approach within two miles of them. How quickly they realize that they are protected! They respond at once.

"These, then, are the rewards of a sanctuary: first, it gives you a wonderland of wild life, a place in town for the children to go to, a place of exhibition, a place that will offset their visits to some other places of amusement which are not quite so salubrious or so salutary in character. Here is a place where they can go with their cameras— and practically every teen-age child in town nowadays has a camera and rejoices in an opportunity to make pictures of wild life. At once the child begins to take a personal interest in that refuge. He becomes one of the unofficial guardians; and in order to bring in more birds, he puts up new bird boxes. He becomes a part owner—in effect, that place is his. He will work for it and take care of it.

"Meantime he is growing up. And what is happening inside? He has learned the priceless lesson that you can enjoy wild life without trying to destroy it. That was unknown a hundred years ago. The only thought then was: Here is a bird; where is the gun? Now the child learns the other side of the story.

"Very soon those children will be voting, and then you will have no difficulty at all in getting as many sanctuaries established as you please, once more restoring the wild life of this wonderful Northland to any extent compatible with agricultural interests. And, mind you, you have a long, long way to go before those interests clash.

"In conclusion, let me remind you once more that we cannot afford to rob our children of their futurity in natural history. That is what we have been doing, and I appeal to you now to strengthen the hands of the men who have charge of the wild life of this country, and to take such steps as are necessary to conserve the game, and once again give the young men of Canada the right to an annual outing with the gun, without fear that they are depleting the game, that they are robbing the country, that they are robbing the children of their fair and joyful heritage.

"I thank you."

The Small Sanctuary

Seton's address to the Canadian Club was enthusiastically received, and many of his suggestions were promptly acted on.

In this talk, among other practical items, Seton spoke briefly on the value of the small sanctuary. It was a subject very close to his heart, and he many times elaborated on the idea. Of course, we had ourselves established several of these miniature reserves; and being of a very practical turn of mind, we could pass on exact information and details of the necessary construction and the approximate cost.

Everyone is familiar with the great refuges of wild life, like Yellowstone, the Kaibab, the Carson, etc., and how they have demonstrated their perfect solution of the game conservation problem. But large areas like these can be adequately handled only by the government.

By "small sanctuary" is meant a protected area of a few acres. Anything from one acre up to ten is easily converted into a successful refuge for wild life; and to insure its fullest usefulness, it *must* be in or close to the town. One acre in the town is of more value educationally than a thousand acres a hundred miles away.

Out of our various experiments in this line, we evolved the following clear-cut plan.

The ideal small sanctuary has certain requisites: a high fence, not less than seven feet, which is poacher-proof, catproof, dogproof, and ratproof; more or less cover of bushes, trees, and grass; a pond with running water; feeding stands; nesting places; hiding places from which observers can watch; and, last of all, on the premises, a comfortable home for the guardian.

These are the absolute requirements; and note that nothing is said about stock for re-establishing species. That, though sometimes helpful, has proved non-essential; for, granted the sanctuary, the wild things find it out and do their own restocking.

SECURING THE LAND

Most men who are landowners are willing to contribute a few acres for us as a sanctuary, which is, at the same time, a pleasure ground for the public. In some cases it has been found that a twenty-year lease is easily secured for a peppercorn rent when a title in fee simple is not within reach. As land used for such a purpose is usually tax-free, it gives the owner a chance to hold it for a distant rise in values.

CONSTRUCTION

Having secured the ground, the next question is the fencing. The cheapest effective fence is made with a combination of posts, 2×4's, sheet iron, and galvanized wire.

A 5-acre plot calls for 2000 feet of fencing; and in times like these the question of financing such a project is quite serious. The answer, leaving out four which we built and financed ourselves, is as follows:

At several places in the Northwest, where Seton was advocating the small sanctuary, he appealed to the Rotarians, the Lions, the Kiwanians, and other service clubs. He set the project with its advantages before them; and asked who would contribute materials for this educational endeavor.

The response he got was encouraging. The lumberman said: "How many posts will be needed?"

"Two hundred," Seton replied.

"All right," was the rejoinder. "I'll contribute them."

Another lumber dealer said: "How many feet of two-by-fours are needed?"

"Four thousand lineal feet," answered Seton.

"All right, I'll contribute that"; but, being a Scotsman, he added:

"Provided the whole amount needed is raised, and the plan put in operation under responsible hands for completion and upkeep."

Next, the leading town hardware merchant said: "What will the galvanized iron cost, and the chicken wire for the whole fence?"

Seton computed: "We need 80 square feet of galvanized iron for each panel, and there are 200 panels; which calls for 16,000 square feet. The chicken wire needed is 8000 square feet."

"Well, I will furnish the chicken wire for one side." Another gave the galvanized iron for one side, and so on.

In this way, the materials for the fence were secured by donations. In each case it was understood that the name of the donor should be put on his gift.

A 2½-room cottage was built at the entrance. Its free rent was the sufficient payment for a part-time man who was interested in the scheme, his principal duty being at night.

The labor was contributed by the serivce club itself.

OTHER ESSENTIALS

The land and the fence secured, the following remained to be provided: a drinking fountain, a variety of shrubs and different kinds of bird boxes and nesting ledges. These are along the lines set forth by the Audubon Society in its pamphlets; but we have been able to add several valuable features, such as a bank for sand swallows, an artificial hollow tree with many nesting holes, and an island nesting place for water birds.

ENEMIES

The worst enemies of the sanctuary are cats, dogs, blacksnakes, English sparrows, bluejays, crows, Cooper hawks, sharp-shins, and sometimes red squirrels. The fence itself is usually a sufficient answer to the four-foots; and, for the rest, the warden must use a shotgun as soon as the marauder appears and begins its destructive work. Very soon the idea gets about among the potential enemies that such destruction does not pay and the slaughter ceases.

RESULTS

The first happy result is found in the great increase of birds in the sanctuary, for they soon learn that it is a place of safety, and species

rare or previously unknown in the region will find and use the place.
In one of our own sanctuaries of 14 acres, we had 76 species nesting.

But by far the most important result is on the growing generation
of our own species. They learn the birds and their habits; and, above
all, the great lesson that it is not only possible, it is joyfully easy, to be
among wild life and to enjoy it without trying to destroy it.

The Hollow Tree

One of Seton's experiments, absolutely unique so far as I know, was
the building of a hollow tree.

In 1908, knowing that a hollow tree in some sort is essential to the
existence of about one fifth of our birds and one fourth of our
beasts, and realizing also that the fate of all hollow trees is to fall
soon to the blow of the ax, he set about constructing an artificial
hollow tree that would provide not only places of refuge for the
wild things but also numerous points of observation for himself.

He decided to build this on an island, since he just then was more
interested in birds and bats than in mammals. Birds especially prefer
a moat about their castle, and an island was the natural choice for
the location.

Six tall chestnut trees with curves in their lower parts were cut and
skinned, giving timbers 10 inches through at the base, and 35 feet high.
These were planted to enclose a 7-foot circle at the bottom and a
3-foot circle at the top. Each of the six uprights was braced four ways
with massive chestnut timbers, on which the bark was carefully preserved. Then over all was made a good roof of boards and painted
canvas.

A ladder inside, some floors cutting it into stories, and many wall
boxes with entrance holes from outside and peepholes inside, completed the tree itself.

It was filled full of stone for 7 feet up and the island built higher
so as to bury the lower part 6 feet deep and make the anchorage
doubly good.

On the roof, he nailed two or three heavy and crooked chestnut
sticks. He cut holes of various sizes, designed for the various birds and
beasts that he hoped to have come. He nailed several jagged hollow

branches at certain points, and the tree was ready for occupancy.

For nearly three months no bird or animal used the tree. But, little by little, first tracks appeared in the vicinity, and then gradually one and another entered and built nests or other living quarters.

Seton, on the ladder installed inside the tree, watched and sketched and collected pellets, etc., for hours of each day. The pellets he sent to the Biological Survey in Washington for analysis. Thus he learned the exact food habits of his tenants.

He sprinkled the floors of the nesting boxes with colored sand so that he could by the tracks know exactly where his birds and beasties went and what they did. In order to know whether one creature was in several boxes, he used different-colored powders. Some had red ocher, some yellow, some plaster of Paris, some lampblack, and others just fine sand. Each morning, after noting the tracks, he sifted and smoothed the sand on the floor, and was ready for a new thrill of discovery.

For over a year Seton make accurate observations, noting every newcomer and following the adventures of each visitor to this welcome addition to the woods. He had given an identifying number to each box, so was able to keep a record that makes exciting reading and a real contribution to our knowledge of the wild things that we so rarely see in their daily domestic lives.

Seton has written in this connection: "The hollow tree is not simply a hollow tree combined with a biological station and laboratory—it is above all things a broad principle. If we wish to save the wood creatures, we must guarantee them their homes. . . . Odd nesting boxes compared with a hollow tree are what a wayside prayer-box is to a cathedral."

It is difficult at this time to give a complete list of all the birds and beasties that used the tree. But I do know that, among others, it comfortably harbored flickers, swallows, martins, starlings, a screech owl, nuthatches, many deermice, coons, a flying squirrel, and wasps.

On one occasion he found a dead mouse in the nest of a screech owl. He took the mouse back to his study and there identified it as the *Microtus pinetorum*, which stands still as the only Connecticut record, and is preserved in the United States National Museum.

For over a year Seton made careful daily records of every episode that occurred in connection with his experiment, proving beyond any shadow of doubt that it answered in fullest measure the ends of its creation. I can assure anyone so minded that he will reap from such an endeavor pleasure and profit that are hard to duplicate in any other way.

Making a Swallow Bank

A source of great joy to us was an artificial swallow bank which we built on a sandy, gravelly hillside of our land while we were still living in the East. Here we dug a straight face some 6 feet high and 20 feet long. Even while we were working on it, two pairs of bank swallows fluttered around or perched impatiently on .some near-dead limbs, twittering "Hurry up there, we want to get busy."

The very next day they were at it and had dug in two holes each over a foot deep. But a drenching rain came and sliced the whole front off the bank, reducing it again to a mere slope on the hillside. So the swallows sought a home elsewhere.

"Now," said Seton, "I will make something that the rain will not wash away." So, selecting a rocky ledge by the lake, he built a masonry wall 6 feet high and 12 feet long, with an 8-foot portion at each end running inland.

In the top front edge of the masonry he set a 2-inch loop of strong wire every two feet. When all was hard-set, he fastened a 2-foot stake in each wire loop, braced it at the top, then laid a row of boards behind this. In the form or box thus made, he put a 6-inch layer of the stiffest clay he could find, well wetted and hammered down. Over this he packed a 3-inch layer of sand, then a layer of smooth clay. On this he laid a roof of boards and rubberoid paper, more or less disguised, but frankly a roof.

The work was begun August fourth; but though it took only one week of actual work, other interests intervened so that it was not finished until September twentieth.

All winter we left up that form or front.

For the sixteenth of April, next year, I find this note in Seton's journal: "Took down the board form from the swallow bank. The brown damp clay with the sandy streaks looks like a section of a bride's cake."

This was the unveiling. We followed it up by cutting away all branches that came too near.

Throughout 1922 the bank was a disappointment. The speedy success of the first sand wall had led us to think that there would at once be a thriving swallow colony in this. But not a swallow came near, nor was it used all summer by any bird.

In the spring of 1923 we one day found three beginnings of a kingfisher den. Later, one of them, that near the middle of the wall, was completed; and in this the kingfisher brood was raised.

Next winter the storms and frost caused a good deal of clay to fall from the front of the bank. The three holes made by the kingfisher were more or less spoiled by this, but the "wampum-bearer" is a stronghearted bird, and in 1925 she made a new den at one end. In this she successfully raised her young; while, in the middle of the bank, a phoebe bird raised two, if not three, broods.

But never a swallow came near, so far as we knew. If only the pernickety little sinners had come frankly forward and told us what was wrong with our bank, or what new feature would please them, we would certainly have tried to make it as they wished. For there is no more lively, lovely sight in birdland than a swarming, teeming bank that is a home colony of the pest-devouring swallow.

We planned to make another bank with a 6-foot wall at each end, a 4-foot wall in front, layers of concrete an inch thick alternating with layers of sandy clay 3 inches thick, the whole bank to be 3 feet wide. Over this we were going to build a concrete roof.

But somehow we never did get to this, so are unable to report on its success or failure.

The Pond

Once we made a dam across a little stream on our land, and so created a pond. After it had been there long enough to be an accepted feature of the landscape we, acting on a new whim, broke the dam and let the waters all escape.

It was a small matter to us, but what a commotion we made in the little wet world we had produced!

We had no idea so many living creatures could congregate in so small a place. There were dozens of turtles of all sizes crawling away on the mud, and several water snakes went wriggling off with them. A number of marsh birds, of course, escaped easily from their ruined homeland, and a score of eels had little difficulty in hiding in the mud.

The shoals of fish and the thousands of polliwogs and insects, however, were everywhere overwhelmed. The bottom of the pond was strewn thickly over with crawling, gasping, wriggling, twinkling swarms, vainly seeking for water—for water, which to them meant life.

But the flood went swiftly through the dam, the few remaining pools were drained; and in an hour the bottom of the pond was like an army battlefield strewn thickly over with the dead. Half a dozen pickerel that had sought refuge in the one spot that still resembled a pool maintained a gasping life for an hour or more, their backs above the shallow dirty water, their gills choking with the mud. But they too at last succumbed and lay on their sides, showing their silvery bellies among the throngs of dead and flabby polliwogs.

A little later we came back and saw the wholesale carnage. We stood before it, thinking. We had undoubtedly been within our legal rights. It was our land, our stream, our pond, our dam. We had made it as we pleased, we had a right to unmake it when we pleased.

Had we? What about the "vested rights" of the hundred thousand lives that we had destroyed while fully within our legal rights? "Sovereign right of man," "heaven-given right of the strongest," were phrases that came up.

We could reason and reason. We could prove we had done no wrong; and then remember that Blackstone says in effect, "No man has the right to take the life of an animal for mere caprice." But words are poor things. They fly by chance to glance and strike like arrows.

Feelings are older and safer guides, and we only know we love to see *life*. We glory in an abundance of it about us, and it fills us with sorrow to see unnecessary wholesale destruction of living beings.

When I hear of a rich man founding a newspaper for his amusement (as has been done many times), and abandoning it with its staff at the next whim; when I hear of a man ousting his uncompensated crofters from their ancestral holdings in order to use the land for other purposes (which also has been done), I think of our dam, and realize that life is more sacred than property, and no technicality of man-made law can shield us from the responsibility of power.

Vivisection

One winter, on a lecture tour, Seton checked into a hotel in Washington; and, while registering, noted an unusual number of women milling about the lobby.

Not long after he got to his room he realized the reason. A call came to him from the president of one of the national associations interested in animal welfare, which organization was holding its annual convention in the city, with headquarters at that particular hotel.

"Oh, Mr. Seton," came a saccharine voice over the phone, "we have just found out that you are in the city, at the very moment when our organization is about to open its convocation in the ballroom of this hotel. We can think of nothing more inspiring than to have you give your views on our work, as the introductory message of the meeting. Would you honor us with a little talk to our hundreds of members?"

"But, madam," Seton replied, "I do not belong to your organization."

"We know that, Mr. Seton—to our sorrow. But you are a friend to animals, and anything that you might say would be stimulating."

"It might be too stimulating," Seton answered warily.

"That I am sure could not be. All the world knows you and your work with animals. You love them very much."

"Perhaps too much to serve your purpose."

"No, no," she broke in. "I can assure you that you will have a most enthusiastic audience."

"But, madam, you might not like what I have to say on the subject. I assure you it would be wiser for you to find another speaker."

"No, no, Mr. Seton," came the silky voice. "Nothing would be more interesting than to listen to your remarks on a subject that is so dear to our hearts."

A moment's hesitation, and Seton replied: "Very well, madam, but the penalty be on your own head."

The woman laughed gently with assurance and delight in having achieved her end.

The members were even then assembling in the ballroom; and Seton, without time for any preparation, but with strong convictions on the subject, went down to the platform.

While being introduced, he found himself facing an audience of some four hundred women, dressed in the height of fashion, apparently a wealthy group with little of the world's real work to do. And three males—all three clergymen.

A brief pause as he looked them over, making a rapid appraisal. Then he slowly began:

"All animals have certain incontrovertible, inalienable, God-given rights."

A burst of applause from the entire audience.

A pause while again he estimated his hearers, then deliberately continued:

"All human beings have certain incontrovertible, inalienable, God-given rights."

Applause, but not so general.

A slightly longer silence before he again took up the thread.

"When animal and human rights clash, of course human rights must predominate."

Murmurs of dissent, a few low growls of displeasure, and a voice vaguely heard above the hum:

"What do you mean?"

"Well," Seton calmly rejoined, "I have a little daughter at home. If my child's eyesight, or limb, or life were threatened, and I could save it by sacrificing the eyesight, or limb, or life of an animal, I would not hesitate to do so."

Then the fight was on.

"You have no right! You cannot do it! You would not dare! You should be stoned!"

"What!" Seton exclaimed. "I have no right to put my child's welfare above that of an animal?"

"No! No! You have no right!" came the general shout.

One woman strode to the front and flourished her fist under his nose. "I would rather see my child dead in his grave than to know that I had purchased his life by that of a dog!"

"Then, madam," Seton quietly replied, "you have no child." He was correct—she was a spinster with a poodle dog.

"I have a child," spoke up another woman, tearfully. "And I could not stand the thought of an animal suffering to give him or me a pleasure, or even a surcease from pain."

"Madam!" and now Seton had to raise his voice in order to be heard above the din. "You are wearing a mink coat. There are over three hundred mink skins in that coat. It represents three days of mortal agony in a trap on the part of every one of those three hundred little animals, in order to give you that unnecessary decoration for your personal pleasure."

She was quieted for a moment now, but up spoke another: "Well, I am not wearing a fur coat, and I feel the same as my sister here does."

"No, madam, you sport no fur coat," quickly replied Seton, "but you are wearing a silk dress. Do you know that thousands of worms had to be boiled alive to give you that superfluous embellishment?"

This one was stilled, hard put to find an answer promptly enough.

Another woman shouted above the din: "I have no fur and no silk, and you cannot say that to me!"

"No, madam, but you are wearing leather shoes. Have you ever been to the Chicago stockyards to see how that leather is obtained?"

A gasp of horror was the only answer to this, but another voice was heard accusingly:

"Does not our Bible tell us: 'Are not two sparrows sold for a farthing? And not one of them shall fall on the ground unless your Father wills it.'"

"Yes," and now Seton himself had difficulty being heard. "But go on with the quotation!"

She could not, so he did it for her: "'Fear ye not therefore, ye are of more value than many sparrows.'"

This, to be sure, did not serve their purpose, and the meeting broke up in a near riot. Seton escaped to his room by a backstage door.

He immediately called the principal newspaper and gave an amusing account of the episode. The next morning Washington was greeted by a headline: "Seton Puts Poodle Dog Women in Their Place."

The president of the association at once called on the editor to give her version of the story, but was politely told that that was now ancient history and the paper could not reopen the controversy.

Years later we were staying in a Midwestern town one night, when a clergyman and his wife came to introduce themselves.

"We were in the audience that day in Washington, when you told the Poodle Dog Women what you thought of them."

"You were!" I exclaimed. "And where did you stand on the question?"

"Oh, we were wholly on your side. In fact, the majority of the audience were on your side. It was only the noisy ones who made the stir."

"Well, why didn't you get up and help the cause which Mr. Seton was sponsoring?"

"Why, he was taking ample care of himself," the cleric replied. "He did not need help from anyone."

In discussing the incident later, Seton said certain things which might have been said at the time of the meeting, but which he was given no opportunity to express. He could have started out with much that would have been quite acceptable to that group. But, by the end of his dissertation, he would have been right back to his unalterable conclusion.

"Aside from sentimental or aesthetic reasons," he claimed, "the extinction of a large or highly organized animal is a serious matter."

In a prior manuscript, he points out that, "first, it is always dangerous to disturb the balance of nature by removing a poise. Some of the worst plagues have arisen in this way.

"Second, we do not know, without much careful experiment, how vast a service that animal might have rendered to mankind as a domestic species.

"The force of this will be more apparent if we recollect how much the few well-known domestic species have done for the advancement of our race. Who can decide which has done more for mankind— the cow or the steam engine, the horse or electricity, the sheep or the printing press, the dog or the rifle, the ass or the loom? No one, indeed, can pronounce on these; yet all, on reflection, feel that there is reason in the comparisons. True, take away these inventions, and we are put back a century, or perhaps two; but also, take away the domestic animals, and we are reduced to absolute savagery, for it was they who first made it possible for our aboriginal forefathers to settle in one place and learn the rudiments of civilization.

"It is quite possible, though of course not demonstrable, that the humble chuckie barn fowl has been a larger benefactor of our race than any mechanical invention in our possession, for there is no inhabited country on earth today where the barn fowl is not one of the mainstays of health. There are vast regions of South America and Europe where it is *the* mainstay, and nowhere is there known anything that can take its place. This is perhaps more than can be said of anything in the world of mechanics.

"Now, domestication succeeds only after long and persistent effort and, in effect, a remodeling of the wild animal by selective breeding. If the early hunters had succeeded in exterminating what are now our domestic animals before their stock was sufficiently tamed, the loss to the world would have been a very serious matter. It might well have been more far-reaching than the loss of any invention; for an idea born of other ideas can be lost but temporarily, while the destruction of an organized being is irreparable.

"Therefore, we today who deliberately exterminate any large and useful, possibly domesticable, wild animal may be doing more harm to the country than if we robbed it of its navy.

"This is the most obvious economic view of the question of extermination. But there is at least one other, a yet higher one, which in the end will prove more truly economic. We are informed, on excellent authority, that man's most important business here is 'to know himself.'"

"Evidently one cannot comprehend the nature of a wheel in a machine by study of that wheel alone; one must consider the whole machine or fail. And since it is established that man is merely a wheel in the great machine called the universe, he can never arrive at a comprehension of himself without study of the other wheels also. Therefore, to know himself man must study not only himself but all things to which he is related. This is the motive of all scientific research.

"There is no part of our environment that is not filled with precious facts bearing on the great problem, and the nearer they are to us, the more they concern us.

"Each advance of science enables us to get more facts out of the same source, so that something that is studied today may yield a hundred times the value that it could or did ten years ago; and if that source of knowledge happens to be perishable, one can do the race no greater harm than by destroying it.

"The Sibylline Books were supposed to contain all necessary wisdom. They were destroyed, one by one, because the natural heir to that wisdom did not realize their value. He did wake up at last, but it was too late to save anything except a fragment. What Tarquin did to the books offered by the Cumaean Sibyl, our own race in America has done to some much more valuable books offered by nature.

"To illustrate: Each animal is in itself an inexhaustible volume of facts that man must have in order to solve the great problem of knowing himself. One by one, not always deliberately, these wonderful volumes have been destroyed, and the facts that might have been read in them have been lost."

It is hard to imagine a greater injury to the world of thought—which is after all the real world—than the destruction of one of these wonderful unread volumes. It is possible that the study of "man" would suffer more by the extinction of some highly organized animal than it did by the burning of the Alexandrian library.

THE VALUE OF LIFE

"While discussing each quadruped in its relation to man, one must keep in mind not only the scientific worth of the creature and its commercial and aesthetic values but also the value of sport. The responsibility of extermination grows greater with each fresh investigation, so that we are compelled to consider seriously the action even of the scientific naturalist who kills and collects. Is he justified? All thoughtful men must set this high value on life, yet realize that every life must be spent. Is it not a candle made to be burnt?

"Stephenson gave his life to the development of the locomotive; Jenner devoted his years and his powers to perfecting vaccination; Wilberforce consecrated his all to the abolition of slavery. In each case the world said, 'Nobly done—a life well spent.' Nothing is more sacred than human life, and still we say 'well done' when it is given to a good cause. But it was not Stephenson's life alone that was sacrificed to the locomotive; his was merely the last, the crowning point of a thousand who went before and gave themselves to the development of the idea that he consummated. Nevertheless, no man pretends to say that all those earlier lives were wasted or could have been better bestowed.

"One great idea is worth countless human lives. And if human lives, why not the lives of lower creatures? One new fact in science is worth unnumbered birds. One new ray of light on our being is cheaply bought by the death of many beasts."

This was Seton's belief and his attitude toward all scientific collecting *in wise and competent hands*. "I believe in it," he says, "just as surely as I believe in amputating a diseased limb. I believe in human and animal vivisection, provided always it is done within reasonable limit that shall insure a movement toward the purpose for which it is permitted.

"Why? To what purpose all this study? It sounds mere platitude if we say we are seeking for the laws of life. A more modest announcement will have more force. We find that by study of the animal we can learn about ourselves. It is like being locked in a house which we have never seen; and yet, by looking at an opposite house of similar lines and magnitude, we may learn of the material and the architect's plan in our own. All this study, then, is light on ourselves from the animal. If we have a minute and profound study of the animal's body combined with a minute and profound study of its environment, we shall have light on the laws of environment, and this means a comprehension of all the unhappy misfits that we call 'Disease.'

"The first step toward remedying an evil is comprehension of it; the man who takes the first step toward an understanding of bubonic plague is taking the first step toward conquering it. As I pointed out more than fifty years ago, he who will explain the immunity of the house sparrow from smallpox, of the white bear and the seal from rheumatism, and of the flamingo and the buffalo from malaria, is on the way to conferring on man a like immunity. Everyone knows that we have learned to conquer many human diseases by study of them in the animals. There is every reason to believe that when our biologists shall have completed the investigation now being actively pursued in their laboratories, we shall be in a position to abolish mosquitoes, not by costly destruction of beautiful lily ponds, but by something much more simple. We shall be able to control and eventually cure cancer by methods which have at least indicated success in the experiments on animals over the years of sincere attempts to learn, years in which it was necessary to sacrifice the lives of thousands of animals in order to confer this inestimable blessing on mankind."

PART SEVEN

FLARES IN THE DARK

THE HUMANITIES

Museum Jargon

Even on the most academic subjects, Seton's sense of humor was always ready. He poked a bit of fun at his naturalist associates in the following.

"I wonder if we naturalists realize that we are in peril of a museum jargon; that is, a special, involved, peculiar, verbose, pompous dialect that seems to us necessary in writing, when we wish to impress our audience with the idea that we are very serious about this. I give some samples from real life.

"One distinguished writer watched some flying squirrels at play until, as he says, 'the last shadows of day had disappeared and darkness admonished us to leave the little triflers to their nocturnal enjoyments.' The context shows that the writer meant 'till nightfall.'

"Another writes: 'I can assert—and that from ocular demonstration—etc.' In plain words, 'I have seen.'

"Yet another says: 'My curiosity induced me to intervene.' Why not simply 'I wanted to see'?

"'In view of the circumstances,' writes one inflated wordmonger, 'the writer is impelled, after a mature consideration of the accumulated evidence in the case, to agree with those who take a partly, if not wholly, negative view of the theory implied.' What he meant was 'I think not.'

"Another cautious writer says; 'The brood probably averages close to about 5 in number.' Wouldn't it be better to say: 'The brood averages 5'?

"'Always biting off the asperities [of the acorns]' is a high-sounding way of saying, 'always biting off the points.'

"'Both combatants were apparently perfectly oblivious of the observer's presence,' says a recent writer who meant 'They seemed not to see me.'

"A favorite phrase is 'It bears a considerable resemblance to,' when, obviously, the author means 'It is like.'

"A pearl of its kind is found in a well-known work thus: 'Negotiating an intervening space of approximately in the neighborhood of about 3 metres.' One can discern on careful study the phrase that the writer meant 'was covering about 10 feet.'

"One of the most frequent occurrences in standard works is 'The basal portion of the hairs is black, the apical section pale ochraceous.' Why not 'Hairs black with yellowish tips'?

"Another modest naturalist covers his retreat in this subterfuge: 'The writer has not personally been privileged to examine the specimens in question.' A little study shows that he meant: 'I have not seen them.'

"In a solemn departmental publication we learn that a certain animal 'is charged with committing serious depredations on the products of agricultural industry.' More of the people would have been reached had the report read: 'It is said to do damage to crops.'

"Still another authority, modestly assuming the third person, says: 'The author has endeavored strenuously to initiate this obviously novel concept of organized investigation.' The paragraph on examination could have been perfectly well rendered as 'I tried to begin in a new way.'

"In a standard work I find this phrase: 'Snow may be falling in quantities sufficient to obstruct the vision.' Had the writer said, 'A blinding snowstorm,' he would have saved time, space, and energy, as well as have given a better picture.

"I shall never forget the printed announcement of a naturalist friend to the effect that 'recent constructive activity had resulted in a duplication of auroligneous specimens of leonine zoology in the environs of our commercial world.' This, we found, meant that there were now '*two* golden lions among the trade signs of the town.'

"A name is the handle of a fact, and the fact is more often useful if the handle to it be convenient. There are two or three methods of providing the handle. The first is the arbitrary, such as Ruskin and others have used. Examples in point are 'Fors Clavigera,' 'Prosperina,' 'Friends,' etc. The objection made to these is that they give no clue to the content. That may be true on first seeing the work, but it is a short-lived condition; and in actual service, brevity of title is a thousand times better than long descriptiveness, which is the next method. As examples of titles that are not titles, and never should have been offered as such, take the following:

"'Synonomy, Description, History, Distribution, and Habits of the Prairie-hare (*Lepus campestris*).'

"Another even worse is: 'Ontogenetic and Other Variations in Gollywogs, with a systematic Review for the Gollywog Group Recent and Extinct.' Imagine quoting that in a reference! Why did not the writer call it simply 'Gollywog Monograph,' then add as much as he pleased in a secondary position?

"That this case is far from unique is shown by the following attempt to put the whole book in the title: 'Preliminary Biological and Ecological Reconnaissance of Certain Parts of the State of Omgush, eliminating such Areas as are adequately Treated in the Reports of the Agricultural Commission.' How much more convenient had he called it 'Field Notes in Omgush' or 'Omgush Notes' or 'Codex Oliver'—anything if only brief and simple.

"Another dreadful phrase that is growing in length and intensity is such as 'An Annotated Check List of the Mammalian Fauna of Borrioboolagah, Within the Limits of Equatorial Nigritia, Excluding however those Portions of Lower Ethiopia and the southeastern Soudan, which Include the Nile Drainage Basin, with Remarks on their Ontogenetic Affinities.' Why not 'Mammals of Nigritia,' and put the rest in the book itself where it belongs?

"Why has the ancient and honorable phrase 'Field Notes' been displaced by 'Biological Reconnaissance'? What good is achieved by these ever-piling-up complications and meticulous distinctions?

"If we are to accept the literal meaning of each name as the test before using it, then not one of our names will stand. A prairie dog is not a dog. A ground hog is not a hog, an elk is not an elk, a flying fox is not a fox, a mountain beaver is not a beaver, a muskrat is not a rat, a jack rabbit is not a rabbit, a cottontail has no cotton on its tail, a musk ox is not an ox, a buffalo is not a buffalo, a flying squirrel does not fly, a mountion lion is not a lion, an antelope is not an antelope.

"And yet each of these names has grown up and established itself in common usage, and therefore is here to stay, in spite of its doubtful connotation.

"The other day, in the magazine *Vision*, I ran across an article by Lorne A. Anderson, which treats this same subject from a different point of view. I cannot do better than close with a sentence from that article. It runs as follows:

"'In promulgating your esoteric cogitations or articulating your superficial sentimentalities and amicable philosophical observations, beware of platitudinous ponderosity. . . .' In other words, talk plainly, briefly, naturally, sensibly. Say what you mean, mean what you say, and don't use big words.

"In short, avoid 'museum jargon.'"

English Names of Our Animals

A further development of a similar idea is in the following article written over fifty years ago:

"During the last few years I have been brought into continual consideration of the English names of our animals, especially of our mammals. I have had occasion to discuss these with many of our best scientific taxonomists, and am surprised to find that these authorities are disposed to apply to English names the same rules as those which dictate the scientific names. This is primarily and rigidly the law of priority.

"In all matters relating to the scientific names, I meekly and respectfully bow my head to the authoritative decisions of this present group, the mammalologists of America. But when it comes to the English names, I am possessed of no such meekness; and, having made the subject a lifelong study, am quite prepared, if need be, to stand alone.

"On this very subject, I wrote some forty years ago [now over eighty years ago] in the *Auk*, and advanced views that I hold even more strongly today.

"The scientific names are, as I have conceded, wholly in control of the scientists; but with the popular names said scientists as such have no more right to disagree than with the English dictionary. The popular names are wholly in the keeping of the people, that is, the genius of English. The scientist has a voice, just as he has a place in the nation; but it is a weak and feeble voice, less potent than that of an unlettered cowboy or farmer, as I think we shall see.

"What is meant by the genius of English I shall try to make plain; and if, among my readers, there be, as I can readily believe, scholars who know the subject a hundred times better than do I, let me crave their indulgence with this explanation. My approach is purely empirical; I never had it given to me academically. Therefore, my theories may be erroneous. Yet to this I add with absolute confidence— my facts, my observations, and examples are *not* wrong; and by them I stand without expectation of contradiction or rebuttal.

"The genius of a language may be defined as the peculiar vital force which, like the life of a tree, gives it its continual growth in certain directions, its digestive power, its peculiar form and development in spite of obstacles and restraints; and, above all, makes it the expression of the mode of thought, the mental growth and psychological peculiarities of the nation to which it belongs.

"In other words, language is a living thing, the expression of a nation's thoughts and growth, done into sounds. Its genius is responsible for peculiarities of pronunciation, stress, idiom, and of accidence, and is the hidden force which determines its tendencies and the direction of the language's changes and growth.

"The instinct of the English language demands among other things

"a. That the word be composed of the sounds represented in or by our alphabet.

"b. A marked rhythm of word and phrase.

"c. A continual forward movement of the accent; till, at last, it is likely to rest on the first syllable, the others being subordinated, sometimes excessively.

"d. The qualifying word must normally precede the word qualified.

"e. A continual trend toward the monosyllable, effected by the dropping of terminal, unimportant parts.

"f. The slow elimination of parts difficult to pronounce, such as *r* at the end of a word.

"g. A continual straining for patness, closely associated with the foregoing; that is, for a word that is short, easily said, and of pleasant sounds or surprising syllables.

"h. A definite unwillingness to accept a new word or sound not composed of familiar elements.

"i. Relationship to Teutonic rather than Romance essentials.

"j. A strong preference toward consonantism.

"k. A continual tendency to degrade and flatten the vowels, so that in time *Ah* becomes A, *Ay* becomes *e*, etc.

"There are other singularities and urges in the English language genius, but these are the special forces to be considered in a study of English popular names of animals.

"As instances of the working of the laws: On early maps of the Northwest, you see a certain lake called *Man-i-tou-wá-ba*. The ordinary attrition of use common to all languages reduced this to Manitobá, the then dominant French influence putting the accent on the last syllable. About 1870 the English settlers began to flood the region around this lake, and the name was applied to the new province then created. The accent moved forward so that when I went to live there in 1882 it was *Manitóba*. The process continues, and today more and more you hear *Mánitoba*, never *Manitobá* except from a Frenchman or other foreigner.

"As illustration of the monosyllabic trend, note the death of various words in the West. *Mountain* is now displaced by *Mount* and *Peak*; *Revolver* is wholly gone in favor of *Gun*; *Caballos, Cayuse, Broncho, Pony* are all gone, with *Horse* triumphant. *Lariata, Lariat, Lasso* are one by one being shifted to *Rope*.

"The strong tendency to transmute a strange word into familiar elements is seen in the growth of the word *Woodchuck*. Originally it was *Otchek*, which the Hudson Bay settlers Englished into *Woodshock*, then into *Woodchuck*, and now even into *Chuck*.

"A still more interesting demonstration is seen in *Coyote*. The original English discoverers of this animal called it *Prairie Barking Wolf*, which, of course, is not a name, but a long description, a temporary expedient pending a real name. In ancient Mexican it was *Coyotl*, which, under Spanish influence, speedily became *Coyóte*, with the accent on the penult. Traveling northward, the word encountered French influence in Louisiana and became *Cóyote*. Going still farther northward, it entered the region of English influence, with the usual results; first, the accent was moved forward; second, the non-essential termination was dropped, so it became the disyllable *Coyote*. Continuing to meet the chemical disintegration of the English mode with its flattening of the vowels, it became *Cayote*, and now even *Kiyute* in the western parts of Canada.

"A hundred examples of this process could be cited.

"In the department of birds, the genius of English is hard at work

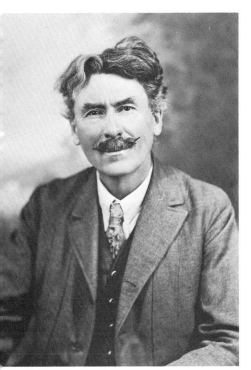

14. Seton, 1921 to 1930

15. Standing Rock Village, showing Seton gratifying the heart of a brave, 1903

16. Seton teaching fire making, 1903

17. Artificial swallow bank.

18. Seton laying cornerstone of the first Boy Scout building in the world, Baltimore, 1911

19. De Winton garage—
an early house in Seton Village

20. Bust of Seton by Clare Dieman, 1923 (Photo by Mark Clayton)

with excellent results coining good names as familiarity with the creature requires. *Parti-colored Rice Troupial* became *Bobolink; Virginia Colin* became *Bobwhite; Carolina Goatsucker* became *Whippoorwill; Virginia Goatsucker, Bullbat; Golden-winged Woodpecker, Flicker; Virginia Horned Owl, Cat Owl; Yellow-bellied Woodpecker, Sapsucker; Black-capped Titmouse, Chickadee; Virginia Cardinal, Redbird.*

"In vain, the scientists scolded the public, tried to make the natives use a foolish and impossible word because it was the first given. The answer was apathetic silence; but all the while the genius of English was at work. It will continue to evolve a good descriptive name for each species as soon as it becomes familiar, that is, a part of our daily lives.

"There are usually four stages in the evolution of a new name, that is, a new word. First, it is slang; next, it enters the dictionary as 'colloquial' or 'vulgar' with a note of apology. Then it comes into general or popular use. Last, the quotations are removed, and it appears as of good usage; it is now a dictionary word.

"This is precisely the history of each popular name for our mammals or birds. Its life begins in the gutter or the pioneer camp and finishes in the dictionary.

"We frowned for long on those who offered English plurals for Latin words; but, as always, the force of our language was irresistible. It is now quite proper to say: fauna, faunas: foetus, foetuses; fungus, funguses; formula, formulas. Thus, in spite of scientists and dictionaries, the spirit of our speech is marching on.

"In summing up, then, the popular English names of animals are as much a part of the language as the conjugation of the verb *to be*. They must be produced by the genius of language, operating on the material at hand, under the inspiration of familiarity with the creature—that is, the need for a name. In selecting these names, the farm boy, the cowboy, and the schoolboy are more influential than all the scientists of the Smithsonian, the Biological Survey, and the museums put together; because these simple folk have, first, a vast majority; and, second, are absolutely, though usually unconsciously, dominated by the spirit of simple English, whereas the scientists have had their minds clouded by theories and poisoned with Latin and Greek.

"Those scientists who wish to further the cause will not try to enforce any mechanical laws of priority, but look out for the right name which, in spite of them, will in time surely be evolved for each species; and by noting, using, and helping it, advance the whole cause of popular natural history."

It is for these reasons that in his *magnum opus, Lives of Game Animals,* Seton has given every English name that has been or might be used, leaving the ultimate choice to the rationality of the language.

A Broader View in Nomenclature

In the serious scientific field, Seton considered the names of the animals as he had those of the human species, with very little difference in point of view. Back in the twenties, he wrote one article in which he says:

"When Linnaeus established the binomial system, he aimed to indicate, in the first name, broad resemblance; and, in the second, specific difference.

"As facts and material accumulated, it was inevitable that we should make changes and refinements; but surely it is obvious to all that the systematists have continually split and reduced, till now we have, in the first term of a binomial, expressed small difference and, in the second, minute or microscopic—yes, in some cases, imaginary—difference. The logical finish of the present trend—a finish even now in sight—is a separate genus for each species, with an array of more or less doubtful geographical races to give color and justification to the method. Frequently these races differ less from the typical form than variant individuals from the same brood differ from one another—often races on such slight grounds that no one, not even the expert, will undertake to name them without full data, especially as to locality.

"There can be little doubt that a study of geographical distribution will eventually teach us the laws that created these races. But the constant degradation in the value of group names tends to blind one to the large aspects that evidence the bigger laws.

"As I pore over Nelson's elaborate monograph of 'The Rabbits of

North America' (Fauna No. 29), the last word in rabbit study, I am dismayed by the conclusions of this gifted naturalist.

"When Dr. J. A. Allen monographed the American *Leporidae* in 1877, he recognized 3 genera and 18 species and varieties; among them, but 1 cottontail with 4 geographical races. With vastly more material comes Nelson thirty-two years later, and announces 97 species and subspecies of hares, and 4 species of rabbits or cottontails with 44 geographical races.

"No doubt these additions are justified by the specimens he had in hand. But it seems to me that it is not a helpful change when one sees the genera *Lepus* and *Ochotona* elevated into families; the subgenera, such as *Sylvilagus*, into genera; geographical races, such as *auduboni* and *nuttallii*, into full species; and a host of slight variants into formally named geographical races.

"Does this fine splitting help or hinder science? It seems to me it does incalculable harm. It obscures or ignores the larger considerations of affinity. It leaves the nomenclature at the mercy of each new monographer, whose training is all calculated to make him magnify unimportant details. It antagonizes the public, and thus prevents the spread of knowledge. It robs nomenclature of all stability, and threatens to bring down with a crash the whole system involved.

"What is the answer to the problem raised? One is not quite prepared to go back to the vast comprehensive genera of Linnaeus. Nor can one afford to lose the results of recent careful studies with the abundant material made available for the first time.

"My own preference is best shown by an illustration. I have on my desk a completed monograph of the Life Histories of the Cats, Wolves, and Foxes of America, north of the Rio Grande. The check list of the U. S. National Museum gives these species as I have listed them in the first column below. It would, I think, afford a far broader view, and would equally conserve the results of modern study, if we used the older names, as in the second column.

	(*Subgenus Felis*)
Felis onca	Felis onca
Felis cougar	Felis cougar
Felis pardalis	Felis pardalis
Felis eyra	Felis eyra

	(*Subgenus Lynx*)
Lynx canadensis	Felis canadensis
Lynx rufus	Felis rufus
	(*Subgenus Canis*)
Canis nubilus	Canis nubilus
Canis latrans	Canis latrans
Canis mearnsi	Canis mearnsi
	(*Subgenus Vulpes*)
Vulpes fulvus	Canis fulvus
Vulpes velox	Canis velox
Vulpes macrotis	Canis macrotis
	(*Subgenus Alopex*)
Alopex lagopus	Canis lagopus
	(*Subgenus Urocyon*)
Urocyon cinereoargenteus	Canis cinereoargenteus

"The objection has been raised that in this case the subgeneric name does not appear in the scientific name; to which I reply: 'Neither does the family name or the order, but they are there in all their force for those who seek full light on classification.' I yield to none in admiration for the fine work that is being done by our monographic naturalists; and yet I feel bound to offer these remarks because they reflect the views, not only of the public, but also of at least a large number of our biologists.

"In brief, shall we accept the principles of broad comprehensive genera that emphasize relationship, or shall we go on at the present speed, till we have a genus established for each and every species?"

A Review

Several burlesques Seton perpetrated, and many a good laugh we had over them. Carrying on the thought in the last chapter, he satirized as follows:

"We are glad to acclaim the superb monograph on the 'Geographical Distribution of Hats, with a Revision of their Nomenclature,' by D. F. Hatteras of Matteawan, N.Y.* This is the most important con-

* Smithereens of Knowledge, Bull. No. 1000.

tribution to integumental zoology in many years, and on a subject only too long neglected.

"Beginning at the foundation, Dr. Hatteras revises the old genus *Capo*, raising it to the rank of a Family, the *Capidae*. As he points out, it is composed of two well-marked subfamilies, the *Capinae* and the *Sombrerinae*. Although their territories overlap a little in the West, they may be defined as Northern and Southern groups respectively.

"The original monotypic genus *Capo* is now and herein replaced by 20 genera and 40 distinct species with nearly 100 geographical races.

"For example, the wonderful *Sombrero* group is represented in Canada by the aberrant forms *Sombrero canadensis policensis*** (sp. nov. nob.), ranging through the Campestrian, but grading rather abruptly into *Sombrero canadensis redriverensis* (sp. nov. nob.) in the Winnipeg country. Farther south, *policensis* merges into the wider-brimmed *jamesorum* (in honor of Jesse James). In the Upper Sonoran, it is displaced by the true *Sombrero stetsoniensis* (sp. nov. nob.), which, curiously enough, finds its type locality in the Montgomery Ward Region of the Chicago lowlands.

"Though aware of its existence, the author wisely refrains from differentiating by name the type which he might well have called *Sombrero stetsoniensis stockyardensis* (sp. nov. nob. nit.).

"Farther south, that is, in New Mexico, we see the first development of the race (species?) *latifrons* (sp. nov. nob.). This in the Panhandle of Texas gives place to the superb *Sombrero texensis panhandlorum* (sp. nov. nob.), and the *cowboyensis* of authors; which name, however, is proven quite untenable, as vague, unidentifiable, and a mere *nomen nudum*.

"We are compelled to admire the conservatism and restraint manifested by Dr. Hatteras. With such material, most of our modernists would have made *stetsoniensis* the name and type of a new genus, so different is it from the *Sombrero* group, with which it intergrades.

"Truly, we ourselves might not have withstood the temptation had

** It is a remarkable fact that the nearest known allies of *Sombrero policensis* are *Sombrero transvaalensis* and *Sombrero anzacensis* (of the subgenus *subsombrero*), found respectively in South Africa and Australia, suggesting that at one time these remote regions may possibly have had some sort of communication with America; perhaps there was a neck of land connecting Cape Cod with Cape Colony.

we been confronted by the dwarfish, skimpy, gray-pelaged *canadensis*, side by side with the gigantic and magnificent *Sombrero mexicanus imperialis* Stetson, with its 18-inch brim, its towering crown, and its load of silver gear. This remarkable species was originally described from the Rio Grande—by elimination, probably Brownsville. This place, then, unfortunately became its type locality. (A series of excellent topotypes have been secured for Matteawan Museum.) It increases in size and intensity of color as one goes farther south, amply justifying the race *Sombrero mexicanus popocatapetlensis* (sp. nov. nob.), and still farther on the dainty, exquisite *Sombrero mexicanus panamaensis* (sp. nov. nob.).

"While dealing chiefly with the exterior of the species, Dr. Hatteras has not ignored the more rigid structure when such existed. He points out also the curious paradox that, in Canada, the summer pelage is paler than that of winter, doubtless owing to the effects of weather bleaching, etc.

"Dichromatism is of frequent occurrence in the Winnipeg area. There the colors are equally divided between the gray and black (i.e., semi-albinism and melanism). On the Plains, the gray prevails, but in California we once more have the black phase in preponderance.

"His elucidation of the soft, brimless forms of the far north is equally inspiring.

"His 600 pages are copiously illustrated with photographs of hats in action, and the distribution set forth fully by maps.

"We repeat that this is one of the most important contributions to the subject that the generation has seen. It deals with a long-felt need, and we can only hope that the gifted author will continue his labors in the field that he has made especially his own. Yes, that he will go further, for there is eager demand for monographic treatment of many cognate subjects—shoes, gloves, belts, etc., and other obscure but important evolutionary forms that belong to the borderland of near zoology.

"We regret to point out that *Sombrero canadensis cinereoargentatus* as a name is preoccupied; therefore we suggest replacing it with the term *Sombrero hatterensis matteawani* (sp. nov. nob.) as a fitting compliment to the near zoologist, our author."

PART EIGHT

A TORCH LEADS THE WAY

LIFECRAFT

What Are God-given Rights?

Concerning the artificiality of modern living, we had many discussions. Seton's attitude was largely as follows:

"We have so beclouded all questions of rights by artificial, unfair social and property laws that it is difficult to show which on our statute books are God-given prerogatives.

"It is quite helpful towards clearing one's judgment if we look at the laws prevailing among the primitive peoples, or even among the higher animals.

"Thus: It is the law in the animal kingdom that the female has absolute choice of her mate among those who offer; and no one may compel her, or influence her choice, by violence. When such things are done among civilized folk—and they are done—all feel that the natural right of the female has been infringed.

"Among primitive tribes, if a woman is cast among a race of strangers, and soon after, say within three or four months, gives birth to a child, no one questions her right to own, train, and direct that child, even though she herself may be allowed no real status in the community. Evidently, then, the right of the mother is a natural, inherent right.

"If some wild beast attacks a primitive family, the right to defend the family belongs to the man, because he is by nature more muscular, better fitted to fight; and, because capability is always coupled with responsibility, to fight is his God-given right.

"Similarly, because the woman cannot care for the children and at the same time go hunting game, her first right implies the duty of keeping the home. Therefore also, because he is able, the man's natural right is to go hunting. And, since he cannot possibly live and multiply without the woman's work in her own department, it is her natural right to share in the game procured, and to share equally, because that is essential to the propagation, and later to the health, of the young she is nursing.

"In the wild animal state, it is well known that the mother has exclusive rights in the den while the young are helpless. As Kipling puts it in his *Law of the Wolves*, 'Den right is the right of the mother—not even the head wolf may enter.'

"But this claim also presupposes exclusive support of the young at that period. As soon as the male is allowed to enter the den and assume a share of the feeding responsibilities, he acquires more privileges. That is, at first, all rights and responsibilities were with the mother; but it is shown to be the part of wisdom to gradually adjust on a basis of near equality, though with a slight preponderance still, perhaps, in favor of the female.

"This condition is closely paralleled among primitive peoples, with this difference: among men, the responsibility of the male for feeding and protecting is extended to the whole life of the young; therefore, with his responsibilities, his rights are increased. He has a place in the home at all times and a say in the upbringing of the young from the first. So with all of the earliest human organizations, the inherent rights of male and female are about equal; some distinct, some common, but on the whole balanced.

"Therefore, in primitive communities where these natural rights have the force of fixed laws, the women have equally with the men the power to say when they shall move camp, when they shall go to war—if indeed they shall go to war at all—what shall be done with the captives, as well as having chief control of the children in the formative stage.

"Let us, then, seriously ponder whether these natural rights as evidenced in the animal world and among primitive races are not more important than artificial social rights. It may be that denying them means inviting dire racial disaster."

The Physical Basis of the Intellect

It is generally admitted in science that the basis of the intellect is, at least in part, physical. Drugs and drinks wholly change our modes of thought, and supply ideas that belong to this or that physical stimulus. A man's mind is always at its best when his physical well-being is at its highest pitch of development and health. In support of this premise, Seton told the following story.

"I shall never forget the tactics of a man who owned some land in the lower part of New York City. This land was needed by certain bankers. The former was alone and poor; the latter were three in number, and with vast resources back of them.

"The bankers requested an interview to negotiate the acquisition by them of the land owned by the little man. He agreed to meet them in conference and settle the matter; but he arranged the date for a Friday a month ahead, and fixed five o'clock in the afternoon as the hour.

"Then he went secretly to a famous sanatorium where athletes retire for training. He cut himself off absolutely from the world; no one but his wife knew where he was. For a month, he took the training of a prize fighter.

"At the appointed hour, he appeared at the conference. As planned, it was five o'clock on Friday afternoon. The bankers were worn out with a hard week in their offices, and at the end of a long hard day. They had not the mental alertness of the little man, who, fresh from an interval without worry, and in the pink of physical condition, every faculty functioning at its keenest, met them at each issue and outpointed them. He sold the property at double what they expected to give, and at ten times what he was prepared to accept. Had it been at ten o'clock of a Monday morning, with their superior experience, they would have had things their own way.

"He is now one of the millionaires of New York. And his fortune was made largely because he appreciated the oft-proven fact that the real basis of the intellect is physical, and can be manipulated by biological means."

Pork as Diet

Seton had always the smallest appetite of any adult I have ever known. He was not pernickety or faddish—he ate any food—but he was satisfied with very little.

One evening at dinner we were discussing food and food tabus among various sects. Having had considerable experience myself among Jews, we gradually came to talk more pointedly in that direction.

As on most subjects, Seton had done much thinking about the basis of the original prohibitions and their far-reaching effects on present-day life.

In the course of our talk he brought out the following ideas:

"Moses was learned in all the wisdom of the Egyptians, so we are told [Acts 7:22]. But of what that wisdom consisted, we are not fully informed.

"The Pyramids and other records show that the Egyptians were profoundly skilled in structural mathematics and observational astronomy. But there is no reason to credit them with attainments in the microbiological or prophylactic therapeutics which are the crowning glory of the modern laboratories.

"Concerning Moses personally, we know that he was a man of superb physique. The implication in the episode that involved the killing of the Egyptian bully is that Moses finished him with a blow of his fist. Furthermore, when he got away into the grazing country of Midian, he faced a whole gang of rough sheepmen in defense of some damsels who turned out to be the daughters of Jethro, the cattle king. Moses, the stranger, was able, singlehanded, to drive off the sheepmen. Thus it was that he won a place in Jethro's household.

"Finally, when he died at the age of a hundred and twenty years, 'his eye was not dim, nor his natural force abated' [Deuteronomy 34:7].

"So we see he set out in life with two great inheritances—he came of a race of brains, and he had a marvelous physique.

"Furthermore, he was a man of tremendous intellectual force; he was gifted with a rare imagination and was the keenest kind of observer. He was trained in the best schools in the world of his day; he mingled with the high society of the Egyptian court. Thus privileged with every opportunity for mental growth, he achieved a consummate knowledge of human nature.

"There is an old saying that solitude is the parent of great thought; and Moses, equipped as set forth, rounded out his possibilities by forty years of solitary contemplative life in the wilderness, before he began to announce the monumental ideas that have left his name like a lonely mountain on a plain—maybe the highest mountain of the whole mental panorama.

"Concerning the laws that he proposed and imposed on the Hebrews, we have the confirmation of the countless savants through the generations that all were on a sound basis; and if our modern translators would substitute the medical terms 'septic' and 'sepsis' for 'unclean' and 'uncleanness,' it would shed a sunrise of new light and afford a complete endorsement of all his dietary discriminations.

"Why, then, did he forbid his people to eat pork?

"Long observation of correlated phenomena, with notation of coincidences, is the earliest approach of man to the understanding of reasons and facts. Thus, there is little doubt that the natives of the Upper Nile, living largely on the flesh of wild pigs which abounded, were tormented with many vague and dire diseases that probably did not appear among the natives of the Lower Nile where such a diet was unknown.

"Moses had every opportunity of correlating these conditions. A vast number of observations established the fact that, first, they had one peculiar item of diet; and, second, they were scourged by a peculiar disease.

"Though we may not follow the mechanics of the phenomenon, it seems convincingly indicated that swine flesh was disease-producing —it was poison, it was black magic, it was unholy, it was unclean, it was not 'kosher,' it was 'tabu,' it was septic. Therefore it was forbidden by the law of common sense.

"This almost certainly was the logic of Moses.

"Modern research has shed much light on this, has offered abundant endorsement of the conclusions reached by the observant, though uninformed, ancients. And here it is well to remember the adage of modern learning: 'That is the best theory which explains the most facts.'

"Science has long known the penalties of eating uncooked swine flesh. The old medicine men called it 'black magic'; the moderns call it 'trichinosis.'

"In spite of the truth of the foregoing, I am inclined to believe that Moses had an even deeper reason for his absolute dictum forbidding pork in any form as an item of diet. Let us approach it from various angles.

"There is a tradition that Queen Elizabeth [I], to determine the relative values of food, set apart three regiments, one to be fed on pork, one on mutton, and one on beef. After a year, they were brought to some sort of trial. The pork-eaters were utterly sleepy and stupid; the sheep-eaters were well-fed but nervous and easily alarmed. The colonel of the beef-eaters, when asked his diet, is thus recorded in answer:

> "'Beef, madam, beef,' as loud as he could bawl;
> 'Beef, madam, beef, and be hanged to you all.'

"The Queen was delighted with his fierce independent spirit, and decided that henceforth beef would be the national flesh food of England.

"I do not know that the story is true, but it is established as a legend that seems to have the backing of long observation.

"An ancient saying in the Orient enshrines this final stage of reasoning, namely: 'You show me what he eats, and I will tell you what he is.'

"After realizing, as we must, the physical basis of the intellect, who can doubt that the nation that admits such a plague-bearer into its daily life must pay the frightful penalty of inevitable, general, and permanent mental disintegration?

"There is another presentation that may not involve the same mechanism, but certainly offers the same conclusions.

"In 50 B.C., the Romans invaded Britain and conquered it. Their method of exploitation exterminated the natives, or drove them to the mountains. The fertile valleys were no longer the happy homeland of the aborigines when, about A.D. 400, the Romans, owing to trouble at home, had to withdraw their armies and their colonists.

"The beautiful valleys of Albion, with temperate climate and joyful possibilities, were deserted.

"Then the Germans of the low country through which flows the Rhine, *viz.*, the Angles, the Saxons, the Jutes, hard put for fertile fields at home, heard of this happy land beyond the sea; and under the leadership of Hengist, Horsa, and others they began a regular migration and colonization of the silent valleys of Britain.

"These Germans brought with them their families, their language, and their habits. Their principal flesh diet was swine flesh, which, under Norman influence, they later called 'pork.' In Britain, it was easy to feed the swine on the nuts of oak and beech that abounded in the forests. The swine needed only a little protection from wolves, and that especially at night.

"The Saxons multiplied greatly so that in the six hundred years that they dominated Britain they fully possessed and populated the country.

"There is no accurate census, but the armies they raised quickly —probably 15,000 under Harold to resist the Normans—as well as the testimony of Domesday Book—indicates that the population of Britain may well have been 1,000,000 when the Normans landed.

"The inhabitants were physically vigorous and well fed. Yet, in all those centuries, they never once produced a man of outstanding intellect, much less a world genius. The few whose names appear on the pages of history as writers, or recorders, were without exception clericals, whose habits and vows enjoined total abstinence from all flesh food—beef or pork.

"In A.D. 1066 the Normans, under William the Conqueror, took possession of England, subdued the Anglo-Saxons, and imposed their own habits on the population.

"Among other changes, they introduced and exploited the use of beef and mutton as flesh foods. The 'roast beef of Old England' became famous as the national dish. And, not long after, as a come-back from this change of diet, we got the period of Elizabeth, the Golden Age of Bacon, Shakespeare, etc.

"Again, the aborigines of Greece were Helots, a race probably of African affinities. Their domestic animals were chiefly swine, and furnished their flesh diet. They had the advantages of temperate climate, numbers, and easy life. Yet there is no evidence of intellectual attainment among them. Later when the Dorians seized the power in Greece, and established the breeding of cattle and sheep, we pass into the Age of Pericles.

"We have not unveiled perhaps the exact chain of events and reactions that is involved. But the observations of scientists and recorders through the ages point the same lesson: when a certain operation is always followed by a certain result, we are assured that they are the cause and effect, even if we cannot trace the mechanism of the operation.

"We have at hand a thousand facts to prove the physical basis of the intellect. We have also many instances such as the foregoing. So, though we cannot with certainty give the reasons, we are compelled to believe that there is in pork diet some principle that is absolutely incompatible with the highest type of intellect.

"Granting that such is the case, we should find the best average of brains in those peoples who totally eschew pork diet.

"*We do!*

"Buddhist and Brahmin, avoiding all flesh diet, unwittingly eliminated the plague-bearer, and have set the world's pace for clear high thinking.

"Innumerable illustrations could be cited to show that the pork-abhorring Jew is a race of brains. When Hitler determined, for sordid reasons, to drive the Jews out of Germany, the world began to realize how many of the musicians, writers, scientists, and great thinkers were Jews.

"In Great Britain, as soon as the legal barrier was removed under Queen Victoria, the nation promptly elected for its real head a Jew, Benjamin Disraeli. He proved one of the greatest and most successful rulers ever given to the Empire. This case was, of course, paralleled by Pharaoh's appointment of Joseph as the administrative ruler of Egypt.

"In America, religious prejudice has barred the Jews from the presidential chair, but many of the administrations in Washington have had a Jew for financial agent, either officially as the head of the Treasury, or unofficially as confidential adviser.

"The Supreme Court of the United States has nine judges appointed by the President, selected in each case for mastery of the profession of law, for outstanding intellect, and for ripe wisdom. Until recently, two out of the nine judges were Jews. If this race had a representation in court proportioned to its population in America, they would have only one thirtieth of a man. In other words, their intellectual power gives them sixty times the official representation that their numbers would justify.

"Illustrations of this kind could be piled up indefinitely. But enough has been cited to show that, as usual, Moses was right. He framed a dietary code that guaranteed to his people immunity from at least one terrible disease; and by the same act established a quality of brains that has placed them in the front rank of the world of intellect.

"The logical inference is that the sooner we abolish pork as a diet —unless safeguarded by the most austere conditions of cookery— the better for ourselves, our children, and our race."

Happy on the Farm

THE SOLUTION OF A GREAT RIDDLE

Some years ago now, we stood on one of the majestic mesas of Arizona, in a Hopi village, with a great crowd of Indians and Whites assembled to witness the Snake Dance.

The Indian agent, a man much above his class, was kind and obliging. He helped us to see the inner workings of many things, and secured for us admission into places that are rarely open to Whites. He showed the historic spots, and led to the towers that gave fine views of the patchwork of farm and field below, with noble mountains butting at the low far sky.

At an appreciative remark from us, he retorted:

"It is all very interesting and picturesque. But we have got to break it up."

"Break up what?" I said, in surprise.

"This village life; the whole thing," he answered.

"Why?" I asked in amazement.

"Because these people have got to go and live on their farms."

"Why?" I repeated. "Aren't they happy and satisfied up here?"

"Perhaps, but see all the time they waste with their festivals and holidays," he rejoined.

"Yet," I answered, "they are wholly self-supporting and care for their own young, sick, and aged."

"Oh yes, but see how unsanitary it is," was his answer.

"Well then, teach them rudimentary sanitation."

"How?" he said scornfully.

"First," I said, "I should establish a sufficiency of toilet houses, and teach their use to the priests, who would welcome and back anything that seemed to give additional importance to themselves and their office."

"Yes," he replied, "and add just so many more opportunities for immorality."

"If a building is to be condemned because it may possibly be used immorally, we must abolish all hotels, bathhouses, gymnasiums, churches, sleeping cars, yes, houses *in toto.*"

"Oh, I had all those idealistic notions about these Indians when I first came," he mused, "but I see now only one solution, and that is, send them out to live on their farms like White folks."

In amazement at his shortsightedness, Seton here launched out:

"Let me show you how far wrong you are. With the single exception that their habits are unsanitary, from our point of view, there is no count against this people. They are peaceful, happy, and contented, not getting one cent of government money; living by farming, caring for their own young, sick, aged, and helpless, demanding no favors of us, asking only to be let alone on their mesa. You would destroy the mesa village and send them to live scattered on the farms over the plains below, to make them more sanitary. If you had ever studied the sheepherder or small farmer who lives that life, you would never again use the word 'sanitary' in connection with that sort of life!

"You would rob these Indians of their independence, of all their social amusements, the joy in life, and reduce them to the awful level of the degraded solitary outcasts of the desert."

Taking advantage of the agent's silence, which implied at least tolerance of our views, we led him to a quiet corner. Seton continued:

"Listen to a chapter of recent history:

"In the late seventies, both the United States Government and the Canadian Government became alarmed at the general stampede of farmers' sons and daughters from the farms. Agriculture would have been in a sad way but for the fact that immigration from Europe filled the gaps. That supply, however, was likely to end eventually, and then what?

"Both governments appointed commissions to study the problem, and each commission made essentially the same report:

"The farm life is so lonely, the hours are so long, that the young

people and the women never have any fun. The women, in particular, are in rebellion. The new generation would rather go to towns
and factories where the cost of living is higher, but where they have
some chance for the pleasures of human society.

"The problem was, how could such a deep-rooted, reasonable,
sane human craving as the desire for companionship be reconciled
with the essentially lonely life of a farm? The answer came in an
unexpected way.

"About this time, a deputation of Mennonites from Russia, forced
out by religious persecution, came to the United States Government,
saying, 'Our people are good farmers; we want to come to your
country and take up land. But we do not wish to live in your
manner. In our way of life, we do not have our homes on our farms,
but in a village, and go forth each morning to the farms, and
return to the village at night.'

"The United States Department of the Interior gave a curt answer:
'Our law requires each to live on his homestead.'

"So, unwillingly, for they had already had enough of monarchies,
these religious refugees went to Canada and made the same request.
In a cabinet meeting, the desire of the Mennonites was considered.
The Minister of the Interior, who is invested with more power than
the United States Secretary, said, 'They are good people; they are
sober and industrious; they will make good citizens. Let us give
them a chance.' Consequently, an order in council changed the law
so the Mennonites could homestead, and yet live in their villages.

"One band after another came to the Canadian Northwest. All
brought a little money, and were steady good farmers. They lived in
their little towns where each man had a small garden and a place
for a horse, a pig, a cow, and chickens. Here they established their
churches and schools. Each morning they set out to the fields and
labored till sundown. Evenings and on Sundays, they had a full
measure of social life. Their way of farming has proven a success.
They are prosperous and contented. They have given a complete
answer to the problem of solitude on the farm.

"The idea has grown in the Northwest. The simple Mennonite
has spread a gospel of practical life; and now most of the small
towns in the Northwest of Canada and the Dakotas are peopled by
farmers whose lands are miles away. They go forth in the morning

to work and come back at evening to town—to eat, make merry,
and sleep. In harvest time they do not return every night; and in the
wintertime they do not all leave their homes every day, but assign
one or more to look after stock if the need be, various groups taking
it month and month about. Meanwhile, the family lives in town,
with church, school, theater, club or sewing circle, and human society. The blank horror of the old farm life is gone.

"The riddle is solved."

The agent in question was not convinced, but the United States
Indian Service did, in later years, accede to some such arrangement.

The Troth Plighting

We have a number of times been called upon to conduct various
ceremonies which usually are confined to the offices of more clerically
trained persons. Where it has been the sincere wish of the parties
intimately concerned, we have generally acceded to their desires. In
this way, we have performed on our own grounds original forms of
baptisms, weddings, and burials; and although we were not in any
way legally endowed with the power to officiate in such capacity,
we have perhaps injected a note of sincerity and variety which
takes the triteness out of the often too familiar phrases of the usual
rites.

Several times we have performed a ritual of marriage at the little
shrine which we built long ago in a corner of our patio. I give here
the ceremony as we worked it out, receiving much suggestive material from a service initiated by our Woodcrafters in England.

At 7:00 P.M., all except the bride and groom assemble in the
patio, facing the shrine (which is in the northwest corner) and the
sunset.

The bride enters through the west gate, the groom through the
north, until they face each other at either side of the shrine.

Seton: "Fellow Villagers, we are met together this evening for the
espousal of two of our members, Mabel Creighton and Cecil Hall.

"As marriage customs vary in different groups, we do not presume to lay down any rule. We think that in a matter so intimate and personal it is for members to form their own opinions, and to adjust the claims of their God and of their fellow men, as they do in other matters of religion.

"Marriage, being the most sacred and important of all human relations, whether for the individual or society, we desire that members will do nothing to impugn its holy office before their neighbors.

"Our members, therefore, have already followed the custom of our country and have completed the legal requirements set up by our government and our civilization.

"Any further ceremony merely binds the couple more closely into an aesthetic and spiritual union, and has no effect one way or the other on the civil rites as already performed; nevertheless is a public announcement of the same.

"Will the parties please read their statements of intent."

Mabel: "I, Mabel Creighton, desire the consent of this assembly to my marriage with Cecil Hall. I have gained knowledge of him and disclosed myself to him so far as I am able. I desire to be used for the purposes of his life and to use him for the purposes of mine. I will not fail to inform him of anything which touches closely either his life or mine; and I solemnly declare my present intention to be faithful to him so long as I shall live.

"If we be given children, I wish to be jointly concerned with him in the nurture of their bodies and minds until they shall be fully grown, and in their liberation from our control as soon as they shall be fit for it."

Cecil: "I, Cecil Hall, desire the consent of this assembly to my marriage with Mabel Creighton.

"I wish to declare my love for her, and my intention to keep the truth whole between her and me, and to be faithful to her as long as I shall live.

"If we be given children, I wish to be jointly concerned with her in the nurture of them in body, mind, and spirit, until they shall be fully grown, and in their liberation from our control as soon as they shall be fit for it."

Seton: "Are there any here who know of any reason against this union proceeding?"

Silence.

"Do you all approve that Mabel Creighton and Cecil Hall shall here and now plight their troth, one to the other?"

All: "We do."

Couple walk toward each other. After a moment of silence:

Cecil: "In the sight of God, and in the presence of this assembly, I take thee, Mabel Creighton, to be my wife."

Mabel: "In the sight of God, and in the presence of this assembly, I take thee, Cecil Hall, to be my husband."

He places ring on Mabel's finger, saying: "Wear thou this ring, as the custom is, for a sign and token of our marriage."

Seton: "Let us commune with the Great Spirit, the Creator and Sustainer of Life! May the Great Spirit bind together this pair in perpetual love and fellowship."

All: "So pray we and fear not."

Seton: "May their lives be linked together in peace and joy, succoring each other in time of need."

All: "So pray we and fear not."

Seton: "May the Great Spirit endow them with power for all the purposes of life."

All: "So pray we and fear not."

Seton: "May their home be built upon the rock of virtue, affording shelter in every need and ministering to their temporal and spiritual well-being."

All: "So pray we and fear not."

Seton: "I now declare in the name of this assembly, in the name of all those interested, past, present, and to come, that Cecil Hall and Mabel Creighton have here and now plighted their troth before this Sacred Shrine, thus uniting their affections and blending their inheritance for the founding of a home.

"In the old days before the White man came, it was the custom of the tribe, in public celebration of the marriage ceremony, to light the first fire for the couple, and the privilege of each friend to contribute a faggot to enhance its brightness. The Sacred Fire is burning within the central spot of this Village, and we invite you each to pick a faggot as you enter."

When all have assembled before the fireplace, Seton continues:

"As the Great Central Fire of all reaches out to the four corners of the earth and kindles blazing lights, so at our sacred symbol fire light we our lamps, one each for Beauty, Truth, Fortitude, and Love. And while these lights are blazing bright, we know that we shall grow."

Each member adds his faggot to the fire; after which, festivities of any sort may follow.

A Burial Service

When we first began to establish Seton Village, we were in need of a permanent helper, a man who could do carpenter work, concrete work, simple plumbing, etc.; but, above all, one who would be patient and tolerant with our more or less unconventional ideas of building. We expected to have to wait a long time for such a paragon to turn up. But instead, with the fortune that is usually ours, he arrived early in our search.

He became so interested in our project that for eleven years he worked seven days a week, rejoicing in the accomplishment of tasks he did not know he could do, in gradually assuming the direction and management of all the gangs of workmen that, on and off, were part of our plan. But that is getting ahead of the present story.

When we knew that he was the man we wanted—and it did not take very long to know—we arranged for him to live on the place with us. Our accommodations for some time were very meager; but he made himself comfortable and happy in a couple of box cars we had bought from the nearby railroad and fitted up for simple habitation.

He was a widower—had been for many years, so that he was accustomed to living alone and doing for himself.

But after a few months he decided to send for his mother, who had lived all her life in Texas and was getting on in years and was perhaps a little lonely.

She came, and soon made a pleasant home of the house he had been occupying. In the cool of the evening she would bring out her little old rocking chair and sit outside the house, spick and span with a starched white apron and a short full cape over her shoulders to protect her from the night air. There was a calmness and sweetness about her that made one feel comfortable and cozy; and as we passed the house on our evening walk about the place, we would stop and talk commonplaces with her for a few moments.

One day the son came over to our house and asked if I would look in on his mother—she was not well. When I saw her I knew he was right—she was indeed very ill. Within two days she had smiled her last smile on earth, and the little house felt very empty.

That evening, again the son came to us. Was there a spot some place on our estate where we would be willing to have her buried? "She said a number of times," he told us, "that she would rather lie under a pinyon tree in Seton Village than in a great marble mausoleum anywhere else on earth."

"Of course," we promised. "We will go out right now and find a place."

We set out—it was sunset—and instinctively climbed a hill. Through dense pinyon and juniper we threaded our way to the top. Here, as if prepared in advance, was a level clear space open to the sky; and as we turned to see whence we had come, we found ourselves looking straight back down into the little village we were building.

We knew it was right, and went back home to report.

"We will start the boys early in the morning to make a trail," we said; for we had picked our way in and out of the trees without any guiding signs to mark a road.

He asked that everything be done by our own employees who were living on the place. So the next day, when they had cleared a path up the mountain, they also dug a grave.

And now came another request from the son.

"Will you conduct the service?" he asked of Seton.

We hesitated at this, then replied: "It would not be an orthodox service, you know. We belong to no set creed, and could follow no regular pattern."

"That is what she wants," he quietly responded. "She said so many times as you passed the door, 'There goes a real man, a man of God.' Anything you say would be according to her belief."

So it was settled.

The funeral was on Sunday morning; and some fifty or sixty persons who knew us all came for the service. When the undertaker arrived, prepared to transport the body in his hearse to its resting place, he was troubled.

"My funeral car is topheavy and could never make that grade."

For a moment we too were dismayed, till our carpenter said: "Can we not use your own truck?"

So, piloted by our own driver, the unadorned truck which had hauled all our lumber, cement, firewood, for months, carried the coffin by slow careful degrees to the top of the hill.

Some cars followed, some friends walked. In due time all were gathered about the open grave, each holding as he had been asked to do a small round stone and a sprig of pinyon.

As the coffin was slowly lowered into the burial place, Seton began:

"My friends:

"We are here assembled to do honor to one of our number who has passed away; to pay the last poor tribute of respect to one who was near and dear to many of us, known and respected by all of us.

"My friends, there are little churches and little groups who preach this or that fine split of doctrine. But there is also a group not affiliated with any of the formal churches, who feel that we are adherents of the oldest church of all, the Church of the All-Father, the Great Spirit, the Maker and Ruler of the Universe, that sense the reality of the Oversoul, the one Great Founder and the End of the world about us.

"This is the oldest of all faiths, and we believe that we have been sent here for a purpose, which the Great Father has never forgotten in the working out of our lives.

"The dear one who has gone from our sight was one of such believers. Of creeds she had no knowledge and no need. She knew her duty as a woman, she did her part, she bore the brunt, she asked no favors but this: that she be remembered as a woman who assumed her woman's part and did her kindly best.

"What were her contacts with the churches we know not, and we care not. But we do know that she carried her share of life, she begot children and dowered them with a mother's care and a mother's love. She failed them never in her duty as a woman, as a mother. For this we honor her.

"We have not sought to inter the mortal remains of our departed friend in what is commonly called consecrated ground; for we feel that all ground is consecrated if we approach it with reverent attitude, realizing that the whole world is the Holy Ground of the

Great Spirit, if we ourselves have the adequate consciousness of His presence.

"My friends, our sister who has gone over the Great Divide had but little sentiment about the place where last she should find her rest. This only was the wish that she expressed: she hoped that she might sleep among the pinyons in a high and beautiful place.

"This is the place we have chosen for her, seeking the exact expression of her wish—among the pinyons in God's own earth, with the sun and the wind in possession of the big wide land, the morning sun and the sun in his westward setting.

"Friends, we know not whence we came into this world, or whither we go when we leave it; but of this we are assured: we are ever in the consciousness of the Great All-Father by whom is measured our past and our future; and without caring to affix a value to creeds and observances, we rest comforted in the thought that, as surely as she has gone from us to a God of love and kindness, she will as surely be received with kindness, understanding, and love."

The stones we had carried up the hill were now reverently placed in an oval about the still open grave. Then all filed by and dropped in the pinyon sprigs we had brought. Seton built a watch fire at the foot of the resting place, and we left to go slowly down the mountain which we had in this wise consecrated in the sight of God. The filling in of the grave was left to the professionals trained for the purpose.

All that day and all that night, for miles about could be seen the little wisp of smoke from the fire which carried our prayers and our assurance of future life to the Great Spirit who dwells in the hearts of all who believe.

Drink It While It's Fizzin'

With all the serious work that Seton was constantly engaged in, with all the responsibilities that were his in the manipulation of his contacts all over the world, there was in him a zest, a gladness of spirit. He was always in full possession of the present moment, he imparted to all about him the joy of living that was so innate in him.

At a banquet for which he was guest of honor, he recited the following attempt at expressing his approach to life in general:

"I was a guileless little boy—
   I hope my meaning's plain—
When just to let me taste of joy
   They gave me some champagne.
I wished to keep that liquid gold
   To gloat and feast my eyes;
But a wise old sinner shouted:
   'While it's fresh, you drink your prize.'

"Remember hence, my simple child,
   This motto wise and pat:
'You must drink it while it's fizzin'
   For tomorrow 'twill be flat.'

"Now listen, all you little girls
   Approaching life's red cups,
Your maiden aunts with snakish curls
   Would frown upon these sups;
They'll prove by scripture, tone and text
   This pace you should not go;
That life's a cup you must not sip,
   For pleasure leads to woe.

"But don't forget, my simple child,
   This motto wise and pat:
'You must drink it while it's fizzin'
   For tomorrow 'twill be flat.'

"And all you proper little boys
   With faces washed and clean,
You're here remote from city noise
   To gambol on the green.

We're young! We'll glory in our youth,
    Forget next day, forsooth;
We're here to drink a loving cup,
    The bumper of our youth.

"And don't forget, you simple kids,
    This motto wise and pat:
'You must drink it while it's fizzin'
    For tomorrow 'twill be flat.'

"There was a little actress
    Who made a little hit;
Before she was but fairish,
    She now was surely it.
Her grandma said: 'Now go it slow.'
    Her manager in town
Said: 'Here's success with brimming cup,
    You better drink it down.'

"Remember then, my simple child,
    This motto wise and pat:
'You must drink it while it's fizzin'
    For tomorrow 'twill be flat.'"

The Tramps

In November 1883, Seton left the prairies and came to New York to "make his fortune." He was a ruddy, round-faced boy with high hopes and ideals. He knew not a soul in New York, had no letter of introduction, had no definite plan, and only two dollars in his pocket.

The whole situation was perfectly normal. He could find good authority for each point, and therein found assurance of victory.

There was but one discordant element: he had two dollars. This was wrong. There was no precedent for more than seventy-five cents, and he felt worried.

This defect in his case, however, was soon put right, and more than right, as day by day went by and no work was found. He was soon down to a roll a day, and a little later was down to half a roll. He used to eat this at noon each day, sitting by the fountain in Madison Square, as that was the only free drink he had discovered in the wilderness.

Half a roll a day for a growing boy with a normal appetite was light eating, and the condition known physically as slow starvation was set up. He was delighted, it was so completely *de rigueur*. In it all, the only dampening thought that came was "Suppose when I get work, my strength should be gone!" But he could recall no authority for this sinister thought, and it died a violent death.

The normal conditions were all carried out punctiliously. To the question "Will you drive a car, shovel coal, or wait on table?" he replied, "Yes indeed."

"Then you needn't worry about the future" was the encouraging but not wholly satisfactory reply.

It was a formative taste of life, and as he sat day by day at that Madison Square fountain with his half roll, waiting for the clocks to strike their permission to tantalize his famishing body, he thought: "As long as I live, I will never say nay to anyone who comes to me and says, 'I am hungry,' be it man or beast."

Time and again have I seen Seton give a dime or a quarter—and sometimes considerably more—to worthless-looking tramps who apparently chose him as a likely target for their begging. At a chance remark of mine one day when we saw one of the recipients immediately enter a saloon, Seton said:

"Yes, I know. I have watched that many times. I know I have bought drinks in this way for many hopeless drunks. But I have seen other things too. Listen:

"Way back in the nineties, after several years in New York, I had not only established myself as an illustrator, paid up all debts, and saved money in the bank, but also realized some happiness in a measure of success.

"One night I came down on the Sixth Avenue Elevated; and a little after 11:00 P.M. got off at 42nd Street, so as to have a walk before turning in to my lodgings on East 9th Street.

"At the same time a tramp came from under the Elevated stairs and approached me. 'Say, boss, don't you want to do something for a fellow that's needing a meal?'

"Acting on the vow I had made to myself when I had been in the same case, I replied: 'Sure. We'll find a restaurant nearby.'

"'There ain't no place near here that would take in a tramp like me.'

"'Well, do you know one that would?'

"'Yes, but you don't have to bother going with me. You give me five dollars or two dollars or whatever you think right, and I'll take care of myself.'

"'No,' I replied, 'I won't do that. We'll go and have a bite together at some place.'

"He sullenly argued till we got to Fifth Avenue, at that time a dark and wholly residential street. At the corner of the old reservoir, under a shade tree, he stopped and said:

"'Ain't ye goin' to give me that cash?'

"'No.'

"'Then take that,' and he handed me one straight for my jaw.

"Fortunately, I was quick enough to catch it on my elbow guard; after which he ran like a rabbit down Fifth Avenue and disappeared.

"Just about a year later, under very similar circumstances, on the same street, that is, 42nd Street and Sixth Avenue, about midnight, another tramp stopped me with the usual:

"'Say, boss, don't you want to help one of the boys that's up against it?'

"'What's up?' I asked.

"'Can't get a job, ain't had a square meal for a week.'

"'Sure I'll help you. I was just thinking about supper for myself. Come on.'

"'There ain't no place round here that'd let me in,' he protested.

"'We'll find something over there,' I said, and pointed to the Grand Central Station.

"He followed slowly, muttering strangely.

"We got to the Grand Central Station. He hung back. 'I don't want to go in there,' he said. 'They've got it in for me!'

"'Well, let's go on to Third Avenue. That's safe enough,' I said and struck out at a quick pace.

"'See here,' said my tramp after half a block. 'I can't walk like that. I've been sailing too close to the wind for a month.'

"'All right,' I rejoined. 'You set the pace, I'll follow.'

"We got to Third Avenue. In those days the streets were lighted by a large arc light at each corner. Under the one at this point, the tramp stopped me and began again:

"'Say, why do you waste your time with me? Why not give me a couple dollars and let me look out for myself?'

"'Where's your restaurant?' I said curtly.

"'It's down there'; and he pointed with his foot down Third Avenue.

"He was keeping alongside with an effort, and mumbling to himself. Suddenly, under the next arc light, he seized my arm and said: 'Say, you ain't one of them damn trailers, air ye? Ye ain't goin' to turn me in?'

"'No,' I answered. 'Do I look like a trailer?'

"He shook his head and muttered: 'Hell, looks don't count'; and he continued to shake his head from time to time, grumbling. We came at last to 14th Street arc light, when he exclaimed: 'Say, ain't you Bob Sylvester?'

"'No, I'm not.'

"'Well, you look like him. You walk like him, and you act like him. It would be just like him to take up with a tramp at midnight.'

"'Where's your restaurant?' I asked. He pointed downtown again with his foot. We came at length to Cooper Institute at 8th Street. Here he stopped, and once more stared hard at me.

"I said: 'Lead on, I'm hungry.'

"'Say,' said he. 'Air you goin' down the Bowery at midnight with a tramp like me? You in slick clothes and a silk hat?'

"'Yes.'

"'Do you know New York City?' he queried.

"'A great deal better than you do,' was my answer, largely bluff.

"The tramp shook his head, utterly puzzled.

"We traveled silently down the Bowery to near Chatham Square. Here was a small dark street leading towards East River. At this, the tramp stopped, and again indicated with his foot, both hands being deep in his trouser pockets. 'It's down there.'

"'Lead on,' I said. The tramp gave a peculiar chuckle, shrugged his shoulders, and led on. In the next block, he stopped at a stairway leading down into a cellar. There were beer and hash signs on it. It was well lighted, and the noise of many voices came up.

"'That's it,' he said.

"'Go on,' and I followed him down.

"To my surprise, it was a rough and ready restaurant; and many men and women, mostly foreigners, were eating or drinking beer. In an iron cage near the door was a big rough-looking man with keen blue eyes; and over them, eyebrows like penthouse roofs. He looked like an ex-prize fighter and was evidently the proprietor.

"As soon as we entered, there was a hush of voices, and the folk at the far end stood up, amazed to see a swell in a silk hat enter such a joint. I noticed the big man in the cage reach out and quietly draw a big revolver.

"Now I realized that I had done a very foolish thing, venturing into such a place. But I knew that I must brazen it out, show no sign of fear.

"On the shelf of the window into the iron cage, I laid a quarter, and casually said to the big man:

"'Can you feed this man for that?'

"To my utter amazement, the big brute with the revolver said: 'Hell, we can load him to the gunwales for a dime,' and he shoved me back fifteen cents.

"I turned toward my tramp, but he was gone. Then I felt someone tugging at my coat behind, and a voice hoarsely said: 'Say, boss, kin I have something?' He was cowering at my back.

"'Go ahead,' I answered. 'The boss says you can eat all you want.'

"He seized both my hands in his and whispered: 'I ain't had a bite for two days, nor a square meal for a week,' and broke down sobbing.

"I am afraid I almost did too, before I got out and away as fast as I could.

"One other tramp adventure is worth remembering.

"On an extended lecture trip I reached Lansing, Michigan, in deep winter. My publishers had arranged an elaborate window display of my books in each city where I was to talk.

"My lecture was at three o'clock. I left the hotel in time to call at the bookshop window en route to the hall.

"As I stood critically gazing in, I saw in the reflection a tough-looking tramp cross the street directly towards me. Then he began:

"'Say, mister. When I seen you looking at all them books, sez I to myself, now there is a man as likes books; and I like books, so he's my kind of a man.'

"I turned and looked closely at him, tough and dirty, and smelling of whiskey. So I said:

"'Now cut out all that stuff and tell me what you want.'

"'Well,' he replied, 'to tell you the truth, I am fy-nancially embarrassed.' He grinned in a disagreeable way.

"I said: 'Is that any use to you?' and offered him a dime.

"He chucked it up, caught it in his palm, and said: 'It's a trifle, but better than nothing. I am proportionately grateful,' and turned off.

"As his road led in the direction of the lecture hall, I thought: 'I'll see what saloon you go into anyway.' He wandered along, looking at various signboards. I followed some twenty-five feet behind. He passed several saloons, then came to a cheap restaurant. Into this he went, and I quietly followed.

"I saw him go to the girl at the desk and mutter something.

"The girl replied: 'No, we don't do that kind of business.'

"He grumbled something else. She said: 'Well, there's the proprietor, talk to him.' The tramp went over to a big fat man at one of the tables. I heard only the man's reply: 'No, no, didn't she tell you we don't do that kind of business? There's lots of hash houses down by the station.'

"The tramp turned away, utterly crushed, and brushed almost into me. I said: 'Hello, what's up? Do you remember me?' A look of recollection came into his sad face as he answered: 'They won't serve me for that'; and in his dirty palm lay the dime.

"In a flash I knew. I drew out a five-dollar bill and handed it to him. 'Try them with that,' I said. 'God bless you,' was all he answered, and I knew I was feeding a hungry man.

"I have kept on feeding them ever since. I know how it feels. If only one in twenty is genuine, I am content."

The Hospital

In March 1933, Seton was in a Southwestern hospital for a repair job on the hernia operation that had been performed in Chicago exactly fifty years before.

He recovered quickly, and as he lay in comfort in a private room, with nurses at call and everything in abundance, he told me of that other experience, which came to him in detail as if it had been but yesterday.

He tells in his autobiography of the difficulties he had at that early date, in arranging for his admission to the hospital, of his profound admiration for the surgeon, Dr. Moses Gunn; but did not in print tell of the conditions in the institution during his recuperation.

After quoting one paragraph from his writing, I give that interlude as he gave it to me:

"On March 20, 1883, I was duly wheeled into the operating room of St. Joseph's Hospital. There, Dr. Moses Gunn and his assistant gave me the benefit of their skill. Of course, during the operation, I was floating among spheres and other worlds with bright streaming spirals that exploded at the end of each windup. I knew nothing of time or life.

"When I came to myself, I was lying in the general ward of the hospital. The place was the reverse of quiet, and the voices which fell on my ear were far from being refined or sympathetic.

"At length I became aware that one or two men near me were betting on my chances of recovery or indeed as to whether I was now alive or not. The last bet I myself soon had the honor of deciding by simply opening my eyes; and I heard one of the gamblers exclaim: 'Just my luck. God damn it! I am always on the wrong horse. But never mind, Jim Jams, I'll drink beer on your coffin before long.' Then ensued a wrangle as to which of these was nearer the grave.

"'Why, you blasted fool, didn't you have a hemorrhage yesterday?'

"'Well, didn't you have two the day before?'

"'Oh, I don't give a damn, the doctor said *you* hadn't two weeks to live.'

"'Why, you damned miserable wretch, he told *me you* might drop off any night.'

"'You're a liar.'

"'And you're a God-damned liar. If I was able to stand up, I'd start you on another hemorrhage.' And so these two continued to abuse each other in feeble tones.

"In an hour or more, I sufficiently possessed my senses to lift my head and look around. The late disputants were on the two beds adjoining the foot of my own; both were in the last stages of consumption. Their argument had exhausted them for some time; but now they were recovered enough to unite in chaffing a third hopeless consumptive.

"This last, though nearly gone, thought no more of his condition than his companions did of theirs. He was gifted by nature with an ugly face, yet an exceedingly white transparent skin; and this was further blanched by the disease till now his blackened teeth almost showed through the thin bloodless lips. Early this morning, he had discovered, by the aid of a pocket mirror, that a tiny pimple had formed on his delicate forehead. His annoyance over the spoliation of his 'beauty' was extraordinary. He could scarcely wait for the doctor to make his ordinary rounds—he wished to have him sent for. He tried to conceal his anxiety in some measure, but the continual use of the pocket mirror and certain timid questions betrayed him.

"'Oh, but I'm Mamma's pretty boy,' said one jeeringly.

"'I tell you, Tubercles,' said another, 'that's no pimple; it's the syphilis. You will be a mass of scabs tomorrow morning. If you had the sand of a baby, you would end your miserable life now; yer no good anyhow.'

"'If it ain't syph, it's smallpox,' said a man with a broken leg and a deeply pitted face. 'I know that's jest how it came on me.'

"And so they talked and jeered till the doctor came and told the man he was a fool; and refused to give him anything to 'preserve his personal appearance.'

"On one side of me was a cowboy who had been frightfully kicked by a mule; on the other was a lad who had been badly vitriolized. They were both great sufferers, but both were good fellows; and, as they were able to move about a little, they did for me any little service that I needed. Fully half the patients were, like myself, bedridden; and they used as messenger a small French boy who, though 'in' with hip disease, could still scramble about on crutches.

"As soon as they saw I was conscious and could answer questions, they proceeded to put me through the mill.

"'What's yer name?' 'Yer age?' 'Yer fightin' weight?' 'What yer in for?' All had to be answered.

"'Say, that lying House Surgeon didn't tell you there was a chance for you, did he?'

"'Yes.'

"'Hm, that's bad—I allus notice that's his way of breaking the worst to the fellows—and yer looking pooty low, I must say.'

"At this moment the riot and hubbub suddenly ceased, and all eyes were turned towards the door. There entered a Sister of Charity who was respectfully addressed as 'Nurse' by some, 'Sister Isadore' by others. She was a remarkably beautiful girl about nineteen years of age, she had a bright sparkling eye, a rosebud mouth, and a style that would have made a most dangerously effective flirt but for an expression of dignity and command that was paramount. Her costume suited her well; and the evident respect she inspired made me the more unprepared to hear her speak in a strong Irish brogue of the type that does not belong to the upper classes. But her personal force was such that, though she was mere nurse of the ward, her influence was felt throughout the hospital; and on the one or two occasions of extremity that arose during my six weeks' stay it was quite observable that the venerable, highly educated Sister Superior quietly subsided to a second place while this unlettered but forceful little Irish girl took the captain's post and successfully passed the threatened dangers.

"Before I had been there a week I had witnessed a deathbed scene for the first time in my life. A young man had been brought in, delirious with kidney disease. He was strapped down to a bed opposite mine; and his ravings continually turned to 'Sadie.' 'Sadie, Sadie,' was all his moan. His relations came and stood around, but he knew them not. 'Perhaps it might do some good if Sadie were to see him.' So she was brought—a young girl, his sweetheart, and she broke down in a paroxysm of grief. The only remark that her agony provoked in the ward was 'Gosh! Wouldn't she make a pile if she could carry on like that on the stage!' and a muffled growl of 'Shut up, you damned cur,' from several.

"Immediately after the entry of poor 'Kidneys,' as he was at once dubbed from the name of his trouble, a tall lanky man walked slowly in and was shown his bed. He at once undressed and lay down. The frightful emaciation thus exposed produced a roar of laughter and a demand of 'What's the matter with you, Fatty?'

"'Fatty' said he was an old soldier, and was down with consumption. But we already had a 'Consumption,' a 'Tubercles,' and a 'One-lung,' so he continued to be 'Fatty' by common consent.

"The boys always made a pot for a sweepstakes when a new and promising patient entered the ward; i.e., betting on who would die first. When Fatty and Kidneys were entered, the little cripple was sent around with the hat. Every man had to put in ten cents or its equivalent. Few had the money; so, besides cash, the hat contained jackknives, plugs of tobacco, pawn tickets, and promises to pay. One who had a pawn ticket for twenty-five cents face value dropped it in and took out fifteen cents in cash, amid a roar of indignation. Nick, the cowboy, was made banker. Then the name of each patient was written on a slip, folded, dropped into the hat, and each man drew his horse.

"In the sweepstakes, Consumption, the beauty already noted, drew Kidneys. I drew Fatty, and Fatty drew me. Next day I said: 'What will you take for your horse, Fatty?'

"'Hell, he's no good. I'll sell him cheap. Will you give me a dime?'

"'No, but here's a lemon. Will you swap?'

"'Done,' said he.

"I was about to throw the lemon, but he said: 'No, don't throw it; I can't see nothin' this mornin',' and Crutches was called on to transfer the lemon.

"So I bought myself in.

"Kidneys was, of course, the favorite, for his hourly raving had now given place to spasmodic muttering and gasping. But one or two that were able to be up had noted strange changes in Fatty's face. I could see something too, and a sudden strange terror of winning smote on my heart.

"'Vot'll you dake vor your horse dis mornin', Satan?' said Gimpy, on the second day.

"'He's yours, Gimpy, if you will wash me.' And Gimpy gladly took my offer; for he was a goodhearted German lad and would probably have washed me anyway. And so I was out of the sweepstakes.

"The next day, Kidneys was clearly dying. The priest came and administered the last rites of the Church to the unconscious man. He occasionally drew himself up in agony, then straightened out with a deep gasp; but the gasps gradually came more slowly and were more feeble. Consumption was watching the scene with unalloyed and unconcealed delight.

"'Guess you might as well hand me de boodle now,' he said to Nick. But Nick was firm. The priest turned next to Fatty and asked him if he could do anything for him, to which Fatty replied feebly: 'Yes, go to hell!' and Father Clement walked out.

"Poor Kidneys was watched so closely that day and evening that no one noticed Fatty in the next bed. The former was gasping and each minute seemed his last. But he was young and strong; and as night came on, he was still breathing hard at intervals.

"About eight o'clock a change was noticeable, the long hard breathing gave place to a low rapid one, the house surgeon was sent for, the dying man gave one gasp, then trembled from head to foot and lay still. 'He's dead,' said the surgeon, and Consumption grinned, and would have hoorayed outright but that the little Sister Isadore stood by. The surgeon then turned to the next cot to speak to poor Fatty. He laid his hand on him, then blurted out, 'Why, this man's dead, and stiff too!'

"This was too much. Gimpy could not restrain himself. He burst into a yell of exultation and claimed the jackpot at the top of his lungs.

"The voice of Sister Isadore instantly and sternly demanded silence. But still I heard Jim Jams in the next bed: 'Ho, Satan, you bloody fool. If you had only laid low, you'd-a won the pot!'

"And the rest grinned over my discomfiture."

PART NINE

DRY TINDER

FABLES FOR ADULTS

A Fabulist

Just as Aesop is credited with the *Fables,* though he probably never wrote them (maybe there wasn't even an Aesop), so we may credit Seton with many animal myths which did not indeed originate with him, but which were put into tellable form by his pen.

Some indeed were conceived in his own imaginative mind, but a number are in essence stories which in one form or another were told to the children by our Red brethren.

Many of these do not even carry a moral, as did those of the ancient fabulist; but each brings with it a message of beauty and devotion to the outdoors, which may be of inestimable value to our young generation today when urban life is apt to keep one's thoughts from some of the more ethereal aspects of living.

The Mink and the Two Fishes

AN INDIAN FABLE

A few years ago a Christianized Indian named Green Tree was preaching to that remnant of the once mighty Iroquois nation that is now living on their reservation on the Otonabee River in Ontario. As he waxed eloquent in his subject, he naturally employed many figures of speech and similes drawn from the everyday life of his hearers.

To illustrate the wiles of the Evil One, he told them a fable which seems to me worthy of being published.

Most of you, no doubt, are aware that the mink is a large ferocious kind of weasel, that can swim and dive and that is very fond of fish for food. So the preacher, choosing the mink as the type of Satan, spoke thus:

"Once as the mink was traveling along the bank of a creek looking for something to eat, he came to a very wide and deep place, in the bottom of which he saw a pike that had made this pond his home. He knew that he could not catch the pike in the deep water, so he went to the edge and called out:

"'Good morning, Brother Pike.'

"The pike replied: 'Good morning, Mink. What news today?'

"'Ah,' said the mink sorrowfully, 'not very pleasant news, my brother. As I passed by where the pickerel lives, I overheard him laughing at you, and calling you "long-nose."'

"'Indeed,' said the pike angrily. 'I'll just go downstream and teach that pickerel a lesson. He shall not miscall me behind my back.'

"Then the wily mink ran down to the next pool where lived the pickerel, and said: 'Good morning, dear Brother Pickerel.'

"'The morning is fine,' said the pickerel. 'But you look sad. What is wrong?'

"'Ah,' replied the mink. 'As I passed by the pike's pond just now, he was laughing and calling you "glass bead eyes," and making great sport at your expense.'

"'Was he indeed?' said the pickerel. 'Then I'll just go up and show him that he is not safe in making sport of me.'"

The mink went upstream where there was a very shallow stony place between the two ponds. Very soon the pike came down and the pickerel came up. They met at this place, and though there was scarcely enough water to swim in, they began to fight. The mink watched till they were tired out; then, suddenly rushing in, he seized them both, dragged them to the shore, and killed them. There, for days afterwards, he feasted on the bodies of these poor dupes of his wicked cunning.

The Birch and the Balsam

Hear now, and I will tell you why the lightning never strikes the birch or the balsam tree.

Long ago, a little Rumor was flitting from tree to tree in the woods of Shebandowan. He had nothing to do but preen his wings and move his broad ears. Though very idle, he was yet a busybody—which often happens.

Just as he was yawning the twentieth time since he perched, the Star Girl came tumbling down from the sky to be the first of the Red race. She came down, not like an arrow, head first, nor like a duck, feet first; but skating and sliding this way and that like a big basswood leaf, till she dropped on a mossy bank.

There she sat very still, holding her little finger where a berry briar had scratched it, glancing through her black hair back to the sky with a sad wistful look.

When the little Rumor asked her whence she came, she made no answer, but gazed up at the sky, and a tear stood in her eye.

The little Rumor was quite touched by her silent sorrow. He was easily touched, though never deeply. And he flew off to tell somebody—anybody—how deep his feelings were.

He had scarcely taken wing when the birch tree whispered: "What news? What news, little Rumor?"

"Oh, such a sad case," answered the Rumor, and his long tongue shot out like that of a snake. "A beautiful child of the stars has fallen down, and sits now silent and sad on a bank, and her finger is bleeding."

"What! All about a scratched finger? She must be seriously hurt, probably wounded elsewhere."

"Yes, that's so. It did seem more serious than a scratched finger. I dare say she has many wounds."

"Oh, this is most interesting," said the birch as the Rumor prepared to flit. "Won't you have some refreshments? You'll find a lot of half-ripe facts on my lower branches, and under those fallen leaves are heaps of juicy innuendoes."

As the Rumor was enjoying his favorite food, the balsam called: "What news? What news, Batwing?"

He answered the balsam: "Oh, such a sad case! A beautiful maiden covered with wounds and weeping her very eyes out."

"Oh dear, has she no friends?"

But the Rumor swallowed a couple of the green facts, and flew off mumbling an innuendo.

The sun went down, and when the Rumor came back to the Star Girl, she was sitting cold and miserable on the bank.

"Would that I had a red light from that star; then should I be warm again," was all she said in answer to the Rumor. And away went the winged one zigzag. He never flew straight, but the birch tree caught sight of him and called: "Ho, long-tongue! What news? What news?"

"Starving and freezing, she—the Star Girl, nearly frozen, crying for red starlight."

"Ah, poor thing," said the balsam. "I will give her two of my limbs that will make the red starlight if she sings the wind song and rubs them as the wind rubs. I know it, for I am a Medicine Tree."

"Little use your red starlight would be," sneered the birch, for she felt the claim of "first finder," and hated the balsam for driving her from the rich ground to the rocks. "I'll give her the magic fringe of my robe that will magnify the starlight into sunlight."

"Oah! Fringe! A mere puff of dust! If she wants warmth, add a few of my cone jewels to the red light. Then you'll see results."

So away went the Rumor to the Star Girl. She rubbed the balsam sticks till a little red star came forth, then she put in the birch fringe, and it blazed. She added the balsam cones and had a warm fire. But the wind was cold on her back, and her finger was sore.

So the little Rumor told the birch and the balsam in the morning.

"Ah, poor tiny child, bleeding to death, and lying on the cold ground. Take her my balsam balm that may heal her wounds."

"She will thank you more if you take her my robe to make a wigwam," said the birch.

"Take her my boughs to make her a soft bed," said the balsam in triumph.

"I will give her also dishes, and sugar, and a canoe to ride in as well as a home. I will wear a white robe so she can find me in the woods in summer; and in winter I will hang my boughs with beads of brown wampum so she may truly know her friend."

Before the balsam could think of anything else to say, the Rumor went zigzag through the woods to the Star Girl. But he was a little liar. His tongue was forked and his flight was crooked. He could not tell the truth, and so he said: "See what I bring you from my grandmother!"

"Tell your good grandmother, whoever she is," said the Star Girl, "I thank her. There is little I can do in return but one thing. The Thunderbird is my brother, and I shall beg him never to strike the one that warmed me when I was cold and gave me so many good things."

So to this day they dispute between themselves, the birch and the balsam fir, as to which is the blessed tree of the Star Girl. Their descendants still give the race of the Star Girl the annual gifts; and the Thunderbird, not knowing which to strike, lets both alone. The pine and the oak and the ash he splinters in every storm, but the birch and the balsam stand unharmed; they never have been struck.

How do I know these things? you ask. Well, I have them as authority you will scarcely deny, the authority for nearly all history. I got this from a little idle Rumor.

Ambergris

Ambergris is a peculiar and mysterious product of the sperm whale. It is found floating on the sea and seems to be inert. It hath neither taste nor smell; it mingleth not with oil, water, or wine. Nevertheless it is vastly prized, for it hath a mystic potency to develop, intensify, and prolong the rarest qualities of flavor and perfume, bringing forth for human joy a thousand sweet and magic aura hitherto unknown.

There are some rare souls like this. They can enter a group, and at their will play ambergris; and, still remaining hid, make each give forth the rarest products of his inmost soul and wit.

The Three Kings of the Brownies

Many a little fable of the woodlands Seton told as the opportunity came to him. And many opportunities there were, for children held him in great love and reverence. Always he could weave a tale for any occasion, and what is dearer to the heart of little ones than this? As a sample I give the following:

In those days there was no winter in the Land beyond the Lakes; and while this was very pleasing to the Brownies of the Wood, it was a source of sorrow to the Snow Fairies that hang the brookside with their white lacework in the far North where they revel.

But their country is small. So they complained to the All-Mother who dwells in the ground.

"The night birds," they pointed out, "have the earth for half the time, and the day birds for the other half. Why should not we hold half dominion on the Land beyond the Lakes, where now there is one long Brownie reign?"

Meanwhile, the Brownies, hearing of this dissatisfaction, hurried in alarm, and begged the All-Mother to leave things as they were, with one unending summer in the Land beyond the Lakes.

The All-Mother replied at length: "You have three kings in the woods. There is the Kingbird with his crest of gold and flame, the Kingfisher with his necklace of white and blue wampum, and the Kinglet with his crown of golden red. As long as these can face the Snow Fairies, the summer shall stay."

Then began the battle, as all know so well. The Snow Fairies, armed with a dawn-chill, tried to slip in by night to frighten the Kingbird. But he fluffed out his feathers and faced them and fought bravely for a long time. And the Brownies encouraged him as well as watched him. The Snow Fairies found that they could not kill the Kingbird; but with the dawn-chill and fog-damp, they destroyed his favorite food. Finally tiring of the fight, he, one black night, pulled his dark feathers over his flaming crest so as to escape detection by the Brownies, and fled away over the river at the end of the lake. So the summer ended according to the promise.

The Snow Fairies, led by Jack Frost, had scored one great victory.

But now the autumn was bright and glorious, and the Brownies watched the other two kings very closely after this. The Snow Fairies realized they must conquer the Kingfisher next. They knew perfectly well that he feared not the fog-damp nor the dawn-chills; he would stay while he had open water. So each night they set to work to seal over the brooks.

But the Brownies worked just as hard breaking the ice all night, and so the Kingfisher stayed.

At length came Indian summer, and there were ten nights in succession without any ice. The Brownies, thinking they had utterly routed the enemy, held a great feast, leaving but one sentinel. Finally, growing ever more careless, they did not even set a watch;

and the crafty Snow Fairies came and sealed up all the ponds and streams with ice. So the Kingfisher flew away over Niagara, and with him went the bright autumn.

Winter was here now—not hard winter, but cold at nights. The Brownies knew it would get no worse if the Kinglet could be kept in the Land beyond the Lakes. The Brownies could always tell where the Kinglet was by his flaming crest. So they not only set a watch to follow him, and persuade him to go back by offering him fine foods when he seemed likely to fly away; they also stationed a sentry at each end of the big lake, and at Niagara, and even at Eri-west.

The Snow Fairies found that the Kinglet laughed at dawn-chills and fog-damp and ice-walls. Though the smallest of their enemies, he was the most fearless. And the campaign failed.

Then, after much effort, the Snow Fairies succeeded in enlisting the aid of the North Wind and the Snow Cloud.

It was a long pursuit and a hard one. They climbed up tree after tree to catch him, and the woody fungus sprang out of the bark of each to help them.

But in the end the Kinglet took alarm and flew away even earlier than he would otherwise have done, over the open lake.

So the Snow Fairies had won, winter really came for part of the year. And it has been so ever since each year in the Land beyond the Lakes.

Fable of the Woods

Another aspect of the same basic idea came to me in this fable:

"How is it, Father," asked a little boy, "that last April I could find nothing in the woods but pussy willows. Every tree seemed to be pussy willow. Then, in a week, I found nothing but spicebush; all the woods seemed spicebush. But it changed at the last of the month, and wherever I looked was red maple blossom. Now there is only dogwood. I look around, and as far as I can see, every tree seems white with dogwood bloom. The willows, spicebush, and red maples are gone. Do they really change one into the other?"

"Nay, my son," replied the father. "Each has its time in which it is the center of all observation and seems to hold the woods. It is like a country school at commencement. There is a throng of little scholars each in his best; each one has a little piece to say and comes forward smiling. For the moment he is the only one observed, all eyes are on him. Then he goes back and is lost in the crowd. Only one can come at a time, and all have their turn, a chance to show what they can do.

"But with the trees, all the year is commencement, from March, when the pussy willows bloom, to November with witch hazel threads of gold. Each says his little piece, seems the only one alive. He owns the hills and woods for a time, then retires to lose himself in the crowd like the scholar who has done his part, whose piece is said and done."

The Fate of Little Mucky

Anyone who has achieved a certain measure of success cannot but be attacked by a class of critics who may or may not be instigated by worthy motives.

In 1904, John Burroughs made such a literary attack on Seton. The bitter denunciation appeared in the *Atlantic Monthly*. It was so unfair and untrue that Seton was amused and made no reply. He felt that the article was an answer to itself.

His personal reaction was voiced in the following little allegory, never hitherto published:

Once there was a race of beings with peculiar laws of growth— they grew big in proportion to what they had done.

In a corner of their land was one who worked away very quietly for half his lifetime, thinking not about growth but about doing certain things that were next his heart.

It so happened that many of his long tasks were finished about the same time; and so he seemed to grow very fast, and became much bigger than his immediate neighbors.

Most of them rejoiced at his success. But there was one who had long schemed and aimed at "being big" without work; and so, by the obverse of the same natural law, had kept on shriveling.

This only thought in his small heart continued to flourish: "I

cannot get anyone to notice me now; but if I can throw a handful
of mud on this tall one that I hate, I shall at least have all eyes
turned my way for a time."

So he prepared a quantity of the nastiest filth he could find; and
by climbing on a hill called Big-serial, he reached high enough to
throw the muck, and the tall worker was plentifully spattered. Everyone turned in surprise, and saw the spindly dwarf grinning with
delight at his success, happy to be for a moment the center of observation.

At first, some of them laughed with the dwarf, and everyone
wondered what the other would do. He would be quite justified in
using his power.

But instead, he went on quietly with his work. The filth was
easily brushed away, because it had no affinities there.

The dwarf grew smaller. People sniffed at him after the first ripple
of surprise and amusement. Furious now, he ran after the worker to
repeat his attack. But, not realizing that he had shrunken to a mere
pigmy, he fell into the hole where he had mixed the muck and was
smothered.

Here endeth the tale of Little Mucky, the envious critic.

Moral: Notoriety is a poisonous substitute for Fame.

The Dream Prince

Seton had, among many others, one marvelous gift. Not only was he
a *raconteur par excellence;* but for any basic thought he could on
the spot weave a story that would embody the idea and make it a
rememberable part of every hearer's life thereafter. Many were the
parables that he fabricated for particular occasions. By their very
nature, they were not written down; and where shortcomings are
apparent in my rendition of them, the blame must rest on my inad-
equacy of presentation.

One which, because it had a very personal message for me, he
called "The Dream Prince."

"Once there was a little girl who loved fairy tales. She read
them, lived and shaped her nature to them, more and more, till all
her heart was in fairyland.

"In her beautiful fantasies, there appeared always her Dream Prince. He was so wonderful that her life grew into one long hungry search for the Dream Prince who would take her by the hand and walk with her in the fairy wood.

"One day as she walked, alone and feeling sad for lack of company, she came suddenly on a boy. He gazed at her very steadfastly, and said: 'Little Girl, I am looking for my Dream Princess—and I think you are she. Will you take my hand and let me show you the Fairy Trail?'

"His eyes were kind, and his manner very gentle and respectful. She liked him. But as she gazed, she saw that he had a pug nose, whereas her Dream Prince had perfect Greek features. In other ways, too, he did not fit her dream, so she said: 'No! Go away! You are not my Dream Prince!'

"The boy went away and she saw him no more.

"But when he was gone, she felt lonelier than ever, and began wishing hard.

"After many days, she suddenly met another boy who came forward, boisterously shouting: 'Ho, Little Girl, come be my Dream Princess!' She was frightened a little, and yet attracted too by his boldness; and when she looked up, she saw that he had a beautiful Greek nose and classical features. She did not quite like his manner, but she remembered how sad she had been after sending the other one away. So, in spite of a sinking and shrinking, she held out her hand. He took it and they walked together.

"Everything should have been worth twice as much now—but somehow it was not. Instead of more gladness, she found less in the pleasant things about. The boy was rude, too. He did not help her in stony places as he did in her dreams; and when by chance he hurt her hand, he merely laughed.

"So she became very sad, and lonesomer than ever.

"One day the boy was running ahead to show his superiority, when he slipped and fell. As he did so, a mask fell from his face, and she saw that all his beauty was put on. He was really very ugly. He was nothing but a tinsel ghoul.

"The girl turned and ran in terror; and never stopped running till she was safe and far away, and quite alone.

"She thought sadly of the snub-nosed Prince. But he was gone, and all her lovely dreams made her sadder and lonelier than ever.

"Now she remembered that she was not the first one to wander in the woods. Others had dreamed and suffered, and sometimes they found comfort one way and sometimes another. But all the wiser ones, she realized, sought strength in work.

"So she prepared a little garden in which to grow chosen flowers, and so find joy. But she wearied of it, and gave it up before any real good had come. She wandered off, lonely and sad, utterly broken. She lay down on a bank, and cried:

"'Oh, I didn't know! I didn't know!'

"She was a long time lying there when she heard a noise; and, looking up, saw not far away a stranger—a boy older and bigger than herself, with a weather-beaten face. She was not afraid. She looked straight at him inquiringly but said nothing.

"Then he spoke: 'Little Girl, when I saw you there on the ground, I thought at first you were a moss bump. Now I see you are a beautiful girl.

"'Little Girl, you have lived always in this woods. I have lived not only here, but in the woods behind, and in the one behind that. And I have lived longer, so I know something you do not know. *I* can read where *you* may be blind. This I read on your face and hand: you have sought your Dream Prince and made a mistake, so were trapped by a tinsel ghoul. That was your punishment.

"'Yes, Little Girl, I also sought my Dream Princess, and foolishly pictured myself as worthy of her. But I was burnt in the fire for my blunder. Yes, burnt in many fires, till I swallowed my wrath and found pleasure in my garden. That is what I am doing now. You also started, but you did not keep on till the radiance came from the ground.

"'Listen now, Little Girl. At the times when I am not working, I feel the same old sadness and hankering. But I have ceased to clamor for my old Dream Girl. I know now that I do not care what shape her nose may be. I know she will come when I have won the right to see her. I have learned that the Dream Princess is *not found* but is made out of one's self and the other one. Half at least of your Dream Prince must be what you construct by glorifying common clay.

"'I am not your Dream Prince. I too weather-beaten and unkempt. I do not know whether or not you are my Dream Princess now. All

I can say is: I offer you this—good fellowship and kindness—that is all. We are both of us very lonely. Will you take my hand and walk with me in the woods?'"

Popular Myth

A quality which made Seton a joy to live with was his absolute honesty. To be sure, in the realm of fiction, or even semi-truth, when it held no ethic purport, he never allowed fact to spoil a good story. He claimed that it was the duty of the real storyteller to leave a tale better than he had found it.

But where natural history or everyday living was concerned, I always knew that I need never think twice about a statement he made. There was never a dissimulation of idea or emotion, never a falsification of incident, never an evasion in the slightest degree from the probity of an event.

One day, as we talked about the moral need for such living, he remarked:

"A total untruth is generally easy to dispose of. 'The lie that is half a truth,' the poet informs us, 'is the dangerous one.' The tiny element of truth in it gives it fighting force and longevity enough to do much evil."

Then, with the innate slant of his mind to matters of natural history, he went on:

"To this demimonde of statement belongs the popular myth; and in every myth that persists from generation to generation, we are pretty sure to find that the fiber of strength is a modicum of fact."

He proceeded to tell me of an experience of his boyhood which illustrated the principle.

"My companions," he said, "knowing my inherent interest, several times told me of a new hummingbird that had appeared. It was as small as the head of an ordinary hummingbird, no bigger than a bumblebee. Its body was green, its throat snowy white, its beak long and curved—at least an inch long. It had big liquid eyes like those of a fawn. Its tail was fan-shaped and of silky brown feathers. Its wings could not be seen clearly as it flew; but hanging from the body under the wings were long filaments like the wires on a Bird of Paradise, and from its head two others like horns.

"Many persons reported that they had seen the creature frequently, but always in the evening, poised in front of a flower, then off with a buzz and lost to view.

"There could be no question of its existence; yet somehow I myself was never privileged to see it. It seemed a cruel wrong that I should always miss what clearly promised to be a real fairy, an elfin bird.

"I could find no description in the books of such a bird; and the summer went by without a clue as to its identity.

"From their accounts, I made a drawing which embodied the details.

"Then one day a friend came to me in triumph. He had *secured the tiny bird.* Corked up in a pill bottle was a creature then new to me. Yes, the velvet body and snowy throat were there, the fantail, the plumes, the big lustrous eyes. But the creature was not a bird at all—it was an insect!

"Now I dimly remembered, and in a few hours' search among my books learned, that this was the hummingbird moth, common in some regions, scarce in mine, but perfectly well known to scientists.

"The myth of the fairy bird had grown all that summer; and it was with a jolt that I had to accept the fact that was the basis for what had given me many joyous hours of delirious dreaming."

Other myths in the natural history world Seton explained on various occasions.

There is a large area of eastern America where both red squirrel and gray squirrel are found. In all this area we find current the tale that there is deadly animosity between the two; that the red squirrel, though smaller, is a more valiant fighter; and, thoughtfully determined to keep down the numbers of his enemy, pursues and emasculates as many male gray squirrels as he can. Possibly it is from motives of clemency that he does not follow the more obvious and simple plan of ending their existence at once.

That is the myth.

These are the facts as Seton pointed them out: The two squirrels are rival species, they need the same food trees and shelter trees, so come much in conflict. The red is an aggressive scold, the gray squirrel likes quiet. Therefore the larger will often vacate a disputed tree for the sake of peace. The red squirrel follows, chattering noisily, but usually at a safe distance.

Now there is in the same region a specimen of botfly or warble scientifically called *Cuterebra emasculator*. This fly lays its eggs in the skin of a squirrel, preferably a gray squirrel, and usually near the anal region. There this bot or grub grows to be an inch long, feeding on the tissues and juices of the squirrel. If, as often happens, it is laid in the scrotum, it develops there and either eats up or atrophies the testicles, hence the name *emasculator*.

This grub leaves the squirrel in early autumn, but the wounds and evidence of destruction are there. Hunters who have shot the gray squirrel so conditioned have had no difficulty in making out a strong circumstantial case to show that the red squirrel has been indulging his taste for refined cruelty, and at the same time blasting his enemy's hopes of posterity.

The myth of the beaver plastering with his tail rests first on the evident trowel shape of the tail, made doubly suitable by its lack of hair; next by the fact that the beaver slaps the water with his tail; and lastly by the marks of his tail appearing occasionally on the mud covering the dam. These facts have started a belief which few persons have questioned or investigated. The fact that all the beaver houses we have seen—and that is hundreds—were in summer covered externally with sticks, not plastered with mud, seems to explode the myth which one hears so persistently.

The earliest published portrait of the American buffalo is a good illustration of a perfectly crooked story out of a perfectly straight witness.

Antonio de Solis described as follows the first one seen by Cortez in 1521:

"The greatest rarity was the Mexican bull; a wonder composition of divers animals. It has crooked shoulders, with a bunch on its back like a camel; its flanks dry, its tail large and its neck covered with hair like a lion. It is cloven-footed, its head armed like that of a bull, which it resembles in fierceness with no less strength and agility." The artist who was commissioned to make the illustration took the description word for word and conscientiously made his drawing.

A charming myth still current in the mountains of Wyoming and Idaho is that of the fantail deer. The hunters have long maintained that there is in those mountains a wonderful little deer. It is no larger than a jack rabbit, its colors are those of a Virginia deer, but its rear end is white; its tail a foot long and six inches wide, brown above, snowy white beneath. When raised aloft, the tail doubles the height of the creature and makes its whole rear aspect pure white. As soon as the tail is dropped, all the white is hidden, the animal is but half the size and appears gray-brown.

Its habit, the hunters say, is to skulk in the densely wooded ravines of the timber belt. Ordinarily it glides about silently like a weasel, under logs and in thickets; it will hide in a hollow tree or lie in a hole in the ground; it will even climb a sloping tree at times. When pursued, it glides away and hides. But when at length startled out, it bounds away with fantail up, and is evidently a snow-white deer. Like a rabbit, it zigzags under logs and into cover; but instead of running a mile or two, it squats as soon as out of sight. At once, by depressing the flag, it hides all white color and turns itself into a gray-brown bump not much larger than your hat. If you do pass near, you certainly will not recognize in this small gray stone the snow-white deer you sought.

That is the myth. Here are the facts so far as we can learn them. The common whitetail deer is found sparingly in all the ravines of the Rockies. Its habits are skulking; it is an adept at hiding; it has a fantail somewhat as described. Sometimes fawns lose their mothers and become miserable little runts, apparently mature, as they have horns. But everything about them is undersized; and occasional examples secured, with many examples not secured but glimpsed, have furnished the ground for the myth of the jack-rabbit fantail.

It is only fair to say, however, that in Mexico there is a tiny deer that comes very near to realizing the creature of the Rocky Mountain campfire story.

"A singular bird myth that came to my knowledge some twenty years ago," said Seton one night, "I have seen in various forms and diverse lands many times since.

"I was traveling across Lake Superior in 1886, when I met among the passengers a Dr. B——. He told me, with all the impressiveness of his professional attitude and dialect, the story of a lame snipe that had repaired its own broken limb.

"The snipe was found in a swamp; it was wounded and sick. On being secured alive, it was found to have a broken leg, evidently the result of a shot. Probably there were other wounds, as it could not fly. But the singular thing was that the broken limb was set, and in splints which consisted of a mass of hardened mud wrapped around vegetable fibers. The artificiality of the setting was very remarkable; but became still more so when it was shown clearly that the bird had set its own limb, using mud and such fibers as it could find. The snipe was set free in a small yard where was mud and cover; and nearly every day it was seen attending to the dressing until the limb was healed, the mud removed, and once more it was a well snipe.

"These, I take it, were the facts: the snipe was disabled and its leg broken by a shot. It hid in the grass of its regular muddy haunts, holding up the broken leg. Nature as usual had poured out plastic lymph on the wound, forming a great bump. On and in this, the mud of the marsh accumulated, as the bird was not using the leg in a way to clean it. In the mud on the bump were also caught vegetable fibers. These, when long, were annoying and painful. The bird tugged at them with his bill, and so removed the worst ones. The lymph and mud mass continued as long as the leg was held up. When it was healed, and could be used again, the lump was reabsorbed, and the ordinary process of use would clean off the leg.

"When last heard, the myth had not yet credited the snipe with the use of a crutch."

"The latest and most satisfactory myth that I have met," he said on another occasion, "came from the Delaware River, and was known as the pigmy gazelle of Oquago.

"There appeared on the Oquago Creek a wonderful little gazelle. It was smaller than the smallest gazelle of Africa; it was, in fact, less than a rabbit. It dwelt on the creek in question, and its tracks showed that it wandered up and down a mile or more. Many of the local trappers went eagerly in pursuit, but it baffled their skill. Wonderful stories of its beauty, its rich fur, its exquisite horns, were circulated in the local papers and other equally unimpeachable records of science.

"Interest grew to fever heat. Finally a professor of the Harrisburg Museum was aroused. A thorough investigation showed that nothing had been seen of the gazelle except its tracks, but these were well known and eagerly shown to the men of science. There could be no question of their genuineness. Each was the track of a hoof that was smaller than the print of a little finger tip; the stride of the track-maker was three or four inches long. Fraud was impossible—no man would or could make miles of these for the sake of a joke. Besides, it was *evidently the real trail of a real animal,* had all the singularities and inevitable accidents of a trail. The wonder grew.

"But the light came. A trapper, Nelson Crane, putting out a line of fur traps, determined to catch or shoot the gazelle. One morning as he went his rounds he saw the unmistakable trail of the pigmy running ahead of him. He followed, and it led him to one of his own traps. This was sprung, the creature was gone, but in the trap—oh, marvel!—was a tiny foot with hoofs unquestionably those that would make such tracks as those of the gazelle. He sent this to Professor H. A. Surface of the Harrisburg Museum. There he and I examined it together, and came to the conclusion that beyond a peradventure it was the foot of a muskrat on which, by some freak development, the two center claws had been expanded into hoofs. The side claws were either dropped or absorbed.

"We have not yet seen the creature itself, but no one who has seen the foot has hesitated to accept the above conclusion."

Salt Mountain Fable

These various examples of the growth of popular myth were not all given me at the same sitting. With the joyous twenty-four-hour-a-day association which we possessed, we often took up a theme which we had discussed before in order to elaborate on it, re-express it, or again revel in the pleasure we had earlier experienced in it. One day, in line with this idea of enduring truth, he gave me the following fable which he had written in June 1907 at Salt Mountain.

Once there was a youth who dreamed in his daydreams that he was to discover Montezuma's Spring and be known to the world. He had tramped the woods and mountains for twenty-five years; and a few white hairs had appeared on his temple when, one day, he discovered the long-sought spring far in the hills beyond, in a vast and terrible swamp.

He had saved the skins of beasts he had killed; and now he filled a bear skin, a wolf skin, and a deer skin, and thus bore the precious water back to the haunts of man.

Everyone knew them for the living waters that they were, and were glad to buy. He was proud to share his burden with all who had understanding; and though he asked no return, the people of the town showered gifts on him.

Finally, though he wasted nothing, the water in the last skin was getting low. One day an evil spirit came and tempted him, saying: "The water from the Holy Spring is low. These folk are willing to buy at a great price. Take therefore the half skinful you have left, and mix with it enough common water to fill the three skins. Thus you will have enough to sell again; and it will indeed have some of the virtue of the true Spring."

Then was the Spring-finder indignant, and said: "Get behind me! Whatever comes, I will never dilute the true waters. And if by chance they are touched by uncleanness or pollution, it shall not be my fault. I may be old, but I know the road." So he left the remaining water with a good keeper and, taking the three skins that he might again fill them at the Spring, set out through the swamps—a long journey—one that eats a great hole in a lifetime.

After many years he returned, sent the full skins to his friend, and went to a quiet place of rest. He knew not how the waters would now be received; but at least he himself was very sure that they came from the true Spring, and he was content.

Santa Claus

In the early 1900s, Seton was a member of the editorial board of the *Ladies' Home Journal*. A number of his stories also appeared in pages of that magazine, so that he was soon considered a friend by countless boys and girls all over the country. Many letters asking advice on various subjects came to him from time to time. One was from a little boy out on the Western frontier. He wrote: "Will you please tell me if there is a Santa Claus—Papa says not."

With his usual integrity, and yet with an understanding of the child's need, Seton replied: "Why, of course there is a Santa Claus, and you will find that Papa wasn't paying attention when he said that there was not. What Papa meant was that there isn't a big fat Santa Claus man that rides on the roof with eight reindeer, and comes down the chimney with gifts to put in the stockings. Papa knows, as do we all, that that kind of Santa Claus was made up to put in picture books.

"But the real Santa Claus is a spirit, the Christmas spirit of love and giving. This is the good principle that God puts into the hearts of men at the same season of the year that He gave His own great gift to the world. However poor or greedy a man may be at other times, the gentle spirit of giving comes into his heart at Christmas. Then the rich man gives to the poor one, and none is so poor but that he gives something. Even the birds and beasts are remembered, and fed by their human enemies.

"And, of course, your own father, who is giving you all the things you need, wants to make your Christmas glad by gifts of unusual number and delight.

"Now, he wants you to find these the very first thing on Christmas morning; so he puts them in your room while you sleep. And to make sure just which are for you and which for your brother, he puts into the stocking of each those that are his proper share.

"That is how it began. But people always want to make pictures of things they love; and so, since the Santa Claus spirit that came in your father's heart was a generous merry soul, the picture-makers made him big and jolly-looking. And since he comes in winter, they show him in warm furs. Because he has so many gifts, they pretend that he needs a sleigh to carry them. Since the best and jolliest Christmas is the white one with the north wind blowing, they tell you that he comes on a gale from the snowland where reindeer are used to draw the sleigh.

"However, all of this is only 'pretend' to make a picture, because we cannot make a picture of a spirit. You will find, if you ask your father again, that he was not thinking of what you meant when he answered you; and he knows perfectly well that Santa Claus is the loving, cheerful, and generous spirit which comes into his heart at Christmastime and causes him to remember his little boy and plans to make him unusually happy that day. For *he* knows— and *I* know—and you will, I am sure, believe—that there is just as surely a Santa Claus at Christmas as there is a God in heaven all the time."

PART TEN

A CANDLE AT THE SHRINE

ASPECTS OF ART

A Versatile Genius

As one reads through the foregoing chapters, one must be struck with the diversity of Seton's interests, the breadth of subject matter that he treated, the all-inclusiveness of his writing. Every incident of a commonplace day, every phase of world events, every aspect of life—all was ink for his pen, food to be served to those who relish a varied menu for the nourishment of the mental body.

He was a practical architect who built many homes. He was a sculptor of rare excellence. He was a portrait painter of masterly skill. But, in most profusion, he is known as a graphic artist of pre-eminence.

All his work was done without a thought of material gain. He never painted a picture for sale; he was merely making a documentary record of something he had seen, to be preserved for the benefit of those students who were still to come.

His technique in this field was innate. True, he studied art under some of the best masters for several years. But this was after he was thirty years of age; and we can with assurance say that many of his best paintings were done before he had had any formal training.

His approach to a picture was never objective. He had no academic plan in mind; he simply put on paper or canvas whatever he saw. For this reason, perhaps, his treatment might take any one of a host of methods, of materials, of techniques.

Some of his birds and mammals, especially in his early years, are so microscopically true to life that one cannot believe they were produced by a human hand. Again, some of his landscapes could be hung in a gallery of contemporary art these days, and would pass for the work of the most modern painter. A line here, a dot there—and the form of the subject, even the mood of a scene, is before one's eyes with a verity that cannot be expressed in words.

He worked in every medium. Very rarely did he determine beforehand whether he would use pencil, charcoal, ink, wash, or water color in a subject he was about to depict. As a matter of fact, he seldom planned a drawing in that deliberate way.

In the field, he might encounter a bird or an animal in a particular attitude. Or, for some reason, he might be in the company of a man or a woman who presented some interesting characterization, or the form of a cluster of trees might appeal to his artist's eye.

Without further consideration of method or medium, he would delve into his pockets for anything that could serve as a canvas.

Sometimes his notebook was available. But often, in his need to capture the essentials of a fleeting detail, he would sketch his impressions on the back of an envelope, on the margin of a newspaper clipping, on the back of another drawing—whatever came to hand at the moment.

One charming drawing of a bird which we have in the Seton Gallery is on the face of a Canadian postcard, with the post office stamp showing through the lines of the sketch!

He never thought of his work as art presentation—although he knew it was good. Each delineation was to him merely a documentary record of what he had seen, but each an authoritative portrait of an experience in his life.

The Century Dictionary

When Seton came of age he was living in Canada in a small backwoods town. He realized that if he was to make a success of his life he would have to get to some metropolitan center, and the logical one was New York.

So, as before noted, in November 1883 he set out. He landed at 23rd Street Ferry, absolutely alone, no friends there, no introductions, knowing nothing of the city, and with two dollars in his pocket.

It was a public holiday weekend, so all business houses were closed, and he could not therefore even look for a job.

There was but one point of interest for him in New York. He

knew that somewhere in the city was a place called Central Park, and they had animals there. Central Park has always had a good zoo.

He hesitatingly approached a policeman and asked: "Can you tell me how I can get to Central Park?"

The officer replied: "Well, you take the trolley that comes down this street, and ride to—"

"Oh," interrupted Seton, "I don't want to ride. I want to walk."

"Hell!" exploded the policeman. "You can't walk. It's miles."

"Oh yes, I can walk."

When he had convinced the man that he really intended to walk, the officer shrugged his shoulders and said:

"Well, there is Fifth Avenue. If you will go long enough and far enough, you will get to Central Park."

So Seton started out. It was several miles; but, with his usual determination, he proceeded until he came to the Park.

He strolled about for some time among the caged animals, until he came to a mule deer in particularly good condition. He sat down at close quarters, and made a careful drawing of it.*

He tramped back to lower Lexington Avenue and soon found lodgings—a small bedroom at two dollars a week. He paid a dollar in advance, sent for his trunk, which was at the ferry; and with less than one dollar on hand, bought two rolls and half a pound of dates. He budgeted his supply of food, which meant that he might eat half a roll at each mealtime.

He had known that in New York was the office of the *Century Magazine,* and they had an art department. So, with but little hope of finding anyone there because of the holiday, he determined to have at least a look at the building. He inquired the way—and, of course, walked.

It was afternoon when he reached the place, quite the most pretentious edifice he had ever seen in his young life. He entered the lobby, and there encountered a man most gorgeously arrayed in a spanking dark blue suit, elaborately trimmed with gold lace across the shoulders, down the front of the coat and the sides of the trousers.

The boy was abashed; he felt that he must be in the presence of

* That very drawing is now in the Seton Gallery at Santa Fe, one of our highly prized exhibits.

some very high official of the government. It could not, he decided, be the President of the United States because he knew that *he* lived in Washington. But perhaps the Vice-President?

It was the elevator boy, but never yet in his life had he seen an elevator.

After an embarrassing pause, he finally screwed up his courage to address the man, and asked if he could tell him where were the offices of the *Century Magazine*.

"On the fifth floor," was the prompt and polite reply. "Get in and I'll take you up."

"Get in! Where?" He saw nothing but a big square hole in the wall.

"In there! In the elevator!" was the rather impatient reply.

Now a new obstacle presented itself in the mind of the stripling. "How much does it cost?"

"Nothing! Nothing! Get in!"

So he was whisked without effort to the fifth floor, where he timidly tapped at the door bearing the inscription CENTURY MAGAZINE. He expected no response, but luck was with him. The door was opened by a fine-looking man who inquired Ernest's business.

"I am looking for the art department of *Century Magazine,* but I presume there is no one working today."

"Come in, young man," was the reply. "I am the art manager, Lewis Fraser, and I happen to be here today doing some extra-curricular work. What is your business?"

The older man's courteous manner encouraged Ernest to continue. "Do you ever look at the sketches of unknown young artists?"

"Yes, indeed," was the quick response. "We look at everything that comes along. Someday we may find something."

Seton now opened his poor little portfolio, full of sketches, everything he had drawn during the preceding months. He took out the one of the mule deer he had done at Central Park the previous day.

Fraser looked at it long and critically. Finally he said: "Young man, I do not know anything about that animal, but I am sure this is a mighty good drawing of it. Perhaps we can do business."

They talked together for some time and Seton showed him other sketches, which apparently impressed him. Finally he said:

"This is a holiday and my associates are not here today. Will you leave these with me and come back tomorrow morning?"

Would he? Seton went away with hope in his heart and joy in his walk.

The next morning he breakfasted on his roll and dates with a drink of water at Madison Square fountain, then retraced his steps to the *Century Magazine* office. He was introduced to the other members of the art department and they discussed many angles of the situation till nearly noon. But when he left to tread back the several miles to Vesey Street, he had in his pocket a contract to do 1000 bird and mammal drawings at five dollars apiece. He did not have to turn these in at once, which would of course have been quite impossible; but he would be paid as the sketches were completed and delivered to the magazine, to be included in the Century Dictionary, then the second undertaking of the great company founded by Roswell Smith.

The Art Anatomy of Animals

Seton spent six years in Paris, not only studying at Julien's Academy, but putting in many hours of each day—or rather night—working on projects of his own. Many of the life studies which still bring forth words of the highest praise from the critics were done during this period. It was also at this time that he did his *Sleeping Wolf.** This won for him the Gold Medal of the Grand Salon (Paris) in 1891.

The Triumph of the Wolves, a canvas 5½×7 feet, was painted at this time and, after much controversy over the subject, was finally exhibited at the Chicago World's Fair in 1893.

* The succeeding history is so fresh and delightful in my own memory, that I give it here, though totally out of chronological sequence. Through the years, the picture was either sold, given away, or otherwise disposed of, so that by the time I became associated with Seton, no one knew where it was. Then, one day in 1963, there came a letter from a gentleman in Toronto who apparently knew Seton's work well and sincerely appreciated it. The letter said that, through some family incidents, he at present needed money. Would I care to buy the original *Sleeping Wolf* which he had acquired some years previously in a vicarious manner? *Would I?* Arrangements were speedily completed; and now after more than seventy years the picture, beautiful as ever, and as originally framed, hangs on a conspicuous wall of Seton Castle in Santa Fe.

In order to do this latter painting, he made innumerable studies of sky and landscape effects, as well as sketches of wolves in all positions; separate drawings of legs, heads, bodies, all elaborately detailed.

This preliminary work, as well as the years he had spent previously illustrating the Century Dictionary, convinced him of the need for a monograph on animal anatomy. There was no work presenting the general principles of comparative anatomy as applied to art.

There had been several treatises on the anatomy of the horse, and one or two on others of the domesticated animals, but these were of little value to the artist. Either they were written entirely from the surgical or zoological standpoint, and internal structure rather than external form made the chief object of study; or the subject was treated obviously with only the dead animal in view. Also they were overburdened with text, and in most cases poorly illustrated.

With his characteristic enthusiasm, he set to work, planning a book which would correct these faults. He spent months measuring live dogs, cats, horses, cows, and birds. He worked always with the living subject before him as well as a dead one on the dissecting table.

He made the most careful analysis of the visible forms and proportions of each species.

Besides the principal bones and muscles, he studied the tendons, the cartilages, the sinew sheaths, the external veins and nerves, the folds of skin, the teeth, the claws, the hoofs, the horns. He analyzed the hair, the fur, the feathers, realizing that every part of the animal was of equal importance with every other part, and each had a bearing on the ultimate true representations of the creature.

With the utmost exactitude, he drew every detail. Eventually these years of close application resulted in the publication by Macmillan of London of the unique volume, *The Art Anatomy of Animals.*

The text of this book is indispensable to the artist who works with animals or birds; yet is clear and readable even for the layman. But the 100 illustrations form the major part of the volume; and all critics agree that the perfection of the draftsmanship makes this a unique contribution to the field of art, whether it be of the human or animal world. It remains the standard and model for every student, yes, even for the few writers who have since treated the subject in an effort to spread the knowledge that on canvas produces an animal that lives after the end of its active existence.

The Arctic Prairies

From his early youth there was a yearning heartache in Seton. He lamented the fact that he had been born too late to have experienced the romance of the Wild West where fences were unknown, to have seen the teeming herds of wild game, to have rejoiced in the primitive lands where White man had never yet set foot.

It was not until he reached middle age that he was able to satisfy that lifelong hunger. It was by that time no longer possible to find such unspoiled conditions in the United States. But in the far northwest of Canada, and even on to the Arctic Plains, it was said that the caribou still roamed in their aboriginal numbers.

So in the May of 1907, accompanied by E. A. Preble of the Biological Survey, he set out on what turned out to be a 2000-mile canoe trip to the region north of Aylmer Lake. He was, as always, equipped with the means of recording every natural history event that came his way on that seven-month trip into hitherto untracked territory.

They journeyed down the Athabasca River to Fort Chipewyan, thence to Fort Resolution on Great Slave Lake, and by way of Artillery Lake to the land of the caribou. They discovered two great rivers which they named Earl Grey and Laurier.

The maps which Seton made on that trip are still said to be the best available, and are to this day used as travel guides to the region.

The Arctic Prairies is a book which will appeal to the sportsman and the naturalist for the wealth of information on the mammals, birds, and flora of this now better-known country. But for the lay reader it is a book crammed with adventure: strange people—White, Red, and half-breed—who lived their lives in this unexplored land,

picturesque scenes of frontier existence, poetry and pathos enough
to satisfy the desire for human interest. And always humor, evident
in both story and picture in his own inimitable manner. It is difficult to find in the literature of adventurous travel a more dramatic
yet sincere narrative; and all told in the unique readable style
that is Seton's lasting contribution to the world's store of knowledge.

What the seven-month expedition meant to Seton is best expressed
in the last page of the book. It reads as follows:

"I had held in my heart the wanderlust till it swept me away,
and sent me afar on the back trail of the north wind. I have lived
in the mighty boreal forest, with its Red men, its buffalo, its moose,
and its wolves; I have seen the Great Lone Land with its endless
plains and prairies that do not know the face of man or the crack
of a rifle; I have been with its countless lakes that re-echo nothing
but the wail and yodel of the loons, or the mournful music of
the arctic wolf. I have wandered on the plains of the musk ox, the
home of the snowbird and the caribou. These were the things I
had burned to do.

"*Was I content? Content!* Is a man ever content with a single
sip of joy long dreamed of?

"Four years have gone since then. The wanderlust was not stifled
any more than a fire is stifled by giving it air. I have taken into
my heart a longing, given shape to an ancient instinct. Have I not
found for myself a kingdom and become a part of it?

"My reason and my heart say, 'Go back to see it all.' Grant
only this, that I gather again the same brave men that manned
my frail canoe, and as sure as life and strength continue, *I shall go.*"

The Lives of Game Animals

In 1904, when John Burroughs' notorious attack on Seton came
out in the *Atlantic Monthly,* many of the most famous naturalists
contradicted his accusation. Among these protagonists, Theodore
Roosevelt, at that time President of the United States, in vigorous
protest to the attack, said to Seton: "Burroughs and the people at
large do not know how many facts you have back of your stories.
You must publish your facts!"

As far back as 1897, Seton had planned to do this very thing. In 1898 he had made the range maps of the big mammals, traveling into every State of the Union and into nearly every Province of Canada. His daily journals, at that time twenty-five volumes of them, contained his observations in minutest detail, with hundreds of sketches to fortify his written notes.

At Roosevelt's insistence, Seton went to work, but it was not until 1909 that his *Life Histories of Northern Animals* was published. This was a set of two quarto volumes, pronounced at the time "the most complete and authoritative mammal work of its kind ever published."

Meanwhile, he continued to gather material, never doubting that in three or four years more he should get out two additional volumes to cover the field.

But the three or four years grew to be ten. Finally in 1919 we definitely abandoned all other pursuits. He now felt that, in order to bring all knowledge on the subject up to date, the *Life Histories* had to be rewritten.

For eight years, seven days a week, we worked, together with one to three secretaries. We did little lecturing during that time, wrote no other books, took no holidays, turned down even social engagements.

The amount of time and energy expended in letters, in checking up newspaper accounts, running down references, etc., would be believed by no one who has not done likewise.

The first volume of this monumental work appeared in 1925, the first of the de luxe edition of 177 sets. It caused a great stir in natural history circles.

In 1926 the second volume was published. For this he received the John Burroughs Medal, an amusing satire on the fact that it was Burroughs himself who really set off the writing of this work when he attacked the authenticity of Seton's natural history articles.

The third volume appeared in 1927; for this one Seton was awarded the Daniel Giraud Elliott Medal by the National Academy of Sciences.

Nineteen twenty-eight saw the publication of the fourth and last volume. Since then, a popular edition has been printed and is going with all the enthusiastic acceptance of the original de luxe edition. The set contains 3000 pages, 1500 illustrations, and 100 maps, all done by Seton's own pen and brush.

With the virtual extermination of many of our large native mammals, the opportunity for a similar work will never occur again, even were there a writer who was capable of such presentation. It is in effect an entire library on the subject, and promises to remain for all time the final word on the mammals of America.

Many of the illustrations in *The Lives,* as it has come to be called, show one element of Seton's work which perhaps is not appreciated by all his readers. That is his sense of humor. His animals, as indeed was his whole being, are a delight to live with. Yet never is there a falsification of character in these charming vignettes.

This trait of portraying an animal with personality sometimes made difficulties for him in the publishing world. When the first volume of *The Lives* was ready for publication, it was sent on for final approval.

In the manuscript, there was a separate Table of Contents for each animal treated. On the page listing this, Seton had put a drawing of the animal in each case. But it was not a realistic presentation. It was a summation of the life and character of the animal, a capitulation of the soul of the animal. Seton called these "synoptic drawings." The publisher was horrified. "A serious work like this that will go down through the ages as the best book on the subject of mammals! It cannot be! We could not put these humorous sketches into an otherwise erudite book!"

Seton's retort was quick and firm. "Then you do not do the book."

The feud went on for weeks. But Seton never wavered. The book would stand as he formulated it, or at least *this* publisher would not bring it out.

He finally won, and the book appeared as he wished it.

Many hundreds of times have I heard learned mammalogists from all over the world comment on these drawings with generous approbation; and I know that the character and personality of each animal is impressed on the mind of the reader in a way that mere words—or even serious representation in painting—would never have accomplished.

PART ELEVEN

RISING WOOD SMOKE

A GOSPEL FOR YOUTH

The Origin of Two Little Savages

In 1898, Seton had first met Kipling. They each recognized the greatness of the other, and a long-lasting friendship was begun.

One day Seton told Kipling of his dream—that outdoor life with simple pleasures and woodcraft pursuits was the proper school for manhood, which Seton always held should be the real aim of education.

Kipling was profoundly impressed, and said: "If you don't get that idea across in a national way, the Chinaman will be sitting astride our necks within fifty years." Then, as they sat in silent consideration, he added: "How are you going to land it?"

Seton replied: "Well, I am writing a dictionary of woodcraft."

"Hell!" Kipling exploded. "Who would ever read a dictionary?"

"Well, what would you do?" Seton countered.

"I'd put it in a novel," he said.

"Maybe you're right," replied Seton. And he began the story of *Two Little Savages* which was destined to be a best seller for generations to come, is indeed selling today as it has through all the years.

But other things came into Seton's life; and the book was still merely in fragments when, in 1899, Rudyard Kipling became deathly ill. He was attended throughout that dread time by his bosom friend, Frank N. Doubleday, known to us all as Effendi. He was then in the early more or less struggling years of his publishing business.

One day, soon after the crisis of his illness was past, Kipling called from his bed:

"Frank, Frank, come here!"

"Yes, Ruddy," and Effendi came close. "What is it?"

"Frank," said Kipling in a weak voice, "you are starting out as a publisher. I want to tell you how to make it a great success. You go down to Seton and ask him to write you a book on American Woodcraft, and you will reach the whole nation."

"All right, Ruddy," replied Doubleday softly. "Now you lie down and be very still." He knew the sick man was yet a little vague in his thinking, and tried to soothe him into quiet.

The next day Kipling turned toward Doubleday as the latter sat at his bedside and said:

"Frank—Frank—did you get the contract from Seton for a book on Woodcraft?"

"No, not yet, Ruddy, but I will as soon as I can. Now go to sleep. The doctor says you must not talk."

And Kipling soon dozed off into slumber.

The following day Kipling was really better, and hopes for his recovery were high.

As he lay in the dimly lighted room, he again turned to Doubleday and said:

"What about that book from Seton?"

Doubleday answered soothingly: "Yes, yes, I'll get it. Now keep quiet."

Then Kipling turned his earnest gaze on the young publisher and said in a voice that sounded perfectly rational:

"Frank, I've been raving, I know. But I am not raving now. I'm all right again. My mind is as clear as it ever was—yes, clearer, for I can see into the future. And I want to tell you this—I'm serious about it. Seton is the coming writer—you are the coming publisher. You go down to his place at once and get a contract for a book on American Woodcraft. He is the only man who can write it. You get it, and it will be a great success for both of you."

"All right, old man!" answered Doubleday. "I'll attend to that soon, but you must lie down and be quiet."

"I won't lie down and I won't be quiet till you go and get the contract."

So Doubleday finally left his charge and sought out Seton in the latter's studio. He related the conversation.

Seton responded: "I can write it. It will take me two years, although much material is all ready now."

The contract was drawn up and Seton began the real work on his

Two Little Savages. As a matter of fact, it took almost four years to complete.

Doubleday published it as arranged for. It was at once recognized as being autobiographical; that Yan was the author himself.

Kipling read it and commented to Seton: "It is far too informational."

"But I have not even at that fully told my story," said Seton.

"Then write another novel."

So Seton wrote *Rolf in the Woods* but still felt that he had not quite delivered his message. This led to the many editions of the *Birch Bark Roll,* issued as the Manual of Woodcraft, which ran through thirty revisions as the years passed.

It is now sixty-four years since *Two Little Savages* first appeared, but the accuracy of Kipling's forecast is shown by the millions of copies sold throughout that time. Olding men still come to me to tell of the influence that that book had on their lives and the reverence in which they still hold what many of them have called the Bible of their boyhood.

But for lack of space, I could tell stories of men who have modeled their lives on Yan in *Two Little Savages;* of men who were influenced to make their life work along natural history lines.

An extract from a letter written by a man we had never encountered expresses a poignancy that has been in the hearts of many others. This man had never met Seton in person, but he wrote:

"For me, the things you have taught have been a religion which, as time has gone on, I have accepted more and more, not as a social form of entertainment, not a popularization of Woodcraft and Indian lore, but something much deeper and more abiding. . . .

"To me, Yan is the symbol and Glenyan the heaven of my religion. . . .

"There is much more to say. I pray that time may spare us both that before long I may see you in person, to talk with you and to drink from the well you have dug so that I too who have known the torment of thirst may acknowledge my debt to you who knew thirst before me."

The sequel to this was visits exchanged between his home and ours, the recital of his life story full of trials and suffering, but a gradual rise to the top, which he credits in every detail to his adherence to the principles set forth, not in print but, for those who understand, between the lines of the book which has been his guide and symbol of life in the fullest measure.

A letter from him written a few days after Seton's passing said: "Of all the letters that I have written, this is the saddest of my life. . . . That the Chief [Seton] is not with us is a fact that fails to penetrate my mind, for he has been a part of me all my conscious life. . . .

"He was a great man, so great that only in the collective mind of all those to whom he was a religion can be grasped the significance of his life. For he was as Prometheus—he gave to all whom he touched the divine fire of understanding, and so enriched us all.

"Of all the beautiful and moving things that have been written in the words of man, none is greater than the simple preface to *Two Little Savages:*

> "Because I have known the torment of thirst,
> I would dig a well where others may drink."

I doubt not that, on reading this, many more memories will be stirred in readers who have lived by that book.

In my estimate, two factors are responsible for its lasting popularity. First is the fact that Seton's literary style was so simple that the reader does not even notice the words or the way they are used. This meets the scientific tests of readability, and leaves the mind open to ideas instead of to language.

The other factor—and this was apparent in all his activities—was the living truth that nothing in his world was static, least of all his ideas. He was indeed conscious of the fact that values change from age to age, and the interpretation of one generation is seldom the interpretation of the next. But with each age that he touched—and he was active through three generations—he changed along with it, reacting with sincerity and warm interest to the eternal youth springing up around him.

In 1897, while at Yancey's in the Yellowstone, he had written: "Here by the campfire, we sit . . . amid the historical scenes, in this ancient land of the Crows, surrounded by landmarks that to the old-timers tell endless tales of joy and sorrow, human suffering and human heroism. Here I am gathering the fragments of their past history, recalling my own early days in the Northwest; and while harkening to wild tales of the mountains and of the past, there comes over me a strange feeling of sadness that almost shapes itself into the question, 'Why was I born too late?' Then common sense reminds me that the glamor of memory and romance is over it all; that twenty years from now, the present will wear the same charm for younger men; and that, after all, the best of all times is the living present."

Such men stay eternally young, even physically; and imbue their world with a vital spirit that can never be destroyed.

The Boy Scouts

Upon such principles as Seton set forth in *Two Little Savages*, he formally launched in 1902 the organization known variously as the Woodcraft Indians or the Indian Scouts, although he had done experimental work with these underlying motivations for some four years before.

In order to launch it as a national movement, the *Ladies' Home Journal* published an article by Seton in each month's issue from May 1902 through November. The magazine ran this series as a department called "Ernest Thompson Seton's Boys."

In 1903 the same periodical published from January through August chapters which in expanded form appeared later that year as *Two Little Savages*.

Groups of boys were organized in many parts of the country, and prominent educators came to see the scheme in operation.

The idea succeeded so well that in 1904 Seton went to England to establish it there. He lectured on the movement at many schools, colleges, and theaters. The first tribe to be organized in England was under the leadership of William Y. Knight at Eccles. This was followed very shortly after at Hove, New Brighton, and Kent Hatch.

In 1906, Seton went again to England, and lectured at many places. It was during this tour that Lord Baden-Powell called on him. The meeting took place on October thirtieth, at the Savoy Hotel in London. The two men spent several hours in discussion about Seton's work with the boys.

Baden-Powell was intensely interested. He said he had been invited to rewrite his book, *Aids to Scouting*, as a handbook for boys. Seton convinced him that it would be advisable to form a separate organization to carry out the purpose. This Baden-Powell did and called them Boy Scouts—an excellent choice of name and a contribution to the movement that has been eminently successful.

On October 11, 1910, a group of prominent men met in New York to organize the Boy Scouts of America. Seton was made Chief Scout, and remained so until 1915 when he retired from active service with the organization. His nominal retirement, however, did not mean an end to his interest or co-operation. He continued to work with the membership in various capacities through the rest of his life; and I am happy to say that to this day the most cordial relationship is maintained between the Boy Scouts of America and Seton Village.

PART TWELVE

BURNING INCENSE

DREAMS COME TRUE

Seton Village

Years ago—many years—as far back as the beginning of our dreams—
we planned that our final home would be in the West, and more
definitely in the vicinity of Santa Fe. We have always felt that this
City of the Holy Faith was the spiritual capital of America, maybe of
the world.

It was necessary to achieve certain objectives before we could
pull up stakes wholly and start a new life; and like so many worth-
while dreams, it took longer than we had anticipated.

However, in 1927 we began to see the fruits of accomplishment,
and we made our first exploratory trip into the land of our hopes.
Twice annually for three years we came again; on each occasion
spending considerable time investigating the possibilities. We sys-
tematically looked at every piece of available land within a radius of
a hundred miles of Santa Fe in every direction. Even when we felt
that for one reason or another a prospect was not what we would
want, we went to see it lest we might someday wonder what we had
missed.

When we first saw the Sebastian De Vargas Grant, we knew we had
found our homeland. Nevertheless, we went right on looking, until
there was nothing else to be seen.

Finally, in February 1930, the land became ours; and on Washington's birthday of that year we made our first camp in a beautiful
spot near the center of the tract. We named the ravine where we
camped that day Ramshorn Canyon, from a pair of rams' horns
which we found there, and nailed up in a tree.

It was one of those heavenly days that come to New Mexico
often, even in February; and we felt our world turn over in the
fullness of our joy. Here would come into being all the hopes and
aspirations of years of planning.

The tract is nearly a square, containing 2500 acres, and is part of the grant made by the King of Spain to Governor De Vargas when the White men first came into the country in 1540. There are intriguing stories of prehistoric Indian pueblos, of buried treasure with maps to fortify the claims, of oil deposits as well as lodes of the precious new minerals that the recent wars have brought into use. There are unspeakable views into the Sandias, the Jemez, the Nacimientos, the Cerrillos, the Manzanos, the Sangre de Cristos, and other lesser ranges. But, above all, there is a spiritual quality about the place that is felt by every visitor, according to his lights.

Now we had our land, but where on this broad estate were we to establish our village?

Each day we drove out from Santa Fe, parked our car somewhere among the trees (occasionally not locating it again for a couple of days), and with the makings of a camp lunch went hiking over the acres.

About noon we would stop in some suitable spot, build a campfire, and broil our bacon or heat our beans. We usually carried with us enough water to make some coffee. One day we had brought with us J. D. Sheets, a well driller, in the hope that he could offer advice on what had to be our first step toward habitation. As we settled ourselves in an arroyo at midday, we remarked as we scouted for wood that some sheepherder had left a little mound of stones when he also had camped here, and we used the blackened rocks for our own fire. The sand about showed still the tracks of many sheep, and we speculated on how long ago they had rested here.

That day we had neglected to bring water from town for our coffee, but there were spots of snow still under the trees; and by scraping off the upper dust, we were easily able to get enough to fill our tin can, and went as usual about the making of our coffee.

We were soon contentedly munching our bacon. When the coffee had boiled, we filled each a tin cup from the can it had been cooked in, and lounged against the little incline in the bank.

As we sipped, I half consciously noted to myself that the coffee did not taste quite as usual; but we had bought our supplies that day in a new little shop on our way out, and it must be a different brand.

I had pretty nearly drained my cup when I was surprised to find that apparently the shopkeeper had allowed some unground coffee beans to get mixed with our purchase. These had settled to the bottom of the cup and were now clearly visible.

I started to remark on the unusual occurrence when it suddenly dawned on me. I went back to the tree where I had gathered the snow for our coffee water, scraped a little beneath the surface, and there found what I had begun to suspect—that the sheep had rested there for some time, probably on the occasion when the herder had made his campfire. In fact, on investigation, we found evidence that this was a favorite spot for roving flocks of sheep, and many a bivouac had been made in this little clearing.

But the coffee had not been too bad—just different!

This is but one incident of many that we reveled in as we wandered day after day, seeking the focal spot for our home.

Even today, after more than thirty-five years, we go out, and in various places come on a tree or bush with a bit of white rag tied to a twig—which was our trail sign: maybe this is the place.

But when we stood together one memorable evening and faced a sunset of unspeakable light, we knew—as we always have known in moments of acceptive decision. No one of the thousands of persons who have since stood on the eminence where is now our "Castle" has ever doubted that we were given wisdom better than our own in the choice. Everything that we had sought together through the years was there in fullest abundance. Every theory of life that we had held was waiting there to prove its truth and rightness, unvoiced but chanting its alleluia to our grateful hearts. The veil is very thin across this point of view.

We returned to the East, arranged our affairs, assembled our goods; and in June were once again in Santa Fe, this time to stay.

The Cabin at Blue Ridge

One idea very dear to Seton's heart was the importance of putting one's self into the building of one's home. On a small scale, the following story, though not actually connected with the building of our own home, illustrates the point:

Some years ago, a new Y.M.C.A. camp was being planned. The director, named Smith we shall say, consulted Seton on the subject of tents. He could get new tents with fly for $160, and these would accommodate each 8 men. If double-decked cots, etc., were added, it made the cost $250 each. How did it strike him?

Seton replied at length: "Here you have 8 young men, all more or less athletic, none with any cash to spare; and you propose to give them a two weeks' outing in a $250 tent that will be useless in 5 years at most. I should say it is all wrong."

"What would you do?" the director asked.

Seton's answer was: "A cabin that will hold 8 men comfortably and will last 50 years. Besides, the tent is a mere thing out of a department store; the cabin that you build yourself is a precious experience."

After a moment's thought, Smith asked: "If one could do it in a week, couldn't two do it in three days?"

"Yes."

"Then I call your bluff. I dare you to prove it, and I will go along as your aide."

So they two got together at the chosen campground on the Blue Ridge in North Carolina, in April 1920, equipped with axes, hammers and saw, nails and roofing paper.

Suffice it here to say that in a little over three days they were finished. They had kept within their budget of time and money.

And what had they got? Something out of the woods, conquered out of the woods, by themselves, a mixture of nature and human enthusiasm, a something which they could not but love, for it was a part of themselves.

They had contacted the wild woods at almost every point without any intermediary. The nails and the paper were the sole exceptions, and to have given this up would have been costly as well as unpractical. So they accepted them, just as they had also to accept the tools which they brought.

What was its effect on the campers, its spiritual power? Its 8 bunks were filled at once, and there was an eager waiting list, so that they had to limit the time each might enjoy the cabin, although the alternative in this case was a comfortable hotel.

The instinctive joy it gave was seen in such expressions as "The real old thing," "Look at those timbers! Honest to God, ain't they?" "I tell you it is good to sit by that open fire and know that it is all real, that you are in a real cabin in the real woods." And, had these men built it themselves, their pleasure would have been tenfold and lifelong.

Could they have gotten any such thrills or memories, or precious contact with the woods, in a factory-made tent, bought in a department store, smelling of mothballs and varnish, without one feature of color or beauty, without romance or memory, and established only because it was less trouble?

The Country House

Deep down in our instincts, nearly every one of us, in a spirit of rebellion against city smugness, means in his early plans to keep his dream place as primitive as possible. He thinks in terms of primitive furniture, primitive fireplaces, primitive hardware, and lists as tabu such annoyances as modern lighting and heating.

These last inhibitions, however, rarely hold out indefinitely. Candles have a pleasing ancestral sound, but electric lights are more convenient and safer. The well sweep gives way to the pressure tank, and the potbellied stove to the central heating system.

But one characteristic of the country house is enduring—it is never finished. Because it expresses an individuality, and because individualities keep on developing, there will be changes in the house every year.

Now that the time had come, and we had acquired our land, we went at the planning with all the ardor of years of waiting and years of experience, but with convictions of unusual strength and clearness. We knew this was to be our final home, and it would embody all the principles not only of architecture but of life itself as we saw it.

Seton held that the fundamental principle of architecture, as of all arts, and indeed of everything good in the world, is Truth. A building must be true to its object, true to its matter, and true to its maker. Or, to be more specific, true architecture considers, first of all, the purpose of the building, and permits no capricious notions to direct the form to the injury of its utility.

"I will not," he declared as we discussed this, "crowd my foot into a boot that does not fit, merely because it seems to the eye to be a beautiful boot."

He harked back often to the builders of the early centuries after the Conquest, and claimed that the buildings that have been preserved to us are masterpieces of that beauty which is but the physical form of Truth.

The next requisite to his mind was that the building be of sound construction. "What pleasure can anyone find in a structure that is evidently doomed to early collapse? It would be like doing exquisite carving on a snow man, or building fine castles of tidal sand. Instinctively all the world resents flimsiness and instability."

Honesty was an essential characteristic of Seton's make-up. It was outstandingly important to him in building. He ranted against the architect—and we knew some of the type—who would say to his client, in effect: "Now, what shall we pretend that this building is going to be? A New England homestead, a Swiss chalet up in the Alps, a feudal castle, or a Greek temple looking out on the sea?"

His answer to this make-believe was more energetic than polite. "I don't want my building to *pretend* anything. It shall be, first of all, a home, strong and weatherproof; later it may be beautiful. But, whatever it is, it shall be honest. I will not put up a box and pretend it is a beam; I will not mark off cement in squares and pretend it is tile or paving stone. If I can afford nothing better than a tarpaper shanty, it will stand up as a tarpaper shanty, honest in the sight of God and man—honest and unashamed.

"There shall not be in my cottage one nail, stick, shred, or brick that is not exactly what it purports to be—and beautiful therefore in its sincerity."

Simplicity Not Crudity

When we were assembling the material for our home, we cut the trees on our own land for the vigas—the strong, naturally round rafters used in the Southwestern architecture based on the old Indian forms of building in that country.

We carefully peeled off the bark of each tree to be used, exposing the sheer beauty of the wood—smooth, creamy white with the soft play of the yellowish-brown grain.

A friend one day remarked as he watched the trouble we were taking to remove all trace of the outer roughness:

"With all your insistence on using natural material of the woods, why don't you leave the trees as you find them? You seem to contradict your own repeated principles."

Seton replied, as he continued to work his drawknife down the long straight trunks:

"Many times have we had to point out the difference between simplicity and crudity. Many of us by nature and by training are devoted to the simple life. But some groups have mistaken simplicity for savagery, and in their enthusiastic desire for the simple life as they see it have been led into some entirely unprofitable boorish customs.

"I can perhaps best illustrate the point by describing three staircases that were made—the first in the factory spirit; the second in the crude spirit; and the third in the spirit of simplicity.

"The first had guard- and handrails turned by machine. Each guardrail was exactly like the next in size and form, but the grain varied so that many were crossgrained and weak, and all were disfigured with paint and varnish—not a trace of the innate and beautiful wood color was visible. The builder and the owner described it as 'very stylish; the latest thing in that line.' But I am very sure that no trained artist would deliberately incorporate this in a picture—and that is a sure test of beauty.

"The second stairway was made by a person who had recoiled from the sandpaper, lathe, and paint pot, and determined to have a primitive stairway, although the house was far from primitive. So he built the guardrails of the ruggedest limbs available in the woods, carefully retaining the snags, bark, and moss. No two of them were alike—but all were a menace to persons using the stairs. Besides, all about were French mirrors and Grand Rapids furniture. To me, it was as silly and ugly an affectation as could well have been practiced.

"The third stairway was in a very rustic cottage in the woods. The handrail was a straight chestnut pole, carefully cleaned, the knots smoothed, its function considered first, last and all the time. The guardrails of the balustrade were of smaller chestnut poles, as straight as could be found, and carefully trimmed, so as to be clear of moss, bark, snags, roughnesses, or weak spots. They were as nearly alike as possible, and yet there was enough variety in color, knots, and slight surface curves so that no two were quite the same. The natural beauty of color was preserved without paint. Last, they were very strong, absolutely reliable as guards, no child could come to grief through failure on the balustrade's part.

"This last was the consummation of simplicity, therefore beautiful from every point of view and commendable to all who saw the honesty and utility of the finished product."

Further Principles

The ugliest line that can be drawn is a long, unbroken, mathematically correct, straight line. Apparently, because it is so ugly, the modern builder tries to use as many of these as he can get in. Brickwork walls, roof shingles, imitation tiles, etc., all attest this dreadful disease.

One day, returning after a stay at a famous and costly hotel in a nearby town, Seton stormed in just rage:

"The only attempt at architectural ornament in each room was a cornice of forty-seven knife-edge straight lines in plaster, costly to make, appalling to look at. And the only beauty spot in the room was where a leakage of sewage from the bath above had stained and crumbled the terrible frieze."

His final principle for successful building was simplicity. "The more complicated, the better" was the rule of the early architects who spoiled so much of the East. The result was a jumble of silly turrets, rope moldings nailed on, make-believe columns one inch thick; not one broad stretch of honest, smooth, dignified masonry.

Much of the above criticism is of course not true of the present-day builders and architects. But the fact that his principles are all adhered to today in the best tradition of modern construction merely proves the rightness of his instincts along these lines.

In our many discussions we looked forward to the joyous adventures we would have in the building of our Shangri-la. We knew
we would have our troubles too—if troubles they could be called
when we really enjoy them—in trying to get our laborers to follow
our radical notions about things they had been taught to do otherwise.

One night we sat in front of the campfire. As we watched the
moon rise over the eastern hills, he told me of a similar difficulty he
had encountered with a previous house.

The first incident was testimony also to the practical streak in him
which was, as he smilingly remarked, his Scottish heritage.

He told the story somewhat like this as I remember it:

"I needed about 25,000 feet of rough lumber and several thousand
lineal feet of 2×4's. These stocks were worth $30 to $40 a thousand
in the market. On my place were a few dead chestnuts, and on
my neighbor's place adjoining, hundreds of these grim relics of the
blight. I bought all I could at old wood prices—$2.00 a cord on
the stump. I bought a mill, cut and sawed all the rough lumber I
needed at a total cost to me of $17 a thousand; then sold the mill
at cost, having all the slabs and sawdust to the good.

"When it came to the roof, the tradition of red tile was strong, but
I found it would cost $30 a square (10×10 feet). So I went to a
slate dealer and found best red slate, $30; best green, $22; best
purple, $18. All too expensive, for the best cedar shingles were only
$7.00 a square.

"But I am deeply prejudiced against shingles, which are frightfully combustible and in any case will not last longer than ten years.
So I said to the slate man: 'Show me the cheapest thing you have.'
He pointed to a pile of culls, all colors, shapes, sizes, and thicknesses,
and said: 'You can have them at $3.00 a square if you take a
carload.'

"'How many squares in a carload?' I said.

"'A hundred,' he replied. I needed but 50 squares, but thought I
saw a chance, and said:

"'I'll take the hundred squares if you will punch them'; (that is,
make two holes in each for the nails), a simple operation when one
has the punching machine. He accepted, and I got the most beautiful
lot of varied gray-green slate imaginable for my roof.

"When the neighboring builders saw how pleasing it was, they got new light. They came and bought the leftover 50 squares for $600 on the ground.

"This is an illustration of what I did all through the work, reducing the cost and enhancing the artistic qualities.

"When it came to laying the slate, I had the usual battle with the trained mechanics (from Greek *mekane*, a machine). But I took away the chalk line and made them lay the slate by eye, reasonably straight, but with constant inevitable variations that effectively stopped any long mathematical edges.

"The outer coat of stucco was mixed in four lots, one each with yellow ocher, red ocher, white and lampblack gray. After a fight, the mason consented to abandon the floating tools, and let it go just as it came from the trowel. By taking alternate trowels of the different colors, I got a lovely terra cotta of endless subtle variations.

"Cement with lime in it is so plastic at this stage that one naturally models forms of animals and of symbols, etc., at salient points. Over each bedroom I shaped the personal totem of the prospective inhabitant, and rioted in the sculpturesque finish of it all."

The uninstructed say of our buildings: "They look so charming, so old." By which they really mean that they have the beauties that are usually associated with strong old buildings—buildings of the Golden Period.

But they certainly do not *look old*. They *are* not old. They are brand new, and we do not want them to look anything they are not.

However, following the principles set forth, they have evident kinship with the structures set up by the honest, simple old builders of the long ago; and in so much have achieved their purpose and our own.

Many years ago, for one of his houses in the East, Seton had written a brief poem.

Because of the differences in material and circumstances, I have, with his wholehearted approval, changed that poem to comply with our conditions. It is now the, shall I say, theme song of Seton Village.

We've clad our thought in stone and steel
    We've built of native pine.
We've made a home that through the years
    Can all our love enshrine.

We do not fear the thunder stroke
    Nor dread the wear of time;
Our deep foundations in the earth
    Give peace and strength sublime.

Yes, more, may God send flush of rain
    And biting blizzards long,
And grind of years and storm wrack strain;
Our bulwark's built for such arraign.
    We've proved our crafting strong.

Progress

That memorable evening when we reiterated to each other our principles of building was in the summer of 1930. Our immediate aim was to provide a simple home for ourselves, and as soon as possible the facilities for a camp-out of the groups we had trained in the East—leaders of outdoor and other youth organizations, not only of America but of the world.

The first of these courses was carried out during July and August of 1932, when we were equipped simply but adequately to house, feed, and teach twenty-five adults the elements of recreational life that Seton had always stood for.

The students lived in the Indian Village we had established at a little distance from our own house. The camp consisted of tepees, wickiups, a few log cabins, a hogan which was our auditorium, a crafts shop, and a dining hall.

In the years that followed we added other houses, built our "Castle," as the natives came to call it, provided facilities for a Children's Camp as well as our Adult Institute. In 1940 we finally had 200 students as the maximum, offered courses which carried college credit, had a staff of 50 experts, a library of 40,000 volumes—in short, a "going concern."

But now the war was on. Neither we nor our students could travel. So we discontinued our school that year and announced that we would not again carry it on.

Our lives were getting too full—even for us who thrived on fullness. What with lecturing autumn, winter, and spring, the school all summer, we had mighty little time to write. So, with real regret, we did not again run a formal school.

Nevertheless, we did not cease to provide facilities for students or other groups interested in our way of life.

Our library has increased until now it contains something over 70,000 volumes. Our Natural History Museum has, available for study, the 2000 bird and mammal skins that Seton had collected during his active lifetime. We have hanging on our walls about 200 of his paintings, with many more still stored, awaiting the building of a real gallery.

The exhibits in our Indian Museum are artistically and uniquely executed; and, though yet far from the ideal we had always contemplated, is still a place for study and interest.

Our campground is freely open to any groups who can come properly supervised and prepared to take care of their own material needs. Our home is the rendezvous of daily meetings of those who are seeking what we can provide.

We have plans for a chapel. It will, of course, be non-sectarian. It will be a shrine and a memorial. It will, we hope, be the epitome of our work, and a haven for those who find value in our teachings.

EPILOGUE

In a physical sense, Seton is no longer here to lead our joyous meetings as he did for so long. But his influence is so deep and strong that even those who never met him feel the impress of his personality in everything about.

His was a fearless spirit, he lived life as he found it; but, in spite of the fact that, in late 1946, he had plans for another book, that he had a canvas stretched ready for a new painting, he knew that his work was finished. He had lost little of his power, especially in the field of art, but somehow he realized that he would not again surpass what he had already done.

He felt, as must all who live long enough to observe, that we are left here until the work for which we were sent is finished. With him, it had been many long years of opportunity to spread what he so aptly termed "the joy of being alive."

I have a big broad plan for the perpetuation of the work he initiated and carried on so successfully during his long full time on earth. But life has taught me that it knows better plans than we can image, so that I try to submerge my own desires, apt to be too insistent, into a calm willingness to accept what comes, and to make the most of it, then wait again. I have discovered that there is a Pattern, larger and more beautiful than our short vision can weave, and I know that what his magnificent spirit has done will never be lost in smallest measure to mankind.

He lives in his books and in his art, in the thousands of boys and girls who follow the path he laid out for youth over half a century ago. But, better still, he lives in all who cherish the spark of the eternal, illuminating sacred fire that was in him.

There is nothing that can dim or change the memories of our life together; and, though I am alone now to walk my road, I have an abiding sense of his nearness, which time does not disturb.

I await with open mind what the years will bring, rejoicing in the privilege that was accorded me—the rare opportunity to walk with a man who was truly great, to live in closest communion with a big soul, one who lived long enough on earth to have achieved peace with himself, to have learned an invincible serenity, and who finally, without regret, in the grandeur of his years, slipped back into that eternity out of which he had for a time emerged.

He has left a light for mankind to follow, a strength for youth to grasp, a hope for those who guide the destinies of children. *end*

The Buffalo Wind has carried him to greater dreams, to broader visions, to larger opportunities, or perhaps to endless sleep. But, because he had known the torment of thirst, he dug a well where others have drunk so deeply that never again can life be the shallow vessel it sometimes has seemed to be.

He needs no visible memorial; but when the practical means are available for building the chapel which he so desired, it will be the joyous gift of Beulah and her mother to the future of the America that he envisioned.

The Buffalo Wind is blowing!

The Buffalo Wind has blown!

INDEX